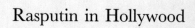

Rasputin in Hollywood

By the same author

The Camden Town Murder
Murder at the Villa Madeira
Not Without Prejudice
The Technique of Persuasion

Rasputin in Hollywood

Sir David Napley

Weidenfeld & Nicolson London

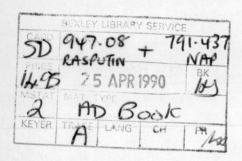
First published in Great Britain in 1990 by
George Weidenfeld & Nicolson Limited,
91 Clapham High Street, London sw4 7ta

British Library Cataloguing in Publication Data

Napley, David, *1915–*
    Rasputin in Hollywood.
    1. Russia. Rasputin, Grigori. Assassination
    I. Title
    364.1'524'0924

    ISBN 0–297–81038–3

Printed and bound in Great Britain by
The Bath Press, Avon

For my wife

Illustrations

Foreword

The case which Princess Youssoupoff, a member of the Russian Imperial family, brought against Metro-Goldwyn-Mayer in 1934 is remembered by all those who practise in the law. Understandably, more than fifty years later, it is less well known to the public generally. Yet in the days before trials, whether arising out of claims for libel or for murder, had become the daily ration for the television viewer, such cases excited extraordinary public interest. The Youssoupoff case was no exception, involving as it did Royalty, the murder of Rasputin, an enigmatic figure whom most people regarded as the incarnation of evil and a few as the embodiment of saintliness, the drama of the Courts of Justice, with the great judge Sir Horace Avory presiding at the age of eighty-three, and the redoubtable and renowned Sir Patrick Hastings appearing for the Princess.

The case raised fascinating questions. Was it defaming a woman to depict her as having been raped? Was it libel or slander thus to depict events in the newly conceived 'talking films'? And what was the story behind the events which led to the film and its production?

This book endeavours to help readers to live through these intriguing events, and to form their own judgement as to the conduct of the case and the justice of the outcome.

I would wish to record my deep appreciation for the help I have received in its preparation. First to all those Publishers who have kindly given permission for me to reproduce extracts from the books which are set out in the Bibliography. Next to my Secretary, Judi Richardson, for having laboriously re-typed my badly typed script. Then to my daughters and my good friend, Gerald Thomas, for having read the typescript and made helpful suggestions. To Oscar Beuselinck of the firm of Wright Webb Syrett for having kindly made available to me a copy of the transcript of the trial. Lastly, and by no means least, to Elizabeth Murray, who gave invaluable assistance with the research, with a degree of skill and application which she always displays and without whose invaluable help the writing could never have been commenced.

Chapter **One**

On the fifteenth day of December 1916, according to the Russian calendar, Russia was fast tottering towards dissolution. The war against Germany had gone extremely badly. Well in excess of four million Russians had given their lives – if 'given' is the apposite word – in defence of their country, to no avail.

The great city of St Petersburg, now called Leningrad, was, on this fateful Thursday, suffering under more than ten degrees of frost. As midnight approached, a car was travelling from the home of Prince Youssoupoff. At the wheel, dressed as a chauffeur, was one Lazavert, a doctor with some claim to being knowledgeable in the field of poisons, and a member of the ultra-right-wing Union of True Russians. His passenger was the Prince himself, wearing a fur coat, a cap with ear flaps, and a heavy scarf around his neck, so that it was virtually impossible to identify him.

Their destination was a small two-storey house at 63–64 Gorokharayd Street, in which was the apartment of Rasputin. Sometimes called 'the Mad Monk', he was certainly not mad and had never been a monk. He exercised more power in Russia than he could ever have foreseen in his early days as a poor and ignorant peasant, despite the clairvoyant powers which he evidently possessed. Born in the 1860s of Russian peasant stock, Rasputin's real name was Grigorii Efimovich.

The Prince had arranged to collect him this night and take him to his home so that Rasputin might meet the Princess. When they reached Rasputin's apartment, the Prince left the car to go and collect him. Beyond the courtyard he was accosted by the porter, who demanded to know who he was and what he was doing there at such an hour.

'Grigorii Efimovich is expecting me,' the Prince replied, ignoring the inquiry as to his identity.

The porter was far from satisfied, pointing out that it was extremely late. The Prince explained that it was by arrangement with Rasputin that he was arriving at that time by the back door. This must have reassured the porter, who presumably, like a good many other Russians, knew something of Rasputin's curious habits, for he allowed the Prince to proceed.

The Prince made his way up the stairs, not without difficulty in the darkness, and rang the bell. The door was opened by Rasputin himself.

According to one account, Rasputin said to the Prince, 'There is no one up, the children are asleep, come in, little one.' Youssoupoff entered, and each of them looked carefully at the other.

By the Prince's account, Rasputin, noticing how wrapped up the Prince appeared to be, asked, 'Why are you trying to hide?'

'Didn't we agree,' replied Youssoupoff, 'that no one was to know that you were going out with me tonight?'

'True, true,' replied Rasputin. 'I haven't said a word about it to anyone in the house. I've even sent away all the *Tainiks*' (the secret police). 'I'll go and dress.'

Rasputin went into his bedroom, followed by Youssoupoff. The only light in the room was a small lamp, illuminating some ikons, so Rasputin lit a candle. He was usually dirty and untidy but, on this occasion, according to Youssoupoff's account, he dressed himself in a silk blouse embroidered with cornflowers, with a thick raspberry-coloured cord as a belt. His velvet breeches and highly polished boots seemed brand new; he brushed his hair and carefully combed his beard. Although the Prince had never before seen Rasputin look so tidy, nothing could eliminate the smell of cheap soap which, according to many observers, always clung to him.

'Well, Grigorii Efimovich,' said the Prince, 'it's time to go, it's past midnight.'

'What about the gypsies?' asked Rasputin. 'Shall we pay them a visit?'

'I don't know,' the Prince answered. 'Perhaps.'

'There will be no one at your house tonight but us?' inquired Rasputin.

'No one will be there you would not care to see,' the Prince assured him. 'My mother is in the Crimea.'

'I don't like your mother,' said Rasputin. 'I know she hates me; she's a friend of Elizabeth's' (the Tsarina's sister). 'Both of them plot against me and spread slander about me too. The Tsarina herself has often told me that they were my worst enemies. Why, no earlier than this evening, Protopoff' (who had been appointed Minister of Internal Affairs in the Russian government thanks to Rasputin's influence) 'came to see me and made me swear not to go out for a few days. "They'll kill you," he declared. "Your enemies are bent on mischief." But they'd just be wasting time and trouble; they won't succeed, they are not powerful enough.'

Rasputin put on his overcoat and they left the apartment, Rasputin closing the door behind him. As they descended the excessively dark staircase, Rasputin took hold of the Prince's arm, to guide him.

'His grip hurt me,' the Prince later recalled. 'I felt like crying out and breaking away, but a sort of numbness came over me. I don't remember what he said to me or what I answered, my one thought was to be out of the dark house as quickly as possible, to get to the light and to free myself from that hateful clutch. As soon as we were outside, my fears vanished and I recovered my self-control.' They went to the car and the 'chauffeur' drove away towards the Prince's home.

When they arrived there, they made their way to the basement. In the room above, friends of the Prince were playing a gramophone. Rasputin took off his overcoat and examined some of the furniture in the basement. The Prince invited Rasputin to sit down, and shortly afterwards Rasputin asked if he might have some of the tea which was in a samovar on the table; the Prince poured out a cup. With it were served cakes and biscuits. What Rasputin did not know, however, was that Dr Lazavert, the 'chauffeur', had inserted into the cakes a vast quantity of cyanide. Earlier that day he had spent some time reducing potassium cyanide crystals to a fine powder, taken the tops off the cakes and filled them with it. He had then placed a liberal quantity of liquid potassium cyanide into two of four wine glasses which he placed on the table. It was his opinion that the amount of cyanide which he had provided in each case was more than enough to kill Rasputin 'several' times over.

In fact, two hundred milligrams – a small quantity indeed – of that poison is a fatal dose. It is the poison of which small pills are made for spies to carry in case of capture. Hermann Goering took it to evade execution, and certainly the Nazis supplied their agents with it. It smells of bitter almonds, but this would have been masked by the ingredients of the cakes. The effect is such that, as soon as it is taken and comes into contact with the moist mucous membranes, it is transformed into hydrocyanic acid and death rapidly results.

The Prince first offered Rasputin an untreated biscuit which he accepted and ate. He then offered him some of the poisoned cakes, which he declined saying he did not want any of them as they would be too sweet for him. The Prince endeavoured to assure him that he would like these particular cakes and pressed him so strongly to try one that he finally assented, took one of the poisoned cakes and devoured it. This would, as the Prince knew, bring about instant death, but, to his amazement, Rasputin appeared to enjoy the cake, continuing to engage in light conversation. The Prince, rather nonplussed, became anxious to ensure that he got some of the poisoned wine into him.

'Do try some of our delicious Crimean wine,' he said.

'No, thank you,' Rasputin replied, 'I would rather not. I am quite content.'

This was far from satisfactory from the Prince's point of view. He poured out two glasses, taking care to use the untreated glasses. Rasputin, seeing the wine in both glasses, relented and drank it, evidently with the greatest enjoyment, whilst the Prince himself drank the second glass.

'Do you make a great deal of this wine in the Crimea?' Rasputin inquired. The Prince said they did, adding that their cellars were full of it.

'It is excellent,' said Rasputin, 'but do you think I could have some of the Madeira?'

The Prince turned to pour the Madeira into one of the poisoned glasses.

'No,' said Rasputin, 'don't bother about that. Put it in the same glass.'

'Oh no,' said the Prince. 'You can't, Grigorii Efimovich, mix two different wines.'

'Really, it doesn't matter, I'll use the same glass,' Rasputin insisted.

According to the Prince's account, faced with this difficulty he reached for the glass, but as he moved towards the decanter containing the Madeira he contrived to drop the glass and poured the wine into one of the prepared glasses, without, it would seem, Rasputin either noticing or even commenting. Rasputin accepted and drank from the glass, savouring the wine, but, to the increasing despair of the Prince, without the vast quantity of cyanide in it having the slightest effect upon him.

There was no facial change such as the Prince had been told would occur, but from time to time Rasputin now put his hand to his throat as though he had difficulty in swallowing. This, at least, was no matter for surprise, for one of the effects of cyanide is to cause a tightness of the throat and the naso-pharynx, which is that part of the throat above the soft palate, behind the nose.

Suddenly Rasputin rose to his feet and took a few steps.

'What is the matter?' asked the Prince.

'Why, nothing,' was the reply, 'just a tickling in my throat. The Madeira's good,' continued Rasputin, 'give me some more.'

In utter amazement, the Prince poured more wine into another of the prepared glasses. Rasputin took it and continued to drink, with no ill effects whatsoever.

Then he sat down facing Youssoupoff, stared hard at him and said, 'Now, you see, you're wasting your time, you can't do anything to me.' As he spoke, his face began to show extreme anger; he stared with hatred at the Prince. Evidently he had decided to try to hypnotize him, for Youssoupoff felt as if Rasputin's eyes were burning into his very soul, and he resisted only with the greatest difficulty.

Rasputin, however, must have changed his mind, for all at once he averted his gaze, saying he was thirsty (as well he might have been), and asked for more tea. He rose from his seat and strode about the room, then he told the Prince that he liked to hear him singing and asked him to play something cheerful on his guitar.

Youssoupoff picked up his guitar, which for some unexplained reason was there in the basement, and, feeling far from happy and not in a singing mood, he played and sang a Russian song.

Contentedly, Rasputin sat down and seemed to be dozing off, but the moment the song finished, he opened his eyes and said, 'Sing another. I'm very fond of this kind of music and you put so much soul into it.'

The Prince was reluctantly about to oblige when, fortunately, there was a noise overhead and, desperate to consult his friends as to what he might now do, he seized the offered opportunity.

'What's all the noise?' asked Rasputin.

'Probably the guests leaving,' said Youssoupoff. 'I'll go and see what's up,' and with that he hurried from the room.

In the room above were the Prince's friends and co-conspirators, the Grand Duke Dimitri Pavlovich, V.M.Pourichkevich and Captain Soukhotin, who, understandably, wanted to know what had happened and whether it was all over.

'The poison hasn't acted,' was the reply.

'It's impossible,' said the Grand Duke in amazement. 'The dose was enormous. Did he take it all?'

'Every bit,' replied the Prince.

A hurried discussion followed, after which the Grand Duke handed Youssoupoff his revolver. The Prince returned to the basement with it. There he found Rasputin seated exactly where he had been before, his head drooping and his breathing laboured.

'Are you feeling ill?' asked the Prince.

'My head aches,' was the reply, 'and I have a burning sensation in my stomach. Give me another glass of wine. It'll do me good.'

Amazingly, another glass of Madeira instantly revived him. Indeed, so well had he become that he suggested they should go to the gypsies, but Youssoupoff said it was far too late for that.

Such, then, is the account of events as given in a book which the Prince later wrote. What is perhaps as surprising as the failure of the poison to dispatch Rasputin, is that the same account states that the purpose of Rasputin's visit was to meet the Princess. By now, however, over two hours had elapsed since his arrival at Youssoupoff's home, and nowhere in the story as the Prince told it does Rasputin appear to have asked why he had not yet met the Princess. Furthermore, if that was truly the purpose of his visit, why did he ask to go and see the gypsies before he had met her? May he not have been attracted to the house by some other inducement?

On a cabinet in the basement there stood an antique Italian crucifix made of rock crystal and silver at which the Prince sat gazing.

'What are you staring at that crucifix for?' asked Rasputin.

'I like it, it's so beautiful.'

'It is indeed beautiful,' said Rasputin, crossing to the cabinet on which it stood. 'For my part,' he continued, as he began to examine the cabinet, 'I prefer this.'

'Grigorii Efimovich,' said the Prince, 'you'd far better look at the crucifix and say a prayer,' and with that he raised the revolver, aimed at Rasputin and pulled the trigger. Rasputin screamed, crumpled and fell on to the bearskin rug. At this, the others rushed down and the doctor, who had remained upstairs, bent over the body. The bullet had been directed at the heart, he said, and there was no doubt in his mind that Rasputin was dead. Dimitri and Pourichkevich lifted the body off the rug to avoid bloodstains, and placed it on the flagstones, then they turned off the light and left the room, locking the door.

In response to what he described as an irresistible impulse, the Prince shortly afterwards returned to the basement. He leaned over the body and tried to feel the pulse, but could not find one. But Dr Lazavert, it would seem, was no more successful in determining death than he had been in prescribing poisons, for when the Prince took hold of Rasputin's arms and shook him, the facial muscles visibly contracted and first the left eye then the other eye opened, enabling Rasputin to convey a look of 'diabolical hatred'. 'I wanted to run away,' the Prince recalled in his book, 'to call for help, but my legs refused to obey me and not a sound came from my throat.'

Then, to Youssoupoff's horror, Rasputin, whom the doctor had pronounced dead, suddenly struggled to his feet foaming at the mouth, and uttered a wild roar, his hands convulsively thrashing the air. 'He rushed at me,' recalled the Prince, 'trying to get at my throat and sank his fingers into my shoulders like steel claws. His eyes were bursting from their sockets, blood oozed from his lips, and all the time he called me by name in a low raucous voice.'

With difficulty the Prince wrenched himself free from the 'dead man's' grasp, Rasputin fell on his back gasping, and lay still for a moment, while Youssoupoff rushed upstairs crying, 'Quick, quick, come down. He's still alive.' He seized a rubber club, which had earlier been given to him, while Rasputin crawled forward on his hands and knees, gasping and roaring. He made a sudden leap to a door, which led into the outside courtyard, and which the Prince had believed to be locked, but it opened and Rasputin disappeared through it. Pourichkevich had, by this time, arrived on the scene and he followed Rasputin through the doorway. Two shots were fired, which missed their target, then two more, and the Prince, who had followed Pourichkevich into the courtyard, saw Rasputin fall into a mound of snow, whereupon Pourichkevich gave Rasputin a resounding kick in his left temple. At last, Rasputin – the power behind the Russian throne – was assuredly dead.

A policeman on duty on the other side of the nearby canal rushed to the scene on hearing the shots. In an endeavour to placate him and send him on his way, the Prince told him that he and his friends had had rather a riotous evening, at the end of which they had amused themselves by shooting at Youssoupoff's dog.

However, Pourichkevich – evidently in no mood for discretion – asked the policeman whether he was a good Christian who loved the Tsar. Having been reassured on both counts, Pourichkevich told the policeman who he was and that he had just shot Rasputin; the policeman should therefore hold his tongue, for the sake of the Tsar and the country. The policeman went to report to his superior. The latter, however, took the whole story as a piece of drunken nonsense invented as a joke by his betters and dismissed it as unworthy of immediate attention; accordingly he did nothing until later that morning.

Meanwhile, on learning that the body had been moved and was now in the house, lying on the landing, the Prince rushed there with his rubber cosh and, in a frenzy, repeatedly beat it about the head, until he himself passed out and was carried away.

At 5.30 a.m. the Grand Duke Dimitri, the doctor, and Soukhotin took the body to the Petrovsky Bridge. There, eluding the sentry, they tried to heave it over the parapet. They could not, at first, do so. On the second attempt, they managed to lift it high enough; over went the body of Rasputin into the icy river. Only when they had achieved this did they realize they had forgotten to weight the body as they had intended.

Rasputin, however, was no more, but he was to prove as dangerous for Russia as if he had remained alive.

Chapter Two

Why did a Russian prince, a Grand Duke and a number of persons in important positions in Russian society conspire together to dispose of Rasputin? Why did they finally, with premeditation, bring about the violent and gruesome death of an ignorant Russian peasant?

Of all the many books written on the history of Russia, one of the best, in terms of accuracy, research and readability, is *The Fall of the Russian Monarchy* by Bernard Pares. The opening words of his book are 'Autocracy really ended in Russia on November 1st, 1894 when the last autocrat died.'

He was referring to the death of Tsar Alexander III, whose son, Nicholas, was destined to succeed him. Nicholas had none of the characteristics which would have made him the natural successor to an autocrat. A man of striking appearance, about five feet seven inches tall, as he grew older he developed a strong facial resemblance to King George V of England. He was kind, exceedingly charming, of great simplicity, and appeared to bear ill-will towards no one. He was also timid, introverted and weak, suffering from what has sometimes been called the 'cushion syndrome' in that he tended to carry the impression of the last person who sat on him.

Nicholas had met Princess Alexandra of Hesse-Darmstadt, a younger daughter of Princess Alice of England and a granddaughter of Queen Victoria, several times when she visited Russia from her home in Germany. An exceedingly beautiful girl, fair-haired and very sedate, Alexandra was shy and reserved, caring little about her appearance. As her mother had died when she was six years of age, she had grown up in England, where her education had largely been directed by Queen Victoria. Deeply religious, she was a devout Protestant.

Although in one of her letters she wrote that she had loved Nicholas since she was a child, it was not until 1891, when she visited Russia to attend the wedding of her sister Elizabeth to the Grand Duke Sergei, an uncle of Nicholas, that Alexandra and Nicholas fell deeply in love.

It was a love which was to endure throughout their lives, with periods of great happiness, but far greater periods of intense sorrow.

By the autumn of 1891 Nicholas was writing, 'O Lord, how I want to go to Ilyinskoe ... otherwise if I do not see her now I shall have to wait a whole year and that will be hard.' Alexandra was expressing her love for him with even greater ardour, but there were difficulties. Despite her great love for him, she could not face adopting the religion of the Russian Orthodox Church. His family, moreover, did not approve of the alliance. Thus, in April 1894, Nicholas and Alexandra met in Coburg, where Queen Victoria had also gone, intending to sort out the difficulties.

Unaided by Albert on this occasion, the Queen pulled all the chestnuts out of the fire, and Nicholas wrote, 'What an unforgettable day in my life; the day of my engagement to my darling, adorable Alix.'

At about the same time, Alexander III, then a middle-aged man, became extremely ill. There was some doubt whether Alexandra would be able to reach Russia before he died, but she arrived at Lividia in the Crimea in October, and the young couple's official betrothal took place in the dying Tsar's bedroom. On 26 November they were married and their happiness seemed complete.

This happiness was not shared by the Russian people. There were many who saw the country as ripe for revolution – and they were not to be proved wrong.

Indeed, the Russian system of government was such that revolution seemed inevitable; the only question was when? Copied as it was from alien countries, it embodied some of the characteristics of the English feudal system. Government officials were granted holdings of land in return for military service. The vast majority of the people were peasants, of whom more than a third were serfs, largely uneducated and illiterate. No relief from their privations seemed possible: once a peasant, always a peasant, with the duties of fighting wars and paying taxes.

Beneath the surface seethed a growing sense of outrage. The small number of intellectuals looked to the example set them by the French Revolution, despite Alexander II's earlier attempts at amelioration. He had granted the peasants ownership of half the land which they had worked hitherto. However, the combination of having less land under their husbandry, and the appetite for more which owning land aroused, caused the more prescient to foresee that the danger of revolution had been increased rather than diminished.

A separate but no less significant danger was the autocratic rule of the Tsars, which probably reached its high water mark under Alexander III. The press was extremely restricted, democracy was unknown in central government, and the local state controllers, whom the peasants hated and whom Alexander II had abolished, were restored. To this was added a period of severe famine. This was intensified by the difficulty, often to the point of impossibility, of moving supplies around the country to the places where they were most desperately needed.

It was immediately after this dreadful famine that Alexander died and the weak Nicholas II ascended the throne. He was neither adequately endowed, nor sufficiently prepared, for the task which faced him. The enormity of his problems, his character and his utter devotion to the Tsarina brought him increasingly under her sway, and when she became subservient to the wishes of Rasputin, the Tsar was brought under his influence too.

Anyone who studies the lives of others cannot but notice the truth of the old saying that no man is an island. The fate of every one of us is inextricably affected by those with whom life brings us into contact.

The first strand that bound together the destinies of Rasputin and the Imperial family was spun on 12 August 1904, when Alexandra, after bearing four daughters, at last gave birth to a son and heir. The royal couple's joy was short-lived, for it soon became clear that the child was a haemophiliac. The finest physicians in the country came to the Palace to examine the baby, but the answer was always the same: there was no known cure.

The next strand in the cord which was to bind the Tsar to the peasant Rasputin was a young woman called Anna Vyroubova. The daughter of Taneyev, head of the Tsar's personal Chancery, she had married a naval officer, but the marriage was never consummated and shortly afterwards she was divorced. The Tsarina felt great compassion for her in her plight and took her as a companion, with the result that she not only became close to the Tsarina but was frequently in the company of her and the Tsar.

In his book, Pares attributes his information in this connection to 'the simple and noble record' of Pierre Gilliard, who tutored the young Tsarevich from 1912 and who, following the Revolution, went into voluntary exile with the Imperial family.

Gilliard tells us that when Anna was seventeen, she nearly died of typhus and, in the crisis, she saw a vision of the favourite priest of the time, John of Kronstadt, who was then called to see her. This made her highly responsive to the alleged powers of proclaimed visionaries. Gilliard described her as 'a child, excitable, with no mind or sense'. She lacked all judgement and saw the world as one divided into 'ours and theirs'.

Russia was at that time a hotbed of gossip, and it was rumoured that Anna Vyroubova had a lesbian relationship with the Tsarina. The wife of a general recorded in her diary that, most nights after dinner, Nicholas left his family to go off and work for some hours, and the two women would withdraw from the dining room through the mauve boudoir to the Imperial bedroom. There was, however, not the slightest ground for believing that there was any truth in the rumour. Certainly when a commission was set up in 1917 to inquire into the events of the Tsar's reign, Anna Vyroubova had to submit to a medical examination, which proved her virginity, and, in turn, disproved later rumours that she had had a sexual relationship with Rasputin.

The next strand in the cord was that which brought Rasputin from the obscurity of his birth in the 1860s to his position of power behind the Russian throne.

He was born into a peasant family at Pokrovskoe in Western Siberia, near the Ural Mountains. His true name was Grigorii Efimovich; Rasputin was his nickname – it means 'dissolute', which was by no means inappropriate. His father had spent a year in prison, supposedly for falling asleep and allowing someone else's horse to be stolen while he was carrying on his occupation as a carter. He was fairly prosperous. Rasputin was born somewhere between 1862 and 1865; precisely when is not known. His daughter, Maria, subsequently wrote a life of her father, but its authenticity is questionable. In it, she says that as a boy he became withdrawn, due to the death of a young brother, and spent most of his time in the yard, where he developed a special understanding with animals. He was also said to possess second sight and an ability to locate missing articles.

On one occasion, if these accounts are to be believed, he was ill with a fever. A horse had been stolen and he declared that one of the peasants, who was better off than most, had stolen it. It was later found when the man's premises were searched, and Rasputin's declaration was thus proved to have been accurate.

In 1917 the Provisional Government set up a Commission of Inquiry to review the events of the reign of the Tsar. The evidence adduced showed that Rasputin, as a youth, had engaged in wild sexual activities and, like his father before him, was greatly addicted to drink. He was insolent, foul-mouthed and lecherous. It was quite evident, however, that he was able to exercise a powerful influence over the opposite sex.

At the age of nineteen, he met Praskovia Dubrovina, who came from an adjoining village. She successfully resisted all his endeavours to seduce her and in 1884 they were married. They were, by all accounts, a good-looking pair, and the marriage seems to have been a success, but it did not change Rasputin. Indeed, he acquired a reputation for being a horse thief. This, however, was to lead to a journey which precipitated a remarkable change in him.

He and some other young men were accused of stealing wood and horses. His two companions were dispatched to Eastern Siberia, and Rasputin, probably wisely, decided it was a good moment to leave the village for a while. He spent three months at the monastery of Verkhoturye, and on his return he appeared greatly changed. His speech was disjointed and jerky, and at least one observer described him as not being in his right mind. He gave up drink and became a vegetarian and a recluse. Moreover, whilst previously he had been illiterate, he now seemed able to read and even, to a limited extent, write.

Some people have suggested that he had become an adherent of a *khlyst* sect, who believed that the greater a man's sins, the greater his suffering and his chance of salvation. After his return to the village, he did not stay long. He set off – as the Russian self-styled holy men were wont to do – travelling around the country. One such trip he made was to Mount Athos, where he was shocked to find that the monks were active homosexuals, to which practices they introduced the novices. Rasputin left in disgust, regarding the monasteries there as places of vice. He remained away from his home for three years. He was unsuccessful in his endeavours to subdue his sexual urges, finding, in the words of Oscar Wilde, that the best way to resist a temptation was to give way to it. However, he liked sleeping with women in order to test whether he could resist the urge to seduce them.

His three-year absence, whilst he wandered the country, had been undertaken at the suggestion of his wife. In January 1896, his wife presented him with a son, to whom he was devoted, but within a few months the child died, and Rasputin was inconsolable. It was then that his wife suggested he should go on a pilgrimage. While he was away, and unbeknown to him, his wife had a daughter.

On his return home Rasputin did no work, he just lazed around the place. At first he passed some time in prayer, which became more regular when he turned a room into a small and rather sparsely equipped chapel, using a few icons and candles.

Rasputin enthralled the villagers with the stories he recounted of his travels; since they had never set foot outside the village, they were unable to judge whether or not they were true or how much he had embellished them. So greatly did he impress them that they knelt and prayed with him; they would then sing and dance, taking off all their clothes in the process.

It was at this time that the unusual powers which he unquestionably possessed began to establish a reputation which extended well beyond his village. He had dark staring eyes which had a penetrating power; he seemed to have a hypnotic effect on those he sought to influence, and all accounts pay tribute to his ability to calm and soothe those in distress to a quite remarkable degree. He dressed shabbily, was dirty in his habits and presented a dishevelled and unkempt appearance. The long robe which he assumed did not look as if it ever came into contact with hot water any more than he did, although undoubtedly he was a frequent visitor to the bath-house.

The bath-house played an important part in Russian social life, and it was one of Rasputin's favourite haunts. He would repair there with young women, sometimes prostitutes, whom he would encourage to wash his genitals, thus demonstrating his iron command of his feelings. He did not, however, strive to maintain the same degree of control on other occasions, and the stories of his licentiousness were legion.

This in no way diminished the growing belief that he was a holy man, which, in turn, aroused the envy and dislike of members of the Church. It was not long before the village priest, who felt he was being pushed into second place, reported what he had heard concerning Rasputin's behaviour to the police, who raided his cellar. They found nothing which they could use against him and Rasputin was able to treat the whole episode with disdain.

The next strand in the rise of Rasputin to power was his visit, during his travels, to the city of Kazan where he made the acquaintance of Bishop Abdrey, the Bishop of Kazan, who was also Prince Ukhtinsky. At first, the Bishop greatly admired Rasputin and, before he changed his mind on learning of his sexual and other questionable habits, he was the means of introducing Rasputin into influential circles in the city. Alex de Jonge in his interesting study *The Life and Times of Gregori Rasputin* says: 'For the first time he entered European houses, saw carpets, gas, electric light, telephones even. He saw people drink tea without sucking it through a piece of sugar they held in their mouths, or pouring it into their saucers to cool it. Yet great though the shift from the peasant world to civilization might have been, Rasputin took it in his stride. As he sat, with his dirty boots, his threadbare overcoat with its bulging pockets, and his straggling beard, in drawing rooms hung with chintz and muslin, at tea tables covered with embroidered cloths, absentmindedly twisting his fingers through his napkin, he did not allow his surroundings to overawe him, and took the veneration accorded to him by his hostess as no more than his due.'

It is difficult to appreciate the awe and respect which in Russia was accorded to holy men or *starets* , as they were called, especially amongst the fanatical religionists, at the end of the nineteenth century. Stories of miracles worked, deadly illnesses cured, and mental incapacities restored by the magical powers of these amazing beings, abounded and were widely accepted. Such had become the reputation of Rasputin when the Bishop of Kazan gave him a letter of introduction to Archimandrite Theophanes in St Petersburg.

Greatly loved and admired, Theophanes was regarded as a man of outstanding ability and religious faith and had not long before become the spiritual adviser to the Tsar. On the strength of the Bishop's introduction, Rasputin made his way to St Petersburg in 1903, where he was invited to lodge with Theophanes, who was always ready to greet new holy men. He, in turn, introduced Rasputin to Sergei Trufanov, known as Illiodor, a fanatical monk, who was intrigued by Rasputin, until he had his eyes opened to the real man behind the façade. Then, years later, he was to take part in an unsuccessful attempt to assassinate Rasputin.

Having made the acquaintance of such persons, Rasputin found himself increasingly in the company of Russian high society. The wife of the First Minister of the Interior, Countess Ignatiev, invited him to her home, where he was treated with all the veneration afforded to holy men. Thus firmly ensconced in society, he returned to his village for a visit, but it was not long before the spell cast on him by St Petersburg, with its promise of power and influence, drew him back again and he took up residence in the Mount Athos monastic hostel.

It was then that he met Madame Lokhtina, who suffered greatly from neurasthenia, a condition which was little understood at that time but which today is recognized as being caused by disease or psychiatric disorder. Whichever it was in her case, Rasputin, after the doctors had failed, managed to cure her, or so she was led to believe. Not surprisingly, she became his devoted disciple, and would kneel before him, addressing him as the Living Christ. Later, she appears to have become increasingly mad.

Theophanes next introduced Rasputin to the Grand Duchess Militsa, and later he met her sister Anastasia (not to be confused with the youngest daughter of the Tsar), so that Rasputin was brought several steps nearer to the Tsar and all that he controlled.

Chapter **Three**

It is not clear how Rasputin first found himself in the Tsar's palace at Tsarkoye Selo.

Most historians seem to agree that the final strand which completed the cord that bound him to the Tsar and Tsarina was the illness of their small son and their belief that, by super-human power, and in a miraculous way, he preserved the child's life.

Certainly by the year 1907, stories abounded of the cures which Rasputin had effected with his miraculous powers. Thus, when the son of Lili Dehn, one of the Tsarina's ladies-in-waiting, was seriously ill, he was summoned to the child's bedside. He knelt and prayed, then he woke the sleeping child and perhaps hypnotized him (whether or not he did so is not known). He then told the mother the child would now recover. It is said that the fever immediately subsided, and the child went back to sleep and was restored to full health. Undoubtedly this story must soon have reached the ears of the Tsarina.

Whatever her actual motivation, everyone appears to accept that Anna Vyroubova played a significant part in Rasputin's introduction to the Tsar and Tsarina.

According to one account, Anna's motives were sinister and it suggests that on 18 July 1907 Rasputin entered the Imperial Palace by a side door. His presence there resulted from carefully laid plans – to which Anna was a party. They were hatched in the home of Countess Golovina, the wife of the Chamberlain to the Court. She, Anna and a number of other influential people were greatly concerned that the Court, as they are said to have put it, was overrun with all sorts of religious fanatics, wild men and wonder workers to the detriment of Russia and her people. It thus became necessary to introduce someone who would have the confidence of the Tsar and Tsarina, but who would report to Countess Golovina and her friends and would also be responsive to their instructions.

Rasputin was suggested as a suitable candidate for the task. This appealed to the bishop who had played such an important part in bringing Rasputin to St Petersburg. Although regarding him as both wild and undisciplined, he evidently saw him as a religious and incorruptible man who, as others testify, was showered with presents, including money, by those who followed him, but took no more than he required for his simple needs and gave the rest to the poor.

Baroness Pistolkors, the morganatic wife of Grand Duke Paul Alexandrovich, is said to have maintained that Rasputin would have his price, and if it were not money, he could probably be bribed by other inducements. V.M.Pourichkevich, a right-wing member of the Parliament, or Duma, and a founder of the Union of True Russians, also favoured the choice of Rasputin, on the basis that since they had dragged him out of the gutter, they could always return him there if he did not serve their purpose. Thus, Anna Vyroubova, who was closest to the Tsarina, was deputed to contact Rasputin and introduce him to the Court.

This decided, the Countess Golovina surprised them all by having anticipated their decision. She told them she had invited him to call that very afternoon and he was expected at any moment. Almost at once, her daughter came into the room to say he had arrived, and there, in the doorway, stood an unkempt man who announced, 'I am here. I, Grigorii Efimovich Rasputin.'

In July, Rasputin was drinking, dancing and copulating with the gypsies, as was his wont. There was the sound of thundering hooves in the distance, followed by the arrival of a number of men on horseback wearing the Tsar's livery, demanding to know, in the name of the Tsar, if a certain Grigorii Efimovich Rasputin were there. One of them told Rasputin that the Tsarevich was ill and he had been recommended as someone who could help. Rasputin asked who had recommended him, and was told it was Anna Vyroubova.

Rasputin fell on his knees and started to pray, covering his face with his hands. Everyone remained silent, whereupon he rose to his feet and said to the messenger, in a loud voice, 'The Tsarevich is dying. I have prayed for him. The crisis is already past. He will recover.' He then jumped on to the horse behind the rider and they galloped off to the Palace. Rasputin had achieved one of his objectives.

It is more probable that Anna Vyroubova, in sponsoring Rasputin, was innocent of any evil designs. She first met Rasputin, it would appear, when she consulted him about her marriage. She had been introduced to him in the home of the Grand Duchess Militsa, shortly before it took place. She had asked Rasputin to tell her whether he thought the marriage would be a happy one. He had told her that the marriage would not last long and that it would not be happy. This prophecy proved to be accurate and thus fortified the favourable impression she had already formed of him. As a result she became his devoted disciple and being close to the Tsarina, was responsible for Rasputin being summoned to the Palace when the Tsarevich became ill and no one was able to cure him. Some accounts, indeed, allege that she fell in love with Rasputin.

One fact, at least, is indisputable. Rasputin found his way into the Palace and, having given every appearance of saving the child's life when all others had failed, won the full and unswerving confidence of the Tsar and Tsarina. It was a remarkable relationship. He showed them far less respect than did their courtiers. He openly detested the Russian nobility, using, according to his own friend, Sumanovich, 'stable language' and taking his food by plunging his dirty hands into his fish soup. Sumanovich also asserts that Rasputin effected his cures by the use of certain Tibetan drugs, which he obtained from a quack doctor called Badmayer; sometimes he used more simple materials; sometimes he used no remedies at all, but created the appearance of doing so, and sometimes he relied entirely on his own willpower.

Bleeding cures were well known to Russian folk medicine, and were passed down from one generation to another. His friend further hypothesizes that Rasputin timed his visits to the ailing child with special care, ensuring that he arrived just as the crises passed, so as to create the impression that it was he who effected the cure. Interesting as these speculations may be, it needs to be noted that if such cures were already well known in Russia, it is odd that none of the attendant doctors knew anything about them. Moreover, it would be exceedingly difficult, and require a not inconsiderable knowledge of medicine and the course of haemophilia, for Rasputin to have known the exact moment at which to make his appearance.

His advent into the highest circles of society did nothing, however, to curb his sexual activities; all it achieved was to transpose his activities from the gypsies (although never entirely) to ladies of position and, in many instances, of previous virtue. Sexual intercourse with Rasputin, he would convince them, was a cleansing process with religious overtones. That they succumbed to one of his appearance, habits and behaviour is surprising.

The Tsarina was unwilling to believe a word of the salacious – though probably true – stories which were carried to her at Court.

When her daughter's governess complained that Rasputin had invaded her bedroom she was unwilling to listen and attributed it to hysteria.

In 1909, the right-wing fanatic Illiodor had been preaching to such effect that he had made many enemies. Indeed, so vociferous had he become that the Tsar banished him to the town of Minsk. Knowing of Rasputin's influence at Court, Illiodor called on him and, as a result, Rasputin took him to see certain of his friends, including Anna Vyroubova, who promptly knelt at Rasputin's feet and kissed his hand. He was next taken to see the Tsarina who, as a result of what Rasputin had to say, suggested they should ask the Tsar to reverse his decree.

This was duly accomplished. It was a grievous error on the part of Rasputin, since Illiodor was destined to become one of his bitterest enemies, who would later join – or perhaps even lead – a plot to kill him. Rasputin's power of prophecy seems to have failed him disastrously at this point. The episode does, however, provide an excellent yardstick against which to measure the power and influence which Rasputin had by now assumed, not only with the Tsarina, but with the Tsar himself.

As his power developed, there were some changes in Rasputin. He trimmed his hair, brushed and combed his beard, and wore blouses of vivid red and blue, one of which was a present from the Tsarina, which she had embroidered herself. He also improved his footwear.

Rasputin's growing influence with the Tsar brought no joy to the Ministers of State. Seblon replaced Lukyanov as Minister of Religion, on the recommendation of Rasputin. Whether Rasputin visited the Palace daily, as one writer asserts, though Pares disputes this, or whether his visits were far less frequent, it seems certain that he often met the Tsarina in the small house near the Palace which Anna Vyroubova had had given to her, and that he often saw the Tsar there as well.

The press ran a campaign against Rasputin, including lurid confessions by his victims and trenchant complaints by their mothers. The Duma debated his behaviour and influence, the mother of Prince Youssoupoff warned the Tsar of the dangers of heeding the advice of this charlatan, but all to no avail. Rodzyanko, the President of the Duma, was so concerned that he discussed the situation with the Dowager Empress. As a result, he sought an audience with the Tsar, telling him that the Dowager Empress had given her blessing to his visit. In the face of this, the President was directed by the Tsar to carry out a full investigation into the myriad allegations against Rasputin.

According to the researches of Pares, one Damensky, an official of the Holy Synod who was close to Rasputin, was required to deliver all the papers collected concerning Rasputin to Rodzyanko. This was reluctantly done, and the papers were handed over to officials at the Duma, only for Damensky two days later to demand their return. Pares quotes from the writings of Rodzyanko: 'He [Damensky] explained that the demand (for the return of the papers) came from a very exalted person. "Who was it?" I asked, "Seblon?" Damensky made a deprecating gesture. "No, someone much more highly placed ..." "Who was it?" I repeated. "The Empress Alexandra." "If that is the case, will you kindly inform her Majesty that she is as much a subject of her august consort as I myself, and that it is the duty of both of us to obey his command. I am not therefore in a position to comply with her wishes."' Here was another example of the extent to which the Tsarina had come under the influence of Rasputin.

Rodzyanko, when his report had been made, sought another audience with the Tsar but this was refused, and no action was taken to remove or even curb the activities of Rasputin. Indeed, when the press fulminations gathered momentum, the Tsar ordered the Minister of the Interior to impose stricter controls on the press.

In 1911 or 1912 affairs (in every sense of the word) had come to such a pass that some action had to be taken.

Rasputin had met a Finnish dancer, with whom he went to a party, ultimately collapsing in a drunken state surrounded by naked women. Reputedly someone took photographs (quite how is not evident since instantaneous cameras with built-in flash had not been invented) and sent the prints to Rasputin. Realizing that someone might show them to the Tsar, with consequences too frightful to contemplate, he decided he would himself show them to him, and did so, saying he was being blackmailed. Nicholas subjected them to close scrutiny and, sighing, told Rasputin he had been foolish and had yielded to temptation. He advised him to leave the capital for a while. Rasputin had no alternative; he returned to his village.

The Imperial family went to a place near the Polish frontier. While they were there, the Tsarevich slipped whilst boarding a boat. He became acutely ill and the doctors gave up hope for him. He was in the most intense pain, and his parents were beside themselves with worry. After their prayers seemed to have no effect, Anna Vyroubova, who was with the Tsar and Tsarina, sent a telegram to Rasputin, to which he replied: 'The illness is not as dangerous as it seems. Do not let the doctors worry him.' From that moment the child recovered, and their faith in Rasputin's powers increased enormously.

The Tsarevich's condition was not such that, if left alone, he would unquestionably have recovered. Following his fall, he had started bleeding internally and a large tumour formed in his groin. He was in excruciating pain, and two surgeons who were called in were unable to open the tumour since they were sure – no doubt correctly – that if they did so he would bleed to death. Indeed, one of the surgeons remarked that only a miracle could save him. Rasputin apparently provided it.

Meanwhile, events of far greater moment were occurring in Europe. Like a vast cauldron it was coming to the boil, and the mixture was being ruthlessly stirred by the German Kaiser. He had established a cordial relationship with Nicholas II, flattering and fawning on him under the guise of sincere friendship. In July 1905, they met by arrangement at Bjorko off the coast of Finland, and the Kaiser persuaded Nicholas to sign a treaty when he had no advising minister with him. It was a term of the alliance that no word of it was to be communicated to the French until it had been made fully effective, when they could have the chance to join if they so desired. When on his return to Russia the Tsar told the Naval Minister to countersign the treaty, Nicholas covered its contents with his hand so that the Minister could not read it. He said he only signed it because he thought it his duty to sign without question whatever the Tsar required him to sign. When, two weeks later, the contents became known to other Ministers, they were emphatic that no such treaty could be implemented without first consulting the French, so that the Tsar was compelled to put the arrangements in abeyance, thus terminating his friendship with the Kaiser.

Bosnia was plunged into the centre of the cauldron when she was annexed by Austria, it having been agreed, long since, by Russia, unbeknown to the Tsar, that such a course had their approval. Then on 28 June 1914, the Archduke Franz Ferdinand, the heir to the Austrian throne, was assassinated at Sarajevo, the capital of Bosnia, and the Serbians, who were closely involved with the Bosnians, were thought to be implicated in the murder.

The Austrian government issued an ultimatum to Serbia which would destroy her independence. Germany declined to intervene, and on 28 July Austria declared war on Serbia. The Russians, expecting that their own land would be invaded, prepared for mobilization, whereupon the Germans expressed their disapproval, indicating that it would precipitate a calamity. This put the Russians on the horns of a dilemma: if they mobilized, they would risk bringing the might of Germany against them; if they did not mobilize, they would most likely have to face an invasion by the Austrian army assisted, as likely as not, by the Germans.

Faced with these alternatives, they decided on general mobilization, and on 1 August 1914 Germany declared war on Russia. On the same day, France mobilized her forces, and on the 3rd Germany declared war on her. England declared war on Germany on 4 August.

Although Russia controlled an empire which stretched from the borders of Poland to those of Japan, containing one hundred and seventy million people, it had an inferior army, a largely illiterate population, was poorly armed and lacked the military capacity of its enemies.

Following his further miraculous treatment of the Tsarevich, Rasputin had returned to St Petersburg even more entrenched with the Imperial family. He was able to exercise his considerable influence in the conduct of a war of which he vociferously disapproved.

Chapter **Four**

There is an old saying that 'you pays your money and you takes your choice,' and this is especially true when it comes to researching the life of Rasputin. Most accounts describe him as a lecherous, ambitious man with some measure of the good which is sometimes found, if you search long enough, in the worst of men. For some, Rasputin was a saintly figure, much maligned and abused.

Certainly, he was bitterly opposed to the oppression, anti-Semitism and corruption which was rife in Russia during his time. He was also bitterly opposed to war. He declared that sovereigns should never make war on each other, said that the Balkans were not worth fighting about, and he sent a telegram to the Tsar reading, 'Let Papa [as he called him] not plan war; for with war will come the end of Russia and yourselves.' This was another of his prophecies which would, in due course, be fulfilled.

As war approached, Rasputin had more personal problems of his own. Early in 1914 came the first attack on his life, which almost succeeded, and his survival seemed to provide the first evidence of a charmed life.

By the beginning of 1914, rumours of Rasputin's wanton conduct had become so widespread that even the Tsar had felt constrained to take action. Rasputin had earlier brought his family to St Petersburg. The Tsar now ordered him to take them back to Pokrovskoe until further notice.

Whilst in the capital, Rasputin's daughter, Maria, had been receiving anonymous telephone calls from a man who told her that he was in love with her and was entranced by her beauty. When, in accordance with the wishes of the Tsar, the family were travelling on a steamer on the way back to their home, Maria was accosted 'by a dark gentleman whose appearance she did not much care for'. He gave the name of Davidson, said he was a journalist and her secret admirer and that he was following her home. Clearly he was really in pursuit of a story which he thought showed promise, having heard of the existence of a plot against Rasputin which seemed worth investigation. As a commentary on the activities of journalists, it shows once again that the more things change the more they remain the same.

What he must have learned was that a woman called Chiona Gusyeva had once been an exceedingly attractive prostitute. She was now grotesque, having been disfigured by syphilis. She was a follower of another alleged mystic, called Illiodor, and believed she was called upon to murder Rasputin. She sought Illiodor's blessing on the venture, which he eagerly gave. Having given it, he evidently recognized that discretion is the better part of valour, shaved off his beard, disguised himself as a woman, and made his way to Sweden, in the hope that he would avoid being implicated.

Having learned that Rasputin was bound for his village, Gusyeva dressed herself as a beggar and went there to await his arrival. A day or so later, her face hidden by a shawl, she approached him in the street and asked him for money. As he put his hand in his pocket, she plunged a knife into his stomach, but Rasputin, being Rasputin, still retained sufficient strength to fend her off and prevent her withdrawing the knife and reinserting it.

The wound was exceedingly serious. It took six hours before a doctor could be obtained. He operated without an anaesthetic, and then sent Rasputin off on a six-hour journey to hospital. The wound had exposed Rasputin's entrails, and the severity of the injury and the manner of treatment meant that death was the probable outcome. Rasputin, however, survived.

Davidson remained in hot pursuit of his story and Maria and in due course prepared a lurid account including further aspersions against Rasputin. It was to little avail; the Palace was alerted to what was afoot and soon forbade any publication of this or any other story of a like nature.

Meanwhile, Gusyeva had been seized the moment after the assault and formally arrested. She asserted that she had resolved to kill Rasputin for abusing his sainthood, heresy and raping a nun. She was imprisoned and later declared insane. It emerged that she had plied her trade in a village where Illiodor had his monastery, and it would seem that it was in reality he who had inspired her to kill Rasputin.

Further misfortunes were to befall. On 15 January 1915, Anna Vyroubova was involved in a railway accident. She was pinned down by an iron girder, sustaining severe injuries to her spine and her skull, and her right leg was broken in two places and crushed. The

Tsarina, who rushed to her aid, took her to hospital. It seemed that she would not survive and the Tsar was called to her bedside. Rasputin did not hear what had befallen her until the next day, probably because he was not on the best of terms with the Tsar, due to his recent conduct.

Pares gives the following account: 'The patient was lying in delirium, murmuring from time to time "Father Gregory, pray for me." The Holy Communion had been administered to her. The Imperial couple were watching by her. Rasputin, without asking leave, entered the room and without a word to the bystanders, took her hand and said "Annushka, wake up! Look at me!" She opened her eyes and murmured "Gregory, That's you! Thank God!" Rasputin turned to the august bystanders and said no more than "She will recover, but she will remain a cripple." He tottered from the room, and fell outside in a faint from which he awoke in a strong perspiration, feeling that all his strength had gone from him. The Empress, writes Mosolov, on returning to the Palace, declared that he had performed a miracle. Rasputin, when speaking of this incident, would say "When I resurrected Anna". She outlived all the other principal characters in this story.'

On 19 January 1915, another attempt was made on Rasputin's life when a troika was driven at him, but once again he foiled the assassins. This was another scheme which bears the mark of having been instigated by Illiodor.

By April, Rasputin was back in trouble once again, and in a fashion which was impossible to overlook. It had become increasingly important for him to observe the proprieties, since it was widely known that he exerted crucial influence within the Palace. With the outbreak of war, the Tsar had seen it as his bounden duty to be with his troops to share their privations and to provide leadership. As a result, the Tsarina was left alone at the Palace, and since she regarded Rasputin as beyond reproach she continued to be very much under his influence. In her correspondence with the Tsar, she left no doubt as to her belief that Rasputin was an emissary from God, and when writing about him as 'he' always employed a capital letter.

Rasputin's latest exploit occurred at a restaurant at a place called Yar where he and his friends took a private room for a party. Soon they were all exceedingly drunk. Rasputin was probably the most drunk of all and was boasting of his great influence within the Palace. He pointed to his blouse, a gift from the Tsarina which she had embroidered herself, and told the assembled throng that 'the old woman' had made it for him. One of the company challenged him to prove he was, indeed, Rasputin, whereupon he opened his flies and displayed his penis for all to see.

This behaviour, which was seen to bring the Imperial family into grave disrepute, soon became public knowledge, and on the advice of his Ministers Nicholas, by then very angry, sent Rasputin packing to his village once again. When the report of his behaviour was brought to the notice of the Tsarina, she burst into tears. Whilst she accepted the accuracy of the allegations, she evidently deplored them and con- sidered – as she wrote to Nicholas – that the 'dirt being spread about one we venerate is more than horrible'. Unquestionably, her judge- ment was clouded by Rasputin's oft-repeated assertion, in his talks with her, that the life of her son was wholly dependent on his presence and prayer – an assertion which, as events had unfolded, had become increasingly difficult to discount.

Until then, the press had been forbidden to write about Rasputin, but public indignation had become so intense that the Ministers took it upon themselves to ignore the royal dictate. They gave permission for accounts to be written in disparaging, although not necessarily untrue terms, but which included the allegation that his known opposi- tion to the war was conditioned by the fact that he was, in reality, in the pay of and working for the Germans.

'How could a dark parvenu,' wrote one journalist, 'make a mockery of Russia for so long? Even if the Senate, the church, the ministers, the Duma itself and the Imperial Council could tolerate such a mockery, how could Russia herself put up with it?'

Was this to be a lesson for Rasputin? Not at all. On his journey back to his home, he again got helplessly drunk, quarrelled with the captain of the steamer, accused a steward of stealing money and then withdrew the accusation, quarrelled violently with passengers, and finished so drunk that he was laid out on the floor of his cabin and had to be carried bodily off the steamer.

Not that any of this stripped him of his power and influence. When his son was called up for the army, he managed to get him a posting as a medical orderly on a hospital train.

By now his influence in Russian affairs was well known. Despite having attracted the displeasure of the Tsar, his relationship with the Tsarina remained exceedingly close and was increasingly resented in high places and even low ones when it became known. Whether or not it was as great as rumour pictured it, or he would himself pretend, there can be no doubt at all that he was still the Tsarina's most revered adviser. Her letters to the unfortunate Tsar, absent with his soldiers, poured out, not always with true attribution, the advice which he should follow, upbraided him when he hesitated to do so, and constantly urged him to follow urgently the advice which had been proffered by 'Him'.

In addition to some very undesirable habits, Rasputin had a number of equally undesirable friends. One of them was a character called Prince Andronnikov. Whilst Rasputin revelled in power for its own sake, Andronnikov's sole purpose in life was acquiring and amassing money. He became almost as close to Rasputin as Rasputin was to the Tsarina – though not quite as close, since one false rumour which constantly surfaced, and persisted, was that Rasputin was her lover as well as her spiritual guide.

Illustrative of the influence which these two men were able to bring to bear was the dismissal and downfall of Sukhomlinov, the Minister of War.

The war was not going well for Russia. The people as a whole were jittery, and ready to believe any explanation which was offered to minimize Russia's manifest deficiencies and inadequacies. There was widespread fear of Germany, and German spies were believed to be everywhere. The presence of a German princess on the throne was not reassuring and the thought of an unwholesome 'Monk' with dirty habits being in the pay of the Germans did nothing to allay public concern.

Rasputin had introduced Anna Vyroubova to Andronnikov who, learning that she was the woman closest to the Tsarina, soon embroiled her in his schemes, providing her with a sum of £10,000, ostensibly to be used for charitable purposes.

He also got into his clutches one Beletsky, a Senator who had been Deputy Chief of Police. Andronnikov's first objective, at the time, was to get rid of the Minister of Internal Affairs, Scherbatov, who, being hostile to Rasputin, was a suitable subject for removal in his eyes as well. The candidate whom they favoured to replace him was A.N.Khvostov, who was well disposed towards Rasputin and as fit to hold office as Caligula's horse. Khvostov first won Anna over to the idea by convincing her of his devotion to Rasputin. She, in turn, persuaded the Tsarina that such an appointment was necessary in view of Rasputin's current state of disfavour with the Tsar. She told her husband Nicholas that Khvostov was 'a very fat young man of much experience and if his body was colossal his soul was high and clean'.

Although Nicholas from time to time expressed to his wife doubts as to the worthiness of some of Rasputin's recommendations for office (one in particular had proved disastrous), and although he must have realized that the Tsarina would have as much difficulty examining Khvostov's soul as the latter would have had trying to examine parts of his own anatomy, the Tsar, with Rasputin surreptitiously prodding in the background, succumbed. Indeed, for good measure they succeeded in getting Beletsky appointed as his Deputy. Thus, Rasputin now had staunch friends not only at Court but outside as well.

The newly appointed Minister lost no time in diverting state funds for Rasputin's use and provided him with a posse of men as a bodyguard at his home. This was ostensibly to allay Rasputin's growing and justified fears that he would be assassinated, and it also enabled Beletsky to keep an eye on what he was about. Rasputin was also given a ministerial car for his constant use, and since the guards lacked one themselves they could only watch him at his home. He was also provided with a personal bodyguard named Komissarov.

Whether by accident or design, Komissarov proved to be almost as objectionable in his habits, and as fond of alcohol, as Rasputin himself, and, not surprisingly, they soon became close friends. The setting now began to take on some of the qualities of an Ayckbourne farce, with Komissarov slyly extracting information as to the secret happenings at Court from Rasputin and passing it on to Beletsky and Khvostov, whilst the unsuspecting Rasputin extracted government information from Komissarov and passed it back to the Court.

Rasputin thus had no difficulty, through these many connections, in getting his way. He secured the removal of two procurators, had an illiterate man made Archbishop of Tobolsk, and secured the appointment to the second most important post in the Church, that of Archbishop of Petrograd, for one Pitirim, a homosexual embezzler.

As can occur with the most profound love affairs, however, this poignant picture of harmony was not to last. Rasputin began to believe that too much power was passing from him to his appointees, and he refused, from time to time, to play their game. They for their part were seriously put out because they considered that, in return for the money and their favour it was Rasputin's bounden duty to do as they bid. What, therefore, was to be done?

Against the background of Russia already painted, no prizes need be offered for the correct answer. Khvostov, in conspiracy with Beletsky, decided that Rasputin must be assassinated. The project was put to Komissarov, who, as one of Rasputin's best friends, thought it a splendid idea – in the interests, of course, of Mother Russia – though he had enough nous to caution Beletsky about the risks of doing Khvostov's dirty work for him. Khvostov remained insistent, however, and as an interim measure it was agreed to start by merely having Rasputin roughed up. Rasputin, it seems, got wind that some unpleasantness was in the offing, and when his intending assailants arrived at the place appointed he was nowhere to be seen.

What followed now resembled the plot of an Italian opera. The Minister, Khvostov, decided there was no future in conspiring with Beletsky (who, in any case, unbeknown to Khvostov, had decided to protect Rasputin). He therefore offered a vast sum of money to Komissarov to undertake the task of killing Rasputin. Komissarov suggested it would be best to use poison and communicated with a number of his criminal contacts, obtaining divers poisons which he proceeded to test on Rasputin's cats.

Komissarov deemed it wise to tell Beletsky of the plot but, knowing that Beletsky no longer extended allegiance to Khvostov, he pretended that it was, in reality, a sham and that the poisons were only coloured water. The cats, however, and Rasputin himself, soon learned otherwise. When Rasputin later returned to his apartment, he found it littered with dead cats. He did not, despite his clairvoyant powers, see this as the prelude to an attack on his own person, rather assuming it to be the petty act of some malicious enemy.

At this point, no doubt, in an Italian opera, the three characters would have broken the story line to sing an appropriate aria. This, however, was no opera. Khvostov, foreseeing no greater success with Komissarov than he had with Beletsky, commissioned one Rzhevsky to kill Rasputin, suggesting that to this end he enlist the support of the villainous Illiodor. Beletsky, having got wind of what was afoot, had Rzhevsky watched. Rzhevsky was found to have perpetrated a financial fraud and was soon persuaded to abandon his mission. Information was also leaked to Rasputin, who complained to the Tsarina that 'Fat Belly', as he called Khvostov, was out to kill him. This should have been the moment in the opera when the Tsarina introduced her contribution in the form of the soprano's aria.

In fact, she took steps to protect Rasputin. Rzhevsky was arrested, and in his possession was found evidence which linked Khvostov directly with the plot. The Minister Khvostov had Beletsky removed to Siberia as the Governor of Irkutsk, which caused the latter to burst into tears. He accordingly appealed to Anna Vyroubova, and in the event Khvostov was dismissed from office and the conspiracy evaporated. Thus the curtain fell on this further unsuccessful endeavour to assassinate Rasputin.

By 1916, Russia was in dire straits. Food was in short supply, there was a lack of firewood, and the air was full of foreboding. The conduct of the affairs of the nation was the subject of constant censure and criticism, all fully justified, and all attributed to the Tsarina's lack of judgement, her intervention being made necessary by the Tsar's absence at the front. In truth, his judgement would have been no better or wiser had it been available. Overall, the feeling remained that the country's misfortunes were due to the evil influence of Rasputin, standing behind the Tsarina.

He, in turn, was showing the ravages of misfortune. He had lost weight, was haggard and drawn and walked in constant fear of assassination. He was prophesying not only his own death but that of the whole of the Imperial family.

Rasputin had earlier used his influence to bring to the notice of the Tsarina the name of Protopopov. Alexandra had lost no time in writing to Nicholas 'I think you could not do better than name him.' Still madly in love with her and responsive to virtually her every wish, the Tsar obediently complied. Protopopov became Minister of the Interior and a fervent supporter of Rasputin, to whom he paid a thousand roubles a month from his own pocket and considerably more from the State's. The guard on Rasputin was lifted at 10 p.m. each night to facilitate the Minister's regular visits to report to him.

As conditions within Russia steadily deteriorated, the news from the front, ironically enough, was marginally better. If the enemy was not, at that precise moment, creeping steadily nearer the capital, revolution was; control of the masses within Russia, in the absence of a firm and determined government, was becoming ever more difficult to exercise. Not surprisingly, the opinion was growing that the only hope of preserving the monarchy was to rid the country of Rasputin.

Chapter **Five**

As we have seen, Prince Youssoupoff played a key part in the murder of Rasputin, but there was no other mention of him in the brief history of the events surrounding Rasputin. Similarly, there is no evidence to show that the Grand Duke Dimitri played any significant part in the political history of Russia at that time, save that he was closer to the Tsar than Youssoupoff had been, was one of those concerned in the murder, and his mother disliked Rasputin as much as he did and warned the Imperial family against him constantly. It is therefore important to know something about these two significant characters in the story.

Felix Youssoupoff, on his mother's side, was descended from the Tartars. The family were reputed to be the richest in Russia. He was born on 24 March 1887, so that by 1934, the time of the civil proceedings against MGM, he was forty-seven years of age. At birth he was small, and so ugly that his brother harshly remarked, 'Disgusting, throw him out of the window.' The Youssoupoffs possessed palaces and vast estates in different parts of Russia, including a summer home in Archangelskoye outside Moscow, which was then, and remains today, one of the show places of the country. It had its own theatre, zoo and glass and porcelain factories in the grounds and was filled, as were all their residences, with vast quantities of priceless treasures and armies of servants.

Whether their residence on the Moika waterway at St Petersburg ranked as a palace or a mere house will be discussed in due course, but to ordinary mortals it had every appearance of being the former rather than the latter. It was vast, bulging with treasure and was, in all respects, a reflection of the limitless wealth which the family possessed. It included a very handsome semi-circular inner court with a colon-nade which led to the garden. The house had been given to Felix's great-great-grandmother, Princess Tatiana, by Catherine the Great.

Felix's mother was the Princess Zenaide, who was the last of the long line of Youssoupoffs, dating back to time immemorial, and when she married Count Felix Soumarakoff she was permitted by the Tsar to retain the family name. Her husband was the illegitimate son of Countess Tienhausen and King Frederick William of Prussia.

The Princess had borne three sons, two of whom had died, and when Felix was born she was hoping for a girl. When she learned that she had given birth to another son and not a daughter, she was devastated, and for the first five years of his life Felix was brought up and dressed as a girl. It was not surprising that he became a homosexual. In his autobiography, he recalls that he used to call out to passers-by in the street, 'Look, isn't baby pretty?' and he recognized that his mother's influence had had a lasting effect on his character.

Christopher Dobson, in a most interesting book which he wrote about him, described him as 'a beautiful, rather than a handsome youth'. His elder brother, Nicholas, who was five years his senior, led a riotous life. According to Felix, he was overbearing and arrogant; he lived, at the age of twenty-one, with a mistress and introduced Felix into his style of life. Felix sang in a soprano voice and would dress as a girl, accompanying his brother on his expeditions. Officers and others would pay court to him, so that, according to Dobson, on one occasion 'he had to flee from their increasingly ardent advances'. The time at which he ceased doing so is not accurately documented, but in his autobiography, *Lost Splendour*, Felix describes his life as a young man as a gay one, using that word in its original and better sense.

On another occasion, Felix's brother got him employment in a night club as a female singer. It ultimately came to the notice of his father, after some visitors to the club had recognized him. His father, a stern military man, was justifiably outraged and went through the roof.

In 1907, Fate dealt a cruel blow to Felix Youssoupoff from which he probably never recovered. His brother, Nicholas, fell deeply in love with the beautiful Countess Marina Heyden, whose father was head of the Chancellery. Prince Serge Obolensky described her as 'much courted, extremely popular, and a great flirt.' She was also engaged to Baron Manteurel of the Horse Guards.

Everyone was against the lovers' wish to bring her engagement to an end so that she could marry Nicholas. He was dragged from her presence and she was forced to marry the Baron. The honeymoon was to be spent in Paris, and Nicholas followed them there, ostensibly to hear Chaliapin sing, which was not at all what he had in mind. The Youssoupoffs sent Felix to Paris to watch over his brother, but he was so concerned at what he discovered that he summoned his parents to follow him. The Baron at first said he would agree to a divorce, but he later changed his mind, and was given such a difficult time by his outraged brother officers that he challenged Nicholas to a duel.

Nicholas accepted the challenge and chose pistols; the duel took place and Nicholas was shot dead. His death virtually destroyed his mother, who changed from a gregarious fun-loving person into a recluse, and Felix was so desolate that he contemplated suicide. In his despair he was helped by the Grand Duchess Elizabeth Feodorovna, the sister of the Tsarina, who built a convent and became its Mother Superior. The sisters became estranged because of the Grand Duchess's constant endeavours to separate the Tsarina from Rasputin. Grand Duchess Elizabeth became Felix's mentor.

In 1909, Felix went up to University College, Oxford. He was evidently a popular undergraduate and participated in London social life to the full, taking a flat in Knightsbridge for lavish entertaining. After three years he got his degree, the purpose of which, he said, 'was to fit myself to be of greater use to Russia and my Emperor on my return'.

It was in 1909 too, on his return to Russia after having travelled to Oxford to make arrangements for his entry into the university, that Felix Youssoupoff first met Rasputin. His family were friendly with Countess Golovina, whose youngest daughter, Munia, had become a great admirer of Rasputin, believing he had been sent into the world 'to purify and clean our souls and to guide our thoughts and actions'. She arranged for Youssoupoff to meet him. He duly went to the Golovinas' house on the Winter Canal on the appointed day, and he later described his meeting with the 'holy' man as follows:

In a little while the door opened and Rasputin came in with short quick steps. He walked up to me, said 'Good Evening, My Boy' and attempted to kiss me. I drew back instinctively. He smiled maliciously and going up to Madamoiselle Golovina and then to her mother, he calmly put his arms around them and gave each of them a resounding kiss. From the very first his self-assurance irritated me and there was something about him which disgusted me. He was of middle height, muscular and thin. His arms were disproportionately long, and just where his untidy crop of hair began to grow there was a great scar, which I found out later was the mark of a wound received during one of his highway robberies in Siberia. He seemed to be about forty, and with his caftan, baggy breeches and great top boots, he looked exactly what he was – a peasant. He had a low common face framed by a shaggy beard, coarse features and a long nose, with small shifty grey eyes sunken under heavy eyebrows.

Youssoupoff did not in the least see him as a holy man; to him he seemed like a 'lascivious, malicious satyr, unctuous, wicked, crafty and sensual'. After recommending Felix to take Miss Golovina as his spiritual spouse, Rasputin left, and shortly afterwards Youssoupoff returned to England.

At St Petersburg in 1913, the Grand Duke Alexander Mikhailovich, the Tsar's cousin, called on Youssoupoff's parents to discuss the possibility of a marriage between him and his daughter Irina. Her mother, the Grand Duchess Xenia, was the Tsar's sister. Felix described Irina as 'a girl of dazzling beauty'. Before the engagement, his friend the Grand Duke Dimitri asked Felix if he really intended to marry Irina. When he assured Dimitri that he did, the latter replied, 'I too intend to marry her and I have never been so serious in my life.' Irina, however, had set her heart on Felix, much to the dismay of Dimitri, whose feelings towards Felix were never quite the same afterwards.

In his autobiography, Youssoupoff relates that his engagement ran into trouble, but he failed to vouchsafe any explanation for this. Evidently, the trouble was that Irina's parents were far from overjoyed at the prospect of their daughter's marriage to an active homosexual. Indeed, so notorious were his activities in the circles in which he moved that to 'do a Youssoupoff' was the colloquial term to describe homosexual conduct. Irina's father sent a Count Mordvinoss to see Felix to ask him whether the stories were true and to give some account of his proclivities. He was then invited to lunch with the parents, and appears to have won them over and secured their consent to the marriage, explaining, untruthfully, that whilst he had been a homosexual, he no longer was.

There was further trouble after the engagement was announced. Youssoupoff wrote of 'disagreeable rumours' about him, but in the words of the popular novelettes Love conquered all, and they were married on 22 February 1914 in the chapel of the Anichkoff Palace.

The young couple left Russia on their honeymoon. In July they were in Germany, where omens of war were everywhere apparent. On 30 July Russia ordered general mobilization. The Youssoupoffs managed, with some difficulty, to return to Russia via Finland.

A daughter was born to them on 25 March 1915.

When war came, Felix's father was Governor-General of Moscow, but as a result of his ineptitude in controlling the anti-German riots he was sacked, which made his wife feel bitter towards the Imperial family.

Not the least surprising part of the story of Rasputin and the Prince is the fact that Youssoupoff took part in the assassination at all. It was, by any standards, a vicious, brutal and sadistic attack, and everything about Youssoupoff seems to have marked him out as an unlikely participant. He clearly had no stomach for the war. He saw no military service, using his rank to stay out of the army at a time when persons of rank might have thought it provided the best possible reason for defending the country. He is described as a flamboyant man of great charm but extremely selfish, lacking staying power and loving the fleshpots.

He was fastidious in his dress, a devoted partygoer and, by all accounts, a shallow thinker. He was a rabid anti-Semite, attributing every misfortune which befell Russia to the Jews, the Germans and the Freemasons. He was clearly embarrassed by, and far from proud of, his homosexuality. Indeed, he is said to have attempted a number of 'cures', and it is at least possible that Rasputin had been invited to assist him in this regard perhaps using hypnosis or other means. Other accounts would have it that, far from endeavouring to eradicate Youssoupoff's homosexuality, Rasputin and he felt a mutual attraction, which Rasputin fostered.

Youssoupoff was neither involved in the political life of Russia, nor was he actively involved in the affairs of the Palace; he appears to have contributed little or nothing to the welfare of his country, save for giving his services to the poor for a short time, following the death of his brother and at the suggestion of his mentor, the Grand Duchess Elizabeth. In short, a more unlikely candidate for a gruesome assassination in a political cause would be difficult to find.

He described himself, as the 'Man who murdered Rasputin', but even that is not strictly accurate. He was the man who attempted to murder him. It is true that, in English law, he was guilty of the murder because all those who actively take part in such a joint venture commit the crime, but it was Pourichkevich who actually shot Rasputin and dispatched him, after Youssoupoff's attempts had failed.

Be that as it may, by August 1916 he had decided that he had to dispose of Rasputin for the good of Russia. He believed that with him removed, the influence which he exercised over the Tsar and Tsarina would disappear, which was correct; and that things would be stabilized and would start moving in favour of Russia and the Imperial family, which was wrong.

He claimed that the decisive factor for him was a conversation which he had with the President of the Duma. 'What can one do,' asked that dignitary, 'when all of the ministers and most of the people in close contact with His Majesty are the tools of Rasputin? The only solution is to kill the scoundrel, but there's not a man in Russia who has the guts to do it. If I weren't so old, I would do it myself.'

The origins of the actual conspiracy are not easy to define. According to the researches of Alex de Jonge, as shown in his book, Youssoupoff's first step was to consult a jurist and Duma member, Malakoff. He told him that Rasputin must either be bought off or killed. Malakoff did not take him seriously, whereupon Youssoupoff said, 'If you will not or cannot bribe him, there is no choice. He must be killed and that is what I have just decided to do.' Later in the conversation, he said that he could not do the job himself, since he was practically a member of the Imperial family and it would be tantamount to revolution for him to do it. He got short shrift from Malakoff, who told him the killing was pointless, since someone else would immediately take Rasputin's place.

In his memoirs, however, Youssoupoff asserts that the first person he approached was a Captain Soukhotin, who had been wounded and was receiving treatment at St Petersburg, and with whom he had become friendly. He says he consulted Malakoff much later.

Certainly, he also consulted Dimitri at an early stage, but since he had married Irina, whom Dimitri wanted, it was clear that their friendship had been greatly strained.

Dimitri expressed willingness to assist but he had to return to the military HQ, although he anticipated being sent back to St Petersburg shortly. In conversation with Soukhotin, it was decided that Youssoupoff would have to establish a relationship with Rasputin in order that an effective plan of action could be devised.

Dimitri was aide-de-camp to the Tsar and had spent most of his time carrying out official duties for him. He was, it would appear, a young man who was easily led, but he too was convinced that it was vital to rid the Tsar of Rasputin's influence and, by that means, the misguided influence of the Tsarina.

Youssoupoff's next task was to arrange for Miss Golovina, who had previously introduced him to Rasputin, to arrange another meeting. They met the following day. He noticed a change in Rasputin. He was now very fat and puffy and was decked out in an embroidered silk blouse and full velvet breeches. He winked, smiled and embraced Felix, asking him when he was going to the front. Since Felix had not the slightest intention of going there (he had joined a military academy known as the Corps des Pages, which was a training ground for higher official posts in the army), he was not greatly pleased by the observation, knowing that Rasputin knew that the front was the last place at which he was likely to be seen.

In his book, Youssoupoff observes that as Rasputin had claimed the gift of curing all diseases, he thought a good way of gaining his confidence would be to invite him to cure his ailments. His particular trouble, he told Rasputin, was a feeling of intense fatigue. It was more likely that he sought a cure for his instability or homosexuality.

However, before much progress was made, Rasputin was called to the telephone and left hurriedly. That evening, Miss Golovina telephoned Felix to apologize on behalf of Rasputin for his hurried exit, inviting him to call again the next day, and to bring his guitar with him.

When he met Rasputin again the following day, Rasputin told him that his hasty retreat had been due to a call from the Palace. His nomination of Protopopof had run into trouble. He explained he had soon rectified this, settling the Tsar and Tsarina's anxieties by simply shouting at them and threatening to leave them if they did not do his bidding.

Felix then sang to the company with his guitar, after which Rasputin promised to take him to visit the gypsies. He then proceeded to embarrass his hosts by explaining to them exactly what went on when he was with the gypsies.

Youssoupoff soon established a close relationship with Rasputin, paying many visits to his home. If his account is to be accepted, it was not long before he was warning Miss Golovina, the devoted disciple of Rasputin, who confided everything she knew to him, that he would be well advised to leave St Petersburg since 'someone will end by murdering him'. It was all very odd. He started to implement his plot by discussing his plan with a minister of the Crown, or at least did so at an early stage; he appears to have discussed it next with a number of others, and then proceeded to warn his intended victim of the danger.

Presumably he was not yet rid of his 'intense fatigue', since he records that Rasputin renewed his promise to rid him 'of his disease' and he returned again to Rasputin's home, where Rasputin exercised his 'hypnotic power', gently running his hand over Felix's chest, neck and head, before kneeling and murmuring a prayer. Precisely what was his state of dress while this was achieved is not described. Felix fell into a torpor, with his body numb, as he gazed into Rasputin's 'glittering eyes'. However, he resisted succumbing to his mastery completely, and when Rasputin pulled him roughly by the arm he came to and departed.

This ritual was repeated on many subsequent occasions, including one when Rasputin offered to make Felix a minister, which he declined, asking, 'What kind of a minister would I make?' and offering rather to help Rasputin secretly.

According to Youssoupoff's account, it was after all these visits that he consulted the Minister Malakoff, and since he was unwilling to assist the conspirators, Youssoupoff, Dimitri and Soukhotin decided the only effective way to deal with the problem was by poison. They also determined that it was better to do the deed at Felix's home rather than Rasputin's, and at this stage they drew in Dr Lazavert. They all decided, he asserted, that no matter what the consequences of their act, they would never disclose their participation in Rasputin's murder. This decision made, Felix was off to see Malakoff again to tell him what they had planned. He wanted no part in it, but providing him with this intelligence seems to have been a curious prelude to their resolve to keep secret their part in the plot.

Dimitri and the other conspiritor, Pourichkevich, had to leave for the front, so events had to await their return. When this time came, they fixed 16 December 1916 as the date when they would carry out the deed.

Chapter Six

Youssoupoff's fellow conspirator V.M.Pourichkevich was a notorious and exotic figure on the right of Tsarist parliamentary politics. He had conducted a sustained campaign against Rasputin and, by 1916, probably because of the influence exerted by Rasputin, had been equally aggressive in his attacks on the Imperial family. He was an unstable man who would show his dislike of the left wing by appearing in the Duma with a red flower protruding from his flies.

His instability flowed over into a constitutional inability to keep a secret. He spoke to Malakoff and told him he knew of his conversation with Youssoupoff; he broadcast the fact that Rasputin was about to be killed; he told a fellow member of the Duma the date the murder would occur and told Sir Samuel Hoare that he and his friends were about to liquidate Rasputin.

By analogy with Dr Johnson's dog walking on his hind legs, the occasion for surprise was not that the conspirators' plans for the murder of Rasputin were so poorly conceived, but that, with such a man involved, they were able to do the deed at all.

A basement room at the Moika Palace was chosen as the best location for the murder and it was necessary to give it a lived-in appearance. Workmen were engaged to lay carpets and put up curtains. Furniture was moved into the room, ornaments, a large Persian carpet and a white rug. Tea was to be available, as well as biscuits, cakes and wines, some intended to be treated with a more than adequate quantity of potassium cyanide.

Somewhat infelicitously, Youssoupoff had chosen for the deed the day before that on which he was to sit his examinations at the Corps des Pages. He spent the afternoon with his crammer, preparing. He then went to the Cathedral of Our Lady of Kazan, where he prayed for two hours.

Shortly after 11 p.m., his accomplices arrived. Dr Lazavert donned rubber gloves, ground the cyanide crystals to powder and prepared a suitable number of the cakes and a quantity of the wine. The table was then put into a state of slight disarray, chairs were pushed back and some of the tea poured into cups to give the appearance of a room that had been recently put to use. It was further agreed between them that the gramophone should be playing upstairs when Rasputin arrived, to create the impression that some sort of a party was in progress up there, and as they had only one record, 'Yankee Doodle came to Town', they would have to play it over and over again for a suitable period of time. Then Youssoupoff and Dr Lazavert donned their overcoats and set off to collect their quarry.

It was not until about 3.30 a.m. that the deed had been done and Rasputin was finally dead. Why it took so long to kill him has never been satisfactorily explained. A later autopsy indicated that a greyish-brown substance had been found in his stomach. The possibility has been advanced that the poison was, for some reason, weak and ineffective. Another theory is that the presence in the stomach of carbohydrates may have delayed the poison's effect. It is recorded that the stomach contained 'a ductile mass, dark brown in colour' and that on his deathbed Dr Lazavert confessed to another White Russian doctor that at the last moment he could not bring himself to break his Hippocratic oath and he had substituted some harmless crystals for the potassium cyanide. Whatever the explanation, one thing remained definite: Rasputin had finally been killed.

When the police eventually called on Youssoupoff later that morning in order to investigate the shooting of Rasputin (which Pourichkevich had admitted to the policeman who heard the shots), Youssoupoff denied all knowledge of it, insisting that Rasputin had never visited his house. He justified the lie on the grounds that he was still bound by his oath not to disclose the identity of the conspirators.

Although he told the police superintendent that Pourichkevich and Dimitri had been guests at his home the previous evening, he withheld the doctor's name when asked to identify his other guests.

In the hope that his part in the assassination would never be discovered, Youssoupoff spent the day cleaning up the house. Perhaps as some indication of his true nature, he shot one of his own dogs through its open mouth to give credence to the story he had told the policeman, and to confuse Rasputin's bloodstains with the dog's. There was so much blood about, however, that even the Russian police saw through the ruse and discounted it. The poor dog had died in vain.

As the river was frozen, they had difficulty in finding Rasputin's body. Bloodstains on the bridge gave a clear indication of where the body had been thrown in, and finally it was found. The autopsy disclosed three shots, other wounds which resembled stabbings, and water in the lungs indicating that Rasputin was still alive when thrown into the water.

As the news of his death sped round Russia, feelings were mixed. Many of the poor greeted the news with despair, for they regarded Rasputin as the voice of the people. The aristocrats, apart from the Imperial family itself, were delighted, although a few believed his murder might bring more trouble than good.

The Tsar, at the earnest request of his wife, who was devastated, at once returned to St Petersburg from the front. Youssoupoff was far from happy, for he was convinced that the Tsarina's first action would be to have him shot out of hand. Dimitri, like Youssoupoff, was desperately trying to distance himself from the whole affair, declaring he certainly had no blood on his hands. Nicholas finally decided upon the action he would take: Dimitri was dispatched, as a form of banishment, to serve with the army in Persia, and Youssoupoff was banished to his estates in distant Kursk.

Rasputin was buried in the presence of the Imperial family and their ladies-in-waiting, the Tsar recording in his diary, 'Just after eight the whole family went to the field where we were present at a sad spectacle: the coffin with the body of unforgettable Grigorii, killed on the night of the 16th by savages in the house of F. Youssoupoff, was let down into the grave.'

There Rasputin's body remained until the Revolution when, in early 1917, it was disinterred and burned.

In 1917, though the Revolution was beginning to take shape, Youssoupoff still managed to return to St Petersburg for two months, taking his wife with him. The objective was to see Kerensky, who had become Premier, to enlist his support in protecting the Dowager Empress (Princess Youssoupoff's grandmother), who had been rudely turned out of bed by soldiers searching her house in the Crimea. With some courage the Princess called on Kerensky at the Winter Palace, where he had now taken up residence with his mistress.

In St Petersburg, as at Kursk, the Youssoupoffs continued to live off the fat of the land as Russia sank into bloody revolution. Before leaving the city, Felix Youssoupoff hid some of the vast art collection in the cellars of the Moika Palace. He took most of the diamonds to Moscow, plastering them into a wall at his palace there.

By early 1917 all hopes of winning the war had evaporated. Food was in short supply and conditions generally were appalling. The time was soon reached when neither the government nor the army command was in control. By March the Revolution was in full swing. The Winter Palace fell to the mob. It was not long before Nicholas abdicated in favour of his son, but to no avail. The Soviets took over, and by July the Imperial family had fled to Tobolsk. Kerensky's provisional government was soon overthrown by the Bolsheviks.

In March 1918, Lenin, who had assumed control, deserted the allies and made peace with Germany. The Germans, who had marched into the Crimea, are said to have invited Youssoupoff to become Tsar – a token one, it is suspected – which offer he declined.

On 16 July 1918, Tsar Nicholas, the Tsarina and their children, together with all the servants who had loyally stayed with them, were brutally murdered. The other members of the Imperial family soon met a similar fate whenever the Bolsheviks could locate them. However, in March 1919, HMS *Marlborough*, dispatched by Britain, arrived at Sebastopol on the Black Sea and rescued as many as they could find and persuade to leave. In April, the battleship sailed carrying the Dowager Empress and many others, including the Youssoupoffs. The ship made for Constantinople and from there proceeded to Malta. The Grand Duchess, the Emperor's mother, was allowed to travel to England in another battleship, but the Bolshevik government, concerned at the arrival in England of those who might be thought to be planning a counter-revolution, would allow no others to follow.

Youssoupoff and his wife were not welcome in England, so they made their way, via Italy, to Paris, where they had many friends. The Youssoupoffs lived in the Hôtel Vendôme. Various valuables which had, from time to time, been left in Europe were used to provide the means to support them. Moreover, a jeweller unexpectedly arrived bringing with him a large quantity of diamonds which they had some time before deposited with him. The difficulty was that Youssoupoff had never had to apply his mind to financial affairs. As a result, it did not occur to him that money was something which, if you spent it to excess, had a habit of running out, and that you needed other sources to replenish it.

In 1919 the Youssoupoffs were to be found in London, in a flat in Knightsbridge. Quite how that was achieved is not clear, but the flat was one which he had occupied previously whilst he was an undergraduate at Oxford. He appears to have kept open house, and for some time his life seemed to be made up of fancy dress balls, parties and a general continuation of his usual extravagant ways.

During 1919, the bag of diamonds which had been brought to him in Paris – said by a newspaper to be worth £15,000 – was lost but was subsequently found.

Following this, the Youssoupoffs returned to France, occupying a fine house in the Rue Gutenburg. In the past, they had been wise in the disposition of their assets, having a villa in Switzerland, jewellery which they had brought with them from Russia and two Rembrandts. It was not surprising, however, with his extravagant lifestyle, that when 1921 arrived, he began to have recourse to pawning some of the jewellery.

While in London, Youssoupoff entered into a bargain with a wealthy art collector under which he sold the two Rembrandts for £100,000, subject to the right to buy them back at that figure, plus annual interest of 8 per cent, provided he repurchased before January 1924. When the art collector, who was American, arrived back in the United States, he wrote to say he had changed his mind and would not proceed unless a further condition was added that if Felix bought the pictures back, he would not resell them for ten years. Because of the state of his finances, this new condition had to be accepted.

Reinforced with this extra fortune, the life of continuous gaiety carried on unabated. By 1923, he was in grave danger of losing his paintings. He approached Calouste Gulbenkian, who agreed to lend him the money to recover the paintings, but the American art collector refused to honour the agreement. Youssoupoff then embarked on his chequered career of litigation; he instituted proceedings against the collector in the United States, and he and the Princess made their way to America to do battle.

There was, however, another and, perhaps, even more important reason for the journey. The Prince was hoping to dispose of jewellery there, where the price obtained was likely to be considerably more than would be realized elsewhere. It was therefore a great shock for him when the American Customs seized all his possessions on the basis of stories spread around that the jewels had been stolen from the Tsar. The American visit was not proceeding according to plan, and it took a decidedly worse turn when, at a dinner he attended with his wife, his hostess introduced them as Prince and Princess Rasputin.

As a result of these misfortunes, the Youssoupoffs lived a hand-to-mouth existence in a small and wholly inadequate flat.

The Prince was able to arrange for Pierre Cartier to give him an advance on the sale of some of the jewels, and thus armed with $75,000 and the rest of his possessions, he returned to Paris. Shortly before that, he was delighted to learn that Cartier, on his behalf, had sold some particularly valuable black pearls which he owned for $400,000.

In 1925, Prince Youssoupoff lost his case against the American art collector. The Supreme Court, with a degree of sophistry which is by no means alien to the courts in that bastion of democracy pronounced that, by the terms of the agreement with the American art collector, the Prince could only redeem the jewels with his own money and not with money provided by a third party.

In 1924, he set up a dressmaking business in London with some Russian friends, which he called Irfe (from Irina and Felix). The venture prospered. He then joined in the promotion of a restaurant called La Maisonette. Irfe now branched out into establishments at Le Touquet, and Berlin, and a second branch in London. By 1927, however, the businesses had gone into decline, and he faced troublesome times. Along came Mrs William Vanderbilt to pay the bills which he was unable to meet, but even she failed to provide sufficient funds to cover future contingencies.

In 1928, he made his next sortie into litigation with some measure of success. Three London newspapers, the *Sunday Express*, the *Daily News* and the *News of the World*, repeated a story which had been published in a Russian newspaper printed in Paris and later denied, that he had been expelled from Paris on account of a society scandal. The redoubtable barrister Valentine Holmes appeared for the newspapers, which withdrew the allegation and agreed to pay Youssoupoff's costs and a sum to be paid to Russian charities in France. By then, Youssoupoff could have made good use of this money himself, and it is to his credit that he so generously donated it.

Meanwhile, he had written and published a book about Rasputin and he was dismayed when the holy man's daughter, Maria, basing her case on the admissions and statements contained in the book, brought an action against him and Dimitri for damages for the murder of her father. She hoped to recover £200,000. It was a new and unwelcome occurrence for Youssoupoff to find himself cast as a defendant to litigation. The case was brought in France and, fortunately for the Prince, the court accepted his French lawyers' argument that the case dealt with political issues in a foreign jurisdiction and dismissed the claim. Since the book had presumably been published in France, this curious decision can only be justified by reference once again to the vagaries of a different body of foreign law.

Youssoupoff's luck appeared to be running out. Piece by piece, his valuable possessions had been sold – the jewellery, the properties, all he owned. His businesses failed, the banks refused to give him credit, and his only visitors were bailiffs, who by then found nothing to satisfy them. By one of those ironic quirks of fate which life so often presents, the Prince, the rabid anti-Semite, was to seek succour from none other than the Jews themselves.

Chapter **Seven**

The events in Europe in 1916 may have seemed remote from those in the United States of America in the early thirties. The famous roaring lion which preceded the opening of films produced by the great conglomerate of Metro-Goldwyn-Mayer gave one of its roars in 1932, and the reverberations reached the ears of Felix Youssoupoff.

Once the film industry became a possibility, it was, for the most part, the new Americans, immigrants from Europe, who established it and subsequently maintained it. One of these was Marcus Loew. His father, Hermann, a Jewish waiter, had come from Austria. In America he married a German widow, Ida Sichel, already the mother of two children. Marcus came into the world in the slums of the East Side of New York.

Marcus, whom his friends called Max, was selling newspapers on the streets at the age of six. For a short time he went to high school, selling his newspapers at night and, during the summer holidays, selling lemons to housewives and saloons. He left school at the age of nine and worked in a map-colouring plant, pulling the maps from the vast presses, which he did for ten hours a day for six days a week. His energy was equalled only by his ambition. Having tried to make a success of a partnership in a small printing business, which was necessarily starved of cash and failed, and having worked in a furniture store, he went to work in a fur factory, where he found himself, at the age of twelve, working eleven and a half hours a day, turning the crank on a heavy fur-cutting table.

Six years later, at the age of eighteen, and with savings of sixty-three dollars, he decided to move into independent broking, buying and selling fur pelts. When, as was not unusual in that trade, he went bankrupt, he found that his creditors were the losers by $1,800. When he told them that, despite the fact that his bankruptcy had relieved him of all liability to repay the money he owed them, he nevertheless would not rest until he had seen them paid, they eyed him with understandable scepticism; they had heard that story before. He obtained employment selling furs for another employer, earning about $100 a week and, as he had promised, repaid every cent he owed.

That promise honoured, Marcus married Caroline Rosenheim, but he encountered further financial problems, so that his fortune was reduced to a sum of seven dollars, as a result of a further endeavour to start another fur business of his own. He turned, once again, to paid employment.

Again he began to prosper, developing his innate ability as a salesman. He had managed to amass some savings when his work brought him into contact with Adolph Zukor and Morris Kohn, Chicago fur merchants, and they became firm friends. Those two were invited to acquire the lease of a penny arcade. This contained numerous forms of amusement, including 'peep hole motion pictures', which showed moving pictures on the insertion of a coin. The venture was a success, and when it was expanding Loew asked whether he might be allowed to invest in it.

From these small beginnings was formed the People's Vaudeville Company, in which Loew was one of the investors, and of which he became the manager for $100 per week, plus a share of the profits to be paid to him in stock. His investment in this company had necessitated the withdrawal of his investment with Zukor and Kohn, and in their place he had Hermann Baehr, who had been the last to employ him as a salesman, and an actor with whom he had earlier become friendly, David Warfield. Before long, Loew bought out the other investors; he opened three more arcades in New York and, in Cincinnati, opened the Penny Hippodrome.

By this time, theatres had elsewhere been opened which showed relatively primitive films. Loew was so impressed with the potential that he began to exhibit them in the Penny Hippodrome. His first venture was a 'bio-graph' called *Hot Chestnuts* and 5,000 people wanted to get into the theatre. This was not to be easily achieved, since the seating capacity was only 110. But the demand was there, and Loew soon turned his other establishments to similar use.

The die was cast and Loew's destiny launched. His next move was into theatre, where he tried out a scheme for showing motion pictures with live actors behind a screen speaking the dialogue.

He had re-established his relationship with Adolph Zukor, and both were also involved with Ludvigh and the Schenks – all to become names to conjure with in the film industry. By 1910, their interests had moved so rapidly ahead that the People's Vaudeville was enlarged into

Loew's Consolidated Enterprises, and it was not long before it was decided that it should be taken over by Loew's Theatrical Enterprises with a capital of $5,000,000.

By 1919, Loew had progressed from his early beginnings selling newspapers on street corners to the control of theatres located all over America. Loew's Incorporated, as a title, was brought back into existence, with a capital of $9,500,000; serving with him on the board were the President of General Motors, the Vice-President of Bankers Trust and the President of Liberty National Bank.

While Loew had been developing his interests, another young man of similar background had been moving along the same road. Louis Burt Mayer had been brought to the United States from Russia by his parents, Jacob and Sara. They had little money, but he too went into the theatre business and from there into pictures, forming en route the Metro Picture Corporation. Metro was short for Metropolitan. Amongst the famous stars whom they had under contract were the Barrymores, and when, in one of her films, Ethel Barrymore played a Russian princess, one of the extras on the lot was Leon Trotsky, who would become even more famous than the Barrymores.

Zukor resigned from Loew's company and formed the Famous Players Company in order 'to make famous plays with famous players'. He produced a number of elaborate films, but Loew decided he was more assured of success with the smaller features which he was producing, starring Mary Pickford. He soon came to realize, however, that more extravagant productions would be required in the future.

Over the years other great combines had been brought into existence. Loew's Incorporated had continued to grow, so that by 1924, following complex and protracted successes, failures and machinations, Loew's acquired Metro Goldwyn Pictures Corporation, with Mayer as Vice-President, and to preserve his full identity with the combine the credit line was introduced 'Produced by Metro-Goldwyn-Mayer'.

In 1934 the MGM studio was under the control of Irving Thalberg, who also became a legend in the film industry; his beginnings and progress through life was another of those stories which would have graced the screen. Born in Brooklyn, New York, he began life with significantly greater advantages than had Max Loew. His father lived in moderately comfortable circumstances, carrying on the business of an importer of lace, but Irving Thalberg was beset by illness which, with some courage, he overcame.

A chance meeting between Irving's mother, Henrietta, and Carl Laemmle, the head of the powerful Universal Picture Corporation, resulted in her obtaining a post for her son in a small secretarial capacity with that company. By a combination of cheek, ambition, determination and undoubted genius for the activities of the film world, he contrived to become an indispensable force within it. He had wrongly believed, with the advent of talking pictures, that they would be something of a passing phase and would not last. He soon realized, however, that he had been mistaken, and in 1928 a not too impressive film was screened at the Astor Theatre, New York, called *White Shadows*, which had a dubbed musical score, one of the cast audibly saying 'Hello', and for the first time the film was introduced by the roaring of the MGM lion.

1929 brought a further milestone, with the production of *The Broadway Melody*, the principal setting for the song 'The Wedding of the Painted Dolls', being presented in full colour.

In 1934, MGM, under Thalberg, by now happily married to the renowned film star Norma Shearer, announced that it was to embark on a great picture which was to feature the three greats, Ethel, John and Lionel Barrymore. The film would be the story of the Russian monk, Rasputin and his violent death. The Barrymores would share the honours: Lionel would play Rasputin, Ethel the Tsarina, and John the Russian Prince who had committed the murder.

If ever a theme needed to be approached with care, this was it. Some of the participants in the historic events were still alive, and to bandy about allegations of murder and intrigue involved the sort of material which causes libel lawyers to jump on their hind legs and cavort around with joy and anticipation.

The film industry, being so closely related to the theatre, had already absorbed the thespian principle that 'it will be all right on the night'. Local difficulties were things to be manfully ignored. The problem which faced MGM was that Ethel Barrymore had a stage appearance to which she was committed, and if her services were to be available filming had to start at once. The fact that the script had not yet reached anything approaching completion was one of the local difficulties.

When the first draft of the script emerged, it left a great deal to be desired. The Russian tragedy had been dressed up with orgies in which the Russian princes took part, a plethora of naked women and, with an appropriate eye on the censor, a large helping of human sin.

The director was one Charles Brabin, who seems to have been chosen because he had Russian ancestry. Another factor in the choice, it has been suggested, is that he was the husband of Theda Bara, probably the original screen sex symbol. He had originally been retained as the director of the great (MGM called it 'fabulous') film *Ben-Hur*, but he had been taken off the picture and another director substituted.

The supervisor of the film, Bernie Hyman, doubted the quality of the first draft, and therefore engaged a series of scriptwriters, one after the other, to write fresh scripts or rewrite the earlier ones. Finally, the choice for this difficult task fell on Charles MacArthur. So many changes were constantly being required, that he had the greatest difficulty in writing fast enough to keep himself a day ahead of the actors.

In addition, all engaged in the production had to cope with the Barrymores, who were regarded as the Royal Family of Hollywood and behaved accordingly. Coping with only one Barrymore could be difficult; coping with all three, who had never before appeared in a film together, verged on the impossible.

At least Lionel had foreseen the difficulty. When told that his siblings were to appear with him, he retorted, 'And who's the poor son of a gun that's got to direct us?' Like Churchill, Lionel could cat-nap. During the filming, when the director called 'Camera' and Lionel was supposed to move on to the set, he stood quite still – he was asleep standing upright.

The film was being made in the early days of 'talking pictures', and Ethel Barrymore, who had established an outstanding reputation as a stage actress, had never before appeared in a talking film. At one point, she was to be depicted at a shrine – on her knees – praying for the life of her son, the Tsarevich, to the effigy of St Gregory. Her lips were seen moving in silent prayer, intended to be inaudible. From the back of the set, Lionel, having forgotten that the picture had sound, proceeded to chat while waiting off camera. Without rising, still with a beatific expression on her face, her lips still moving as if in prayer, the first lady of the stage, inquired in a loud, well-modulated voice, with appropriate American expletives, who the hell was making all the noise. When the scene was finished and the cameras halted, she came to her feet so urgently, and in such anger, that she twisted her ankle. What she told her brother Lionel is not a matter of record.

Her movements were so redolent of the stage that for much of the time her arms obstructed the camera's view of the acting on the set. When the director endeavoured to correct her, she maintained that she had done it correctly and had stood in the correct position.

When asked to play a scene in a particular way – it having been explained that a Tsarina would not do it the way Miss Barrymore wanted to do it – she would retort, 'Oh wouldn't she! You forget I knew Her Majesty personally. It is exactly as she would have done it.' This was, in some respects, accurate. True, Miss Barrymore had never been at the Imperial Court in Russia, but she had met the Tsarina whilst the latter was in London to attend the funeral of Queen Victoria. When the Tsarina was told that there was an actress present who bore a striking resemblance to her, she asked for Miss Barrymore to be presented to her, after which, it is said, they became friends. John Barrymore, also, had met the Grand Duke Alexander and Prince Youssoupoff. With the Barrymores available, acting and working out the story, it sometimes seemed that scriptwriters were a superfluous luxury.

To do justice to Lionel Barrymore, he clearly demonstrated that the ultimate quality of a performance is a reflection of the care and dedication which is put into it. He had made a study of the times and incidents, reading voraciously. Thus, the final version of a script for one scene showed Rasputin wearing sandals. When Natalie Bucknell, the head of the research department, realized that an error had been made, she walked on the set to tell Lionel, but immediately saw that he had ignored the script and was wearing boots, as was Rasputin's habit.

So the filming progressed – or almost progressed. The script, with true American refinement, called for the use of the word 'graft'. 'That's not a word they would use in the Russian Court,' complained the Barrymores, with justification. It was changed to 'dishonesty'. One of the scripts also called for the film to open with Rasputin between two beautiful blondes. However, there were three Barrymores, all entitled to equal treatment and all expecting it. The scene had to go. As a contemporary writer said, 'These Barrymores are so busy protecting the good John Barrymore profile, the good Ethel profile (Oh yes, she has her best side too!) and the good temper of Lionel Barrymore that they are the only ones on that set who actually act as if nothing unusual is happening.'

To those unfamiliar with the film industry, all this might have seemed to spell disaster for the film. To Hollywood, however, nothing unusual seemed to be involved. True, MGM evidently treated the subject as something which had happened marginally before anyone had discovered America. They were amazed to hear that the Imperial family were relatives of the Royal Family in England. Someone had to be brought from the British diplomatic service before, the Barrymores apart, they would accept this, whereupon, according to the struggling scriptwriter, MacArthur, they began to treat the Tsar and Tsarina as if they were 'Mr and Mrs Hoover'.

Disaster, however, was again to hit Charles Brabin. Having been struck down by *Ben-Hur*, he was now worsted by Rasputin; he was dismissed as director, his Russian ancestry notwithstanding. In his place came Richard Boleslavsky, whose name would look well on the credits since it definitely had a Russian ring. In truth, he was an émigré Pole, an actor who had once acted with the Moscow Arts Theatre. He fared no better than his predecessor. The sorry story merely repeated itself. So much so, that the studio joke was that the film should have its title changed from 'Rasputin' to 'Disputin'.

But this was Hollywood, where nothing was impossible. Moses could be made to ascend the mountain once again and return with the tablets; Ben-Hur could make what would, perhaps, be his positively last appearance winning a chariot race; and, later, Errol Flynn would be made to win the Second World War single-handed. The filming was concluded, and the film was ready to be shown.

Chapter **Eight**

As Hollywood had learned, the great secret of depicting history on the screen is never to allow history to get in the way of a good picture.

In America, the film was given the title *Rasputin and the Empress*. Because it was thought that the British would resent the mention of royalty in a film title, it was renamed, for English consumption, *Rasputin, the Mad Monk*. In terms of accuracy, this was par for the course: as already noted, Rasputin was not mad and he was not a monk, and the British could not have cared less whether the word 'Empress' appeared in the title or not.

The serious dialogue had something of the quality of Gilbert and Sullivan about it, and the storyline bore about as much relation to what occurred in Russia in 1916 as, to quote those two gentlemen, 'the flowers that bloom in the spring'.

One fact of history that could not be ignored was that the Prince and Princess Youssoupoff were both alive, as were others who had been concerned in the events depicted in the film. This problem, MGM decided, might easily be circumvented; they invented two fresh characters. As a thin disguise of Prince Youssoupoff, they had 'Prince Chegodieff', who would, in due course, slay Rasputin. How precisely they came to use that name has never been satisfactorily explained. MGM implied that they had invented it as being a name which no one at the relevant period could have possessed. They also said that their difficulty had been that they were dealing 'with a country where the ordinary public records and books of reference had, to a large extent, been destroyed or otherwise rendered inaccessible owing to subsequent political changes'. The second part of the explanation was assuredly correct. The first part is rather more difficult to swallow. There were, in fact, alive at the time a Prince and Princess Alexis Pavlovich Chegodieff, who had moved in the highest circles of the Imperial Court, he having been Governor of Erivan and Lublin. Prince Chegodieff took MGM to court in 1937 and, with the help of Norman Birkett, KC, extracted agreed damages from them. The Chegodieffs did not take kindly to the suggestion that he had murdered Rasputin and she had been raped or seduced by him, particularly since they had not been connected with him in any way.

This, and MGM's subsequent problems with the Youssoupoffs, had come about because the supervisor of the film, Bernie Hyman, required what he called 'shock progression'. What he meant by this was to be inferred from his imperative requirement that there should be a scene in which Rasputin would violate one of the beautiful ladies of the Court. In one of the innumerable script changes which occurred, the person to be carnally known by Rasputin was altered from a lady-in-waiting to the Princess Chegodieff, who was to be given the name Princess Natasha (the real Princess Chegodieff was called Elena). The part was played by that talented and lovely English actress, Diana Wynyard.

The film opens in the Cathedral, presumably at St Petersburg, where, in the presence of the Tsar and Tsarina, Mass is in progress in celebration of three centuries of Romanov rule. Also present is the young Tsarevich, played by a small boy called Tod Alexander, who had no Russian connections apart from the name Alexander. He came from Iowa, and an added difficulty had been to adjust his accent to the kind of English which the Russians would have spoken had they not habitually been conversing in Russian or French. (As a writer at the time sagely observed, whilst it is easy to take little boys out of Iowa, it is almost impossible to take Iowa out of little boys.) With him are the Tsar's four young daughters, Olga, Marie, Tatiana and 'Stacia'.

Prince Paul is manifestly distressed. The strain clearly shows itself on his more photogenic profile, which he displays. He alone of all those present knows that the Grand Duke 'Sergei' has just been assassinated. It is made clear that Sergei was the father of Paul's beloved betrothed, the Princess Natasha, and the uncle of the Tsar.

Prince Paul (who the ardent cinemagoers, of course, knew was in reality none other than John Barrymore) approaches a bearded man, who already looks less than pleased, and says, 'Highness, I regret to tell you the Grand Duke Sergei cannot be present.' This reflects the high water mark of diplomatic discretion. The bearded man may well have been surprised that this unimportant piece of intelligence should be thus imparted to him, but it avoids the direct assault on his susceptibilities which might result from at once telling him the truth.

However, behind that beard is one with the highest level of intelligence. He must immediately have known that only one thing would have kept the Grand Duke Sergei away from High Mass in celebration of three centuries of Romanov rule, so he at once asks, 'Is my brother dead?' thereby rendering clear what the relationship was between them.

'God rest his soul,' says Prince Paul. 'His Highness was assassinated this morning by a terrorist. A police courier brought the news to the Spassky Gate and one of my captains conveyed it here.' The Prince must therefore be in the army and have some senior rank. We shall shortly learn that he is the Colonel of the Imperial Chevalier Guard.

By some means, the news of the assassination seeps through to the congregation. Prince Paul looks across to his beloved Natasha, who is bearing her grief with dignity but with tears running down her face.

It further emerges that the bearded man is the Grand Duke Igor, Governor of Moscow, who will doubtless seek to exact revenge. In real life the Grand Duke Sergius, called Sergia, was the Governor, and he was not at all the sort of fellow whom the lovely Natasha would have had as a father. According to Bernard Pares, he did not have a friend or admirer in Russia or elsewhere and his cousin, Alexander Mikhailovich, wrote of him, 'Try as I will, I cannot find a single redeeming feature in his character.' He was, in fact, married to the sister of the Tsarina.

The screen story moves to an anteroom in the Palace, where Paul is in hurried conversation with the lovely Natasha. She soon reveals how well she knows, and is impressed by, Father Gregory. Paul is outraged. 'Don't listen to him,' he tells her, '... I wish you'd give up your visits to him. Oh, I know you think it is your duty, and you're interested in these alleged cures of his ...' He is interrupted and says, 'What is it, Yougooff? Yes, at once. Order my car.' He then goes off, after telling Natasha that he suspects that Igor has already begun his plans for revenge.

It is now necessary to demonstrate what a fine, upright fellow Prince Paul is. On his return to barracks, he comes across a platoon of his regiment, the captain in charge of which is informing the crowd that anyone caught with arms will be shot. That was an ambiguous comment, since everyone in the crowd had arms, and legs as well, and they were much in evidence. Standing upright – and very upright at that – in his car Paul says, 'Captain Raminoff, I rescind the order. The squad will dismiss.'

At this moment across the square, the bearded Grand Duke Igor comes and it is learned that he gave the order in retaliation for the assassination of his brother. Paul protests, and Igor reprimands him and tells him that he will be reported to the Tsar, whereupon they both go in Paul's car to achieve that end.

On arrival at the Palace, they come upon the Tsar and Tsarina surrounded by their children. When the Tsar hears of Paul's countermanding of the Grand Duke's order, he is understandably very cross, but the Tsarina intervenes: 'The Grand Duke talks of killing as if it were his right. He forgets that in the eyes of Europe today, such actions put our country back twenty years.'

The day is saved by the manifest humanity of the Empress, and, as Paul leaves, she makes the very wise comment: 'You know, Sergei was ten men. You will have to be a hundred, Paul. We need you. Who is there to help this poor country?'

Whilst the audience is engaged in trying to fathom what on earth she is talking about, there comes from Paul the obvious answer: 'The Tsarevich, Highness. There is one for whom the mass of the people do care.'

By happy chance at that very moment a vast crowd of people has arrived outside the Palace, every one of them clamouring for their little Tsarevich to appear on the balcony. Everyone within the Palace, however, is agreed that the mood of the mob is such that it would be too dangerous for the little ailing child to risk an appearance, but while the adults are busy talking, the little man makes his own way on to the balcony. True, he forgets the speech which he has been taught always to use on such occasions, but he at once resorts to an extempore effort in which he tells the crowd how pleased he is to see them. Quite why this ugly crowd had wanted to see him in the first place is never disclosed, but having seen him, and heard he was pleased to see them, they are clearly content and disperse.

'Your Highness,' says Paul, 'did I not tell you the Tsarevich will save Russia?'

'If only he is strong enough, he will,' replies the Tsarina.

They continue to discuss the physical strength of her small son, when another of those remarkable coincidences occurs. At the very moment when Paul is reassuring her that with his lifestyle the little Tsarevich is unlikely to receive a blow or a shock, the little chap begins to run, and trips over himself, to their joint consternation. Although there is nothing to see as a result of the fall, he soon begins to bleed internally.

As the crisis develops, Paul is dispatched to Vienna to bring back a doctor who has made a study of haemophilia. (Until the arrival on screen of Dr Kildare, Hollywood always brought doctors specially fitted to deal with crises from Vienna, so they had no difficulty adjusting to the true facts.) When Paul returns with Dr Wolff, he meets Dr Remezov, the Imperial physician, who tells him he has been dismissed. There is, however, no question of keeping Dr Wolff from the door. They are both admitted to the sickroom, where they see the pitiful figure of the small boy, and sitting beside him on the bed an exceedingly grubby monk with very dirty habits. The audience have no difficulty in guessing that this is Father Gregory Rasputin, for it is indeed he. He is gazing at the child with mesmeric eyes. As Rasputin rises from the bed, the Tsarina asks him, in a pleading voice, whether her child is going to live.

The *Picturegoer Weekly*, which recounted the story of the film in 1933, broke off the story here. The box at the end of the first instalment read: 'Next Week, Vividly depicted against a background of court intrigue, the rise to power of the sinister Rasputin makes thrilling reading. And then – War.' The readers of *Picturegoer Weekly* must have rushed for sedatives to carry them over to next week and the next thrilling instalment.

It is now essential that Rasputin should answer the mother's question. What then is his reply? He strides across the room, gathers up from the night table an array of bottles of medicine and throws them all out of the window with a resounding crash.

What irreparable damage the mad film monk might have done had he not been interrupted will never be known. Certainly, he has skilfully avoided answering the Tsarina's difficult question, for at that moment, with a cry of pain, the little child calls from his bed 'Little Mother.'

Rasputin strides to the bed to tell him 'It's no good calling Mummushka, she's gone,' adding with tenderness, 'She's gone to buy you a beautiful white elephant with purple eyes, and a shining silver house on its back.'

After some further dialogue of a similar calibre, Rasputin mesmerizes the child with a watch and sends him to sleep. Finally, when Paul and Dr Wolff express doubts as to whether Rasputin has really cured him, the Mad Monk commands the small boy to rise from his bed and walk across the room to him, which he does. (This scene was also the highlight of a rather better film of the book, *The Outsider*, in which the actor Harold Huth carried out, with greater realism, the same routine.)

A series of incidents reveals how bitterly Prince Paul feels about the growing power of Rasputin. In the latter's presence, he tells the Tsar that Rasputin is an ignorant peasant, an impostor and not the saint and prophet the Tsar believes him to be. The Tsar remains adamant. He points out that the very life of his heir is at stake. In an unguarded moment, Prince Paul tells him, 'My love for Russia must come first.'

The Tsar, close to tears, replies, 'I love my son. I accept your resignation from the Imperial Guard, Prince Chegodieff.' Paul is out of a job. As he salutes and leaves the room, he notices that the Tsar puts his arm around Rasputin's shoulder.

It may have been about this time that Bernie Hyman reviewed the latest addition to the script and demanded his 'shock progression'. Paul is in a state of some desolation. The Tsar has not sent for him, and Natasha is still under the influence of Rasputin. As if this were not more than the most stoic Russian prince might bear, his lame servant, Petrushka brings him a note from Natasha. It reads, 'Dearest, I'm no longer fit to be your wife,' and at the bottom she has added, 'Please come to the Hospital as soon as you get this.'

Getting to the hospital is portrayed for Paul as no small undertaking. He is at his home in Moscow and the hospital is some four hundred miles away in St Petersburg. Moreover, it is now winter and the film graphically depicts all that a Russian winter can be. Is our intrepid hero to be frustrated by wind, ice and sleet? Never. No longer an officer in the Guards, he makes the journey across Russia in a straw-strewn cattle truck, dressed as a peasant with a woollen cap on his head. Although no longer an officer, he is still a prince and not, presumably, short of a rouble or two. However, his bravery in making the journey at all makes him pictorially as moving as Captain Oates walking to his death in the snow in the famous painting *A Very Gallant Gentleman*.

Eventually Paul arrives at the convent where, whenever they can, the Tsarina and Natasha work as nurses. It has already been made clear that Russia, having decided to mobilize, has brought about war with Germany. Natasha has been through an awful ordeal, which is conveyed more than adequately by her wan appearance and the expression on her face; the Tsarina looks no better.

As Paul embraces Natasha and their lips meet, she whispers, 'Paul, Her Highness asked me to send for you.'

Paul at once responds, 'If you knew how thankful I am. All these weeks I have been distraught with anguish. Of course, it's that monster Rasputin.'

Natasha begs him to sit down and listen, before seeing the Tsarina. When he does so, she tells him of the power which Rasputin now wields: all the ministers in Russia have been appointed by him, he having dismissed all the previous ones. She tells Paul that she found Rasputin hiding in the bedroom of the Grand Duchess Marie, whereupon he assaulted her and hypnotized her, and when his beard scratched her face, she woke from a deep trance with the knowledge that she had been violated.

She says, 'Naturally he denied it. He threw me across the floor. When I saw his face ... Paul I've never seen anything so fiendish. Her Highness must have noticed it.'

Rasputin must have turned over in his grave as the Tsarina explains, 'Natasha has gone through so much for me. Thank Heaven my eyes have been unveiled before it's altogether too late! I can never believe in Father Gregory again. I have sent for you, for I believe you to be the only man in Russia who can deal with him.'

This hardly speaks well for the millions upon millions of people in Russia besides Prince Paul, but, needless to say, it is enough for him. Within minutes, our hero has given instructions for the opening of his St Petersburg home. With no less delay, Smarov, the controller of the Tsar's household, is instructed to extend an invitation to Rasputin to attend a reception at Prince Paul's home. Bernie Hyman must have known that Rasputin would be the last person to smell a rat, on receiving an invitation from the Palace to go to the Prince's home. What, therefore, did Rasputin do? He sat down and wrote a letter of acceptance. If history is correct, however, he must at least have got someone else to write it for him.

With the help of Dr Remezov, the Imperial physician, Paul places cyanide in cakes and wine.

'Enough cyanide in those,' comments the doctor, 'to kill a dozen men.'

'Let's hope the reverend Father will enjoy himself,' Paul laughs.

Then turning to a waiter, since the reception appears already to be in progress, he says, 'Get along, Petrushka ... Feodor ... whatever your name is. Take that to Father Gregory and make sure he helps himself.' And in an aside to the doctor, 'The only hired man here whose character I couldn't vouch for. I'm not sure I was wise to trust him.'

The two men move to the reception to see the most vital action in the plot. The *Picturegoer Weekly* graphically described the scene: 'The two men had barely reached the still-room door when they were overpowered by a couple of armed guards.'

'By whose orders?' Paul snaps, feeling his revolver being whipped from its holster.

'Father Gregory Rasputin.'

'Take me to him at once.'

When Paul enters flanked by his captors, Rasputin has accepted a chocolate cake and is biting into it.

'So,' he shrills at his host between mouthfuls, 'you plotted to murder me tonight. That waiter fellow gave the game away with his eyes. I knew what he was thinking, but you can't kill me.'

He takes Paul's revolver from one of the guards. A dozen hands go up to restrain him as he levels it. Someone parts the shaggy, greasy hair to murmur in his ear.

As if this were not enough to stretch credulity to the limit, the film continued, as *Picturegoer Weekly* correctly related, with a strange and totally inexplicable comment by Rasputin, in the circumstances: 'I understand you have a marvellous cellar, Prince Chegodieff, full of rare wines and huge pantries. Suppose you show me over them, while we get to know one another better?'

'Certainly,' replies Paul.

The two of them go downstairs to the main cellar, where there is a sofa and table.

'How does it feel to die?' asks Rasputin, whilst he again levels his revolver at Paul.

'You ought to know,' says Paul, 'you've been poisoned. You're turning green.'

'Swine,' shouts Rasputin, raising his revolver again to Paul's face. There is then a shot. It misses Paul, who dashes across the room, throws himself at Rasputin, removes the revolver and throws it into the fireplace. Rasputin has been thrown to the floor. Paul seizes a poker from the fireplace and batters Rasputin's head. When someone starts knocking on the door, Paul makes for the french windows (which are evidently to be found in all Russian underground wine cellars). Rasputin has struggled to his feet and followed Paul outside. With one leap, our hero rushes at Rasputin, bowls him over and drags him towards the adjoining ice-covered canal. There he thrusts Rasputin into the ice and, for good measure, his head is crushed between two blocks of it.

Before his final dispatch, however, Rasputin cries, 'Kill me ... kill me ... but look out ... when I die ... Russia dies' – words Paul will never forget.

Not surprisingly, it is not long before Paul seeks an audience with the Tsar. The Tsar is very stern, in the presence of General Orloff, to whom he hands a document.

'See this order is carried out,' he says to the General. 'There is no justification for murder on the part of Prince Chegodieff. My ministers have demanded his death. But I cannot take a life that has been devoted to my service in the past. I order his banishment. You understand, Prince?'

The General takes the order and departs. No sooner has he left the chamber than the Tsar grips both of Paul's hands. The Tsarina assents with a smile; the little Tsarevich jumps into Paul's arms, throwing his arms round his neck.

The Tsar politely asks Paul what he is going to do.

'Highness,' replies Paul, 'you know of my English blood. I have relatives in Yorkshire. I have even written to ask if I can get a commission in the Yorkshire Regiment. It will not be the same as fighting for Russia, but at least it will be for Russia's allies.'

'Take Natasha with you,' says the Tsarina. 'She is killing herself with work at the hospital here. You need her more.'

The film ends in Soho Square, London. There we see Lieutenant Paul Chegodieff of the British army. He has acquired an artificial leg, having, presumably, lost his own in the British army. With them is Dr Remezov, who imparts the knowledge that the Imperial family has been horribly massacred – which, at least, was accurate.

They are inconsolable, but Natasha reminds Paul of the Empress's parting words to her before she left Russia: 'Find happiness, Natasha.'

'Natasha ... beloved,' says Paul, and the film ends.

It might be thought that Bernie Hyman's – to say nothing of MGM's – first mistake was ever to release such a film, which bore so little relation to the true facts, and which so distorted history to the accompaniment of the most appalling and incredible dialogue. If so, Bernie Hyman was about to make his second mistake. He composed a preface to the film, which duly appeared, and which he would later have cause to regret.

It read: 'This concerns the destruction of an empire, brought about by the mad ambition of one man. A few of the characters are still alive. The rest met death by violence.'

Chapter **Nine**

The film opened at the Astor Theater, New York, at Christmas in 1932, and at the Empire, Leicester Square, London, the following year. It was well received by the cinemagoers but had a mixed reception from the critics.

The *New York Times* reviewer believed the film was 'further distinguished by the knowledgeful guidance of Richard Boleslavsky'. He also thought he had 'worked out his episodes in an impressive fashion, particularly the fight between Prince Chegodieff, as Prince Youssoupoff is known here, and the "Mad Monk."'

The most significant aspect of the review was the fact that the reviewer had been immediately satisfied that the Prince portrayed was indeed Youssoupoff. No one seems to have discovered this particular review in the subsequent litigation in England. Of that part of the film which depicted the reluctance of Rasputin to die, the comment is made, 'As is surmised, it is learned later that he had taken the precaution to protect himself with a steel jacket' – although, in truth, there was not an iota of evidence that such was the case. All the Barrymores 'gave equally fine performances. Lionel Barrymore leaves no stone unturned to give a vivid idea of the repellent monk. Yet he never overacts.' Avid followers of the silver screen may or may not have agreed with the last sentence.

The review in *Photoplay* magazine was equally fulsome: '...you can't miss this offering. We urge this in spite of liberties taken with history.' The *Hollywood Spectator* took a different and less enthusiastic view: 'When historical subjects are distorted quite beyond recognition there is no conceivable basis upon which a defense may be constructed. History, at its purest sources, is closely allied to truth. And truth is a thing with which even the hierarchy at MGM may not safely tamper. *Rasputin and the Empress* will leave an impression on the American mind, which fifty years of education cannot efface. It not only twists events and principals but it grossly misrepresents characters. From beginning to end it is a concoction of myths ... Nor is there the usual excuse that truth would have been duller than the preposterous fiction dished up in its place ... Metro-Goldwyn-Mayer, by sticking to history, not only would have produced a truer picture, it would have produced a more interesting one.' The *New York Herald Tribune* said of the film, 'It achieves one feat which is not inconsiderable, it manages to libel even the despised Rasputin.' In the MGM studios, some wag suggested MacArthur would get the Academy Award for the best original historical story of the year.

Much the same reaction was to be found in England. *The Times* believed the story of Rasputin had been told 'at its most melodramatic', and whilst not falling over himself with enthusiasm, the reviewer had nothing unkind to write and applauded the Barrymores. The *Observer* wrote: 'The present slightly insolent version of European history provides a playground for the three Barrymores. In the absence of any complexity of character in Rasputin, who is just plain Hollywood Bad Man, the interest resolves itself into a betting on the number of close ups "hogged" by each Barrymore from the others. Richard Boleslavsky directed, presumably on the ground that there ought to be something Russian about a Russian film.' (Unhappily, it failed even on that score, since, as already noted, the director was not a Russian.)

Picturegoer Weekly, having earlier serialized the whole exciting story of the film, wrote: 'A rather disappointing and highly melodramatic story ... Lionel Barrymore's portrayal of the name part is highly artificial and his mannerisms are accentuated. John Barrymore ... who finally assassinates him in a hectic knock about fight, is also an offender in this respect ... Diana Wynyard plays Princess Natasha ... with grace and dignity ... Ethel Barrymore, the third of the famous royal family of Broadway did not appeal to me very strongly as the Tsarina, but Ralph Morgan made a pathetic weak figure of the Tsar.'

Such are the peculiarities of Hollywood that the film did exceedingly well at the box office and made a great deal of money for MGM – and when one writes of money, one writes of Fanny Holtzmann.

She was a highly charismatic lawyer. Five feet two inches in height, she had long, wavy bobbed hair, and used her hands in a delicate way, conveying a demure air, which somewhat belied her sharp and acute mind. She was born in a large house on Eastern Parkway in the Brownsville section of Brooklyn. Although some Americans would have regarded that location as being 'on the wrong side of the tracks,' her family were known locally as 'the royal family of Brownsville'.

This, however, was royalty of a different order from that of the Barrymores. Her grandfather lived to be ninety-six, but, unlike Max Loew, who founded a series of theatres, Holtzmann Senior founded a series of synagogues. Indeed, he was known as 'the Republican leader of the bearded vote in Brownsville'. When Theodore Roosevelt passed through Brooklyn, he would visit Fanny's grandfather as one of his valued supporters.

His granddaughter said of him, 'Anyone who was a Socialist or a Democrat he considered as ungodly, almost anarchist, and he would not let him get up and read in the synagogue. So they would depose him and he would go and found a new synagogue.' Fanny's father, Henry, 'taught school' to immigrants. He had six daughters and three sons, and his wife used to say that she 'gave birth to a bar association, because those who did not become lawyers married them'.

Fanny Ellen Holtzmann was born in 1903. She was educated at Public School 144, which, of course, has a different connotation in America: it was a state school. She attended high school for only three years, but with great diligence studied law at night, passing the bar examinations in 1923, at a very early age. She came third in the bar examinations and, by special dispensation, was admitted in a couple of weeks instead of the usual two months. She was a young woman in a hurry.

Once admitted to the bar, she started to practise at West 44th Street, having made a special study of the law of copyright, and continued to do so until her death from cancer in 1980. She had difficulty acquiring the right to occupy this office, because she was female, very young, and Jewish. It was a building occupied by lawyers: Woodrow Wilson and Bainbuck Coldy had offices there, and Justice Cardogo had the office above the one she wanted. Through the influence of her older brother, Jacob, she succeeded in gaining occupation. At her death, the light green, dusty suite contained the same carpets, tables and chairs which she put there when she first opened it, although meanwhile, she had secretaries working permanently at Claridge's Hotel in London, and at the Beverly Hills Hotel near Hollywood.

She was a friend of King George of Greece. When a London news-paper reported that she 'broiled chops for him', she was indignant. 'I don't go to London to broil chops for anybody,' she declared roundly. 'When the King of Greece comes to see me, he broils his own chops.' Occasionally, she was invited to tea by King George and Queen Mary. 'I behave to the King', she was quoted as saying, 'as I would to my own grandfather, with dignity and respect, and I let him do the talking.' She also became close to the Grand Duchess Xenia of Russia.

Fanny had a great love of England. On one occasion, when she heard that a show called *Jubilee* was about to be produced, sending up King George and Queen Mary, she immediately intervened – without instructions from anyone – and succeeded in persuading the producer to change the locale of the show to a Ruritanian Country.

Fanny was a gregarious person. She related that her brother was wont to say she took longer than anyone he knew to walk down Madison Avenue, where she had an apartment – 'Here she comes, kissing her way down the avenue' – because whenever she met any of her numerous acquaintances, she would embrace them. Largely as a result of her part in the Youssoupoff libel case, she achieved some international notice, although she had a very busy and extremely lucrative practice before that. She numbered George Bernard Shaw amongst her friends, and her clients included Gertrude Lawrence, Noël Coward, Fred Astaire, Constance Bennett and the writer Louis Bromfield. She was a talented painter in oils, examples of which lined her walls and she studied sculpture with Jacob Epstein. She went to the founding conference of the United Nations in San Francisco as counsel to Chiang Kai-shek. By some means which have never been revealed, she made contact with Prince and Princess Youssoupoff. The Youssoupoffs had already approached a number of New York lawyers, but they had declined to bring proceedings, regarding the case as 'too flimsy'.

The first shot was fired in the litigation battle in 1932. The film had been shown in America, and, although the Youssoupoffs had not seen it, the events it depicted had been relayed to them. By means which are not known, they were introduced to a firm of American attorneys, Neufeld & Schlechter of New York, all others having refused instructions. They wrote to MGM on behalf of the Prince, claiming that the film constituted a libel because 'the incidents surrounding the historic drama and the manner and method of the killing of Rasputin were neither fair nor true'. They did not indicate precisely what they required, other than that they would be pleased to confer with MGM's representative. The film company did not agree and replied on 19 January 1933 repudiating their complaint. No claim had been made at this stage on behalf of the Princess.

The Prince's claim does not appear to have been pursued. Doubtless he was advised that he was batting on a sticky wicket. The only possible libel would have had to be the allegation that he had murdered Rasputin: how he did it would not make a great deal of difference. The truth was, however, that he had murdered him, or, more correctly, made a very good attempt at doing so, and truth, in regard to any allegation made, is a complete answer to a claim for damages for libel. Distorting the way in which he did the deed would not constitute libel.

The scene then moved to Europe, to Menton, on the Riviera, where both the Princess and Fanny Holtzmann chanced to be. Whether this was the case, and they met socially, as the Princess was later to imply, or whether Fanny Holtzmann, with or without the Princess's knowledge, had deliberately sought her out, is not recorded. What is certain is that it was there that they met.

Nothing more transpired until 2 March 1933, when the same attorneys wrote to MGM, this time on behalf of the Princess. They asserted that the character Princess Natasha was 'a thinly disguised impersonation of the real Princess Irina Youssoupoff' and that 'the whole world is apprised of the alleged desecration' of their client. They said the damage suffered by their client in the United States and abroad was incalculable, demanded the withdrawal of the film from exhibition, 'as complete as possible a nationwide and worldwide apology', and immediate action showing a determined effort to rectify the great wrong done.

The policy of MGM was to defend libel actions, since claims of that nature were fairly common.

Following the showing of the film in London at the Empire, Leicester Square (it was also shown at the Dominion Theatre, Tottenham Court Road), there was a meeting between the Youssoupoffs and Fanny Holtzmann in Paris. How this came to be arranged is not known. It was to be suggested by MGM that Fanny Holtzmann was the inspiration behind the ultimate litigation. At all events, the New York attorneys were dropped and Fanny Holtzmann took over in their place.

Her first step was to send a cablegram to J. Robert Rubin, the Vice-President of MGM. Rubin was an attorney who had originally been in private practice, and had been an Assistant District Attorney and Deputy Commissioner of Police for New York City before becoming counsel to MGM.

The cablegram read: 'My friends Prince and Princess Youssoupoff want me substituted in action against Metro. Hesitate, knowing nothing, not having seen the film. Remaining Hotel Lotti until tomorrow, Thursday. Can you cable me status of case etcetera? Needless to say this cable and your reply confidential. Regards. Fanny Holtzmann.'

Back came the reply: 'Neither Prince nor Princess Youssoupoff have sued us. Once threatened suit but they have absolutely no grounds and we would consider no settlement but defend to the limit. As to taking their case you must act entirely as you think fit.'

Fanny's cable was a curious tactical move. There would have been no need to write to the proposed or actual defendants to inquire as to the state of her own clients' case, for when she took over the papers this would have been evident from them. Manifestly, she must have thought that telling them that she, the redoubtable Fanny Holtzmann, was about to take the reins would bring MGM running to the negotiating table. Rubin did not have to be very bright to see through this ploy, and his reply was predictable.

This move having failed, Fanny Holtzmann came to London. Having conferred with the Prince and Princess, she made an appointment to see a Mr Eckmann, the managing director of the MGM company in London. Her request to him was almost impertinent: he should cable to America for authority to settle 'as it was only a question of money'. She had no response to this request, so on 29 September 1933 she called on him again, repeating that the whole matter could be settled by a payment, which MGM were obviously not of a mind to make.

If they were to collect the money which she had said could end the matter, Fanny Holtzmann and her clients now had no alternative but to take action. Accordingly, attorneys in America were instructed and a firm of solicitors of good repute, Langton & Passmore, were instructed in England. The guiding spirit seems unquestionably to have been Fanny Holtzmann and her enthusiasm knew no bounds. Writs were issued claiming damages for defamation in America and England, but not before Fanny had made a final call, this time on the chairman of the English company, who was also the solicitor who represented MGM in England. She told him that 'the film company would get a pain in the neck but they could still settle by a money payment'. Proceedings were taken contemporaneously in Austria, Germany, France and Italy, and also against 288 cinemas which had shown the film.

There was more than a touch of irony about the scenario thus presented. When it came to finding a champion, a mentor and someone who could produce the money, Prince Youssoupoff's anti-Semitism was temporarily put on one side and Fanny Holtzmann became his lawyer, friend and negotiator. He was prepared, for the sake of expediency, to put his true feelings out of his mind, and she, in the spirit of the best legal traditions, must have been prepared, had she thought of it at all, to ignore years of appalling cruelty inflicted on Jews in Russia. It was not a new phenomenon: the house of Rothschild had learned the lesson generations before.

The plaintiff in the action which began in London was the Princess. As we have seen, the Prince could not make a claim for damages merely because the way in which he had carried out the murder had been distorted.

The case clearly involved a number of interesting legal problems, and to understand them it is necessary to know something of the law of defamation. An actionable defamation may be one of two kinds, namely libel or slander. In very general terms, libel is contained in written or other permanent material; slander in the spoken word. To succeed in an action for slander, it is necessary to prove that the plaintiff or claimant has suffered financial loss, with certain limited exceptions, one of which alone would be relevant to the Princess's case, namely where the spoken words impute unchastity to a woman, which resulted from the passing of the Slander of Women Act 1891.

Libel is actionable without proof of special damage; the mere publication of the defamatory material is enough in itself. The thinking behind this is easily understood; a libel is a permanent record to which others may from time to time have access, whilst the spoken word is transient and is thus only within the cognizance or memory of those who hear it. The exceptions, such as allegations of unchastity, are, however, regarded as so serious and damaging of themselves that the normal requirements ought fairly to be mitigated.

What then was the position in regard to a talking picture which was not merely spoken but also recorded on film for all time? Into which category did it fall, or did it fall within both? In either event, what was the law applicable? Was it necessary for the Princess to prove she had suffered special damage or not? In 1935 these questions had never been satisfactorily resolved.

Then there was another question. Had the Princess really been defamed? To assert that a woman had willingly had intercourse with a man was defamatory beyond doubt, but was it defamatory to say of her that she had been raped, since the first essential of rape is that it has occurred without the woman's consent? Certainly this was the case in the 1930s. Whether it remains so today, in the permissive society, may one day be argued.

Not everything unpleasant which is written or said about someone is defamatory. The test has long been whether the words were such as to subject the person to 'hatred, ridicule or contempt', or, more generally, were the words likely to bring the person concerned into disrepute.

Around the time of the Youssoupoff case, the House of Lords provided an alternative test: did the words tend to lower the plaintiff in the estimation of right-thinking members of the community generally? How, it might be argued, could any of these tests apply to a woman who was depicted as having been violated wholly against her will? She was thus a person for whom right-thinking members of the community would feel sympathy, compassion and indignation; they would hardly regard her with contempt, or think any the less of her, because she had been the unwilling victim.

And what if she fell into neither category but had been seduced? Suppose, although unwilling, she had been taken to the point where she just gave in? Was that a further distinction to be drawn? The case bristled with difficulties.

Was it relevant to inquire whether MGM intended Princess Natasha in the film to be a thinly disguised portrait of Princess Youssoupoff, or was it immaterial? Although many of the other questions were uncertain at the time, that point was at least fairly well understood. It was largely immaterial. The test to be applied was whether reasonable people acquainted with the plaintiff would take the material to be referring to him or her.

Finally, a libel has to be published; everyone who repeats or republishes it is equally liable to pay damages, hence the many actions against the cinemas which showed the film.

The first step after the issue of a writ is for the plaintiff's solicitors to deliver a statement of claim to the defendant's solicitors. This is a document which defines the issues which arise for determination in the proceedings; it does not, however, set out the evidence on which the plaintiff will rely at the trial. It merely exists to restrict the ambit of the inquiry at the trial and to acquaint the defendant with the case he will have to meet. It is generally settled by junior counsel. One of the advantages of a barrister becoming a silk, i.e. a Queen's Counsel, is that he no longer is allowed to draw pleadings, which can be a tedious pastime. It is one of the many anachronistic rules, of a trade union nature, which have survived over the years, and it is said to be justified by the fact that it thus gives the senior barrister more time to concentrate on other more important work, even if he has none, which for some silks is the case.

As the Princess's junior counsel, her solicitors, Langton & Passmore, selected Henry St John Field. He was educated at Rugby and at Balliol College, Oxford, and was called to the bar in 1908, when he was twenty-five. He was, thus, at the time of the case, a very senior junior, having been practising as such for twenty-seven years, apart from the four years when he was away fighting in the First World War. In fact, he took silk the year following the trial, in 1936. It provides an interesting commentary on legal times; today juniors tend to become silks in not far short of a third of that period. He acted as a 'devil' to Henry McCardie who, later became a renowned, if rather controversial, High Court judge. As a devil, St John Field would have prepared drafts of pleadings for McCardie, noted cases, researched the law and the like, for the most part without financial reward and as a means of learning his job. He was regarded as an exceedingly busy and experienced junior at the time of the Youssoupoff case. He became Recorder of Warwick in 1937, and accepted an appointment as a County Court judge in 1943 (because he suffered from a heart condition, it is said), dying in 1949 at the age of sixty-six.

In the Youssoupoff case, despite his undoubted erudition and experience, St John Field seems to have slipped up with his pleading, and his leader seems not to have noticed the error, since at a late stage of the trial it had to be amended. In the pleading, St John Field had alleged that the film depicted the Princess as having been seduced by Rasputin. As already observed, that might have restricted the scope of the Princess's complaint. Moreover, the jury might well come to the conclusion that what the film suggested was that she had been raped. Thus, at a very late stage, after legal argument, the judge allowed the statement of claim to be amended so that the claim that she had been 'seduced' had added after it 'or ravished'.

The next stage in the course of civil proceedings is for the defendants to deliver a document called a defence, which answers the claim and further defines the issues. The line decided upon by MGM was vigorously to deny that the Princess had been libelled; to argue that Princess Natasha was an invented character, who could not be confused with the Princess Youssoupoff in any way; and further to contend that it was not a libel to present a woman as having been raped.

The solicitors for each side devoted considerable time to searching out witnesses. The plaintiff sought witnesses who knew her and her husband, and who would say they had no doubt that Princess Natasha was really Irina Youssoupoff; the defendant sought witnesses who would say that they also knew the Youssoupoffs and it had not occurred to them, and never would have occurred to them for one moment, that the film was about Princess Youssoupoff.

Meanwhile, there would be a number of what are called interlocutory applications to the court, one seeking an injunction to restrain further showing of the film, others to obtain further particulars of the claim and defence and then a hearing to fix the arrangements for the trial.

The solicitors for MGM in England were the firm of H.S. Wright & Webb, who operated from a delightful old house on the corner of Bloomsbury Square. They had acted for the English MGM company for some time, and Wright was also the chairman of the English company.

Fanny Holtzmann spent some time in London, giving whatever assistance she could behind the scenes. She also arranged, through friends of the Youssoupoffs, for them to stay, during the trial, at Frogmore House, in the grounds of Windsor Castle. She decided, however, that her presence in the court could prove counter-productive and sailed for America a few days before the trial opened.

The lines of battle having been drawn, the time had come to bring up the big guns before the main battle commenced.

Chapter **Ten**

The 'big gun' engaged for the plaintiff, Princess Youssoupoff, was Sir Patrick Hastings, KC. He was not only a wise choice, but at that time, given adequate resources to retain him, virtually the inevitable choice for such a *cause célèbre*, as the case promised to become. Norman Birkett, KC, later Lord Birkett, held Hastings in the highest possible esteem and described him as the greatest cross-examiner he had ever heard. Hastings was, in no sense, a great lawyer, and certainly not a great orator, but he had the uncanny ability to cut through the wood, despite the trees, and concentrate on the vital point in a case.

'Pat' Hastings, as he was always known, was born on St Patrick's Day, 17 March 1880, the son of a solicitor, who claimed to be descended from an illegitimate child of the Earl of Huntingdon. Certainly, my recollection of him, on the rare occasions when, as a very young man, I was privileged to instruct him, was that he had no trace of aristocratic bearing. My recollection is that he looked as though he had come straight from hard work on an Irish farm. His mother was an artist, and she was described by her granddaughter as 'ugly, untidy and quite enchanting', so it may be that he took after her.

His father did not restrict himself to practising law. He would, from time to time, engage in commercial ventures, and although there were times when they lived a prosperous life, 'bankruptcy', wrote Hastings in his autobiography, 'in my family was not a misfortune, it was a habit, and, moreover, a habit which occurred with remarkable regularity'.

His education began at a private boarding school and, since it fortunately coincided with a period when there was some money around, he moved on to Charterhouse. 'I hated school', he later said, 'and was lonely and miserable there.' After two years he had not progressed beyond the fifth form, but then the money ran out again, and he left school at the age of sixteen. Without his father, the family departed to live cheaply on the Continent. At the age of nineteen, he joined the Suffolk Imperial Yeomanry and soon found himself sailing for South Africa to fight the Boers; he remained there for two years.

On his return to England, and against all advice, he joined the Middle Temple. He had no money and had to pawn his war medal, and as he was forbidden by the Inn to engage in trade, he decided to try his hand at journalism. One job, with the *Daily News*, at a pound a week as the assistant to the drama critic, did not last very long, so he turned to writing the drama notes for the *Pall Mall Gazette* and, in addition, acting as political secretary for a Liberal candidate.

Immediately after being called to the bar, Hastings walked into the Temple and saw the only barrister he knew by sight. Fate was indeed kind: without hesitation, the barrister offered Hastings a seat in his chambers, which he gratefully accepted. However, progress at the bar depends now as it did then, on being in busy chambers. He knew he would have to make a change, and he searched about for other chambers where he might be welcome. Fate was again kind: he approached Horace Avory, one of the greatest of criminal lawyers, who had been a Treasury junior at the Old Bailey and had earned great distinction in the process. When Avory turned him down, Hastings lost his temper, which made Avory laugh (Hastings said it was the only time he ever saw him do so) and he changed his mind. This was to be the making of Pat Hastings.

Two years after his call to the bar, he had married, which perhaps shows his adventurous spirit, since he was finding it difficult enough to maintain himself. By the end of his first year, he had earned sixty guineas, and £200 by the end of his second. In his early days Herbert Easton was a great help to him. A young solicitor of roughly his own age, he had been impressed by Hastings' ability when Hastings found himself substituting for a more senior barrister who had, as too often occurs, returned his brief at the last moment. Easton's firm still continues, with a fine reputation, and he and Hastings became life-long friends.

In 1910, Avory was appointed to the bench of the High Court, and Hastings was once more uncertain as to his future. The adventurous spirit surfaced again.

'What are you going to do?' asked Avory.

'I'm going to take over your chambers myself,' came the reply.

'Don't be a fool,' said Avory. 'To begin with, the Inn won't let you have them.'

Avory asked how, in any case, he would be able to afford the rent. Hastings said it was doubtful whether he could do so.

Avory thought for a moment. 'I suppose that means that I pay it and you owe it.'

'Yes,' said Hastings, 'I suppose that is about the size of it.'

Avory agreed and, as Hastings had no furniture, gave him his, adding, 'But I'm damned if I'll give you my books.'

And so it was. It is a warming story, because Avory was frequently regarded as a sour, cruel and humourless character, with little of the milk of human kindness, and his generous behaviour in this instance gave the lie to his public image and reputation.

From that time, Hastings' career advanced with leaps and bounds. He became a King's Counsel in 1919, and was returned as a Labour Member of Parliament for the Wallsend Division in 1922. Politically, his interests were always to the left, although, to quote the *Dictionary of National Biography*, 'his opinions mellowed in later years'. Tall, thin and dark-haired, with blue eyes, he had an upright carriage but looked untidy. Although he had an aggressive and abrupt manner, there was an underlying kindness.

Within two years of entering Parliament, due to the dearth of notable lawyers in the Labour Party, he became Attorney-General. Around the time he became a Labour Member of Parliament, he was living in a superb Georgian house in Curzon Street, Mayfair, with twelve servants, although his entry into the House did not assist his conduct of his practice.

In 1924, Hastings faced what some would regard as the greatest professional disaster of his life, but which Conservative voters at the time regarded as his greatest triumph – he brought down the Labour Government, although, in truth, he probably carried the can for others.

The Communist periodical the *Workers' Weekly* published an article urging members of the armed forces not to turn their guns on the workers in a military or class war. The Director of Public Prosecutions considered this to be actionable under the Incitement to Mutiny Act 1797, but needed the consent of the Attorney-General before a prosecution could be launched for that offence. John Campbell was charged, having said he took full responsibility for everything which appeared in the journal. This was far from pleasant for many of Hastings' parliamentary colleagues, some of whom were so far left it was often difficult to know where their Socialism ended and Communism began. Jimmy Maxton, for example, asked in the House why this man was being prosecuted for writing expressing his own views.

Hastings was forced to look more closely at the matter. It transpired that Campbell was not the editor of the *Workers' Weekly* but only acted as such when the editor was away, although what difference that made, if he had authorized the article, is difficult to fathom. It also appeared that he had a distinguished war record; both his feet had been blown off and he had been decorated for conspicuous gallantry. Again, praiseworthy as that may be, it hardly seems to afford any defence to the charge of incitement to mutiny, but it might have won the sympathy of the jury. Under pressure from the Prime Minister, Ramsay MacDonald, who unjustly blamed him for the prosecution, Hastings withdrew the charges; the case against Campbell collapsed and so did the Labour Government.

Hastings was re-elected at the next general election, but he had been suffering from a kidney complaint and, at his wife's urging, he resigned his seat, terminating his political career. This enabled him to concentrate all his energies on the bar, and he established himself as the leader of the common-law bar. He was one of the few barristers to become a household name. In addition to his legal career, he maintained an intense interest in the theatre. He wrote half a dozen plays, the most noteworthy of which was *The Blind Goddess*, which was also made into a film. He also wrote several books. In addition he was a good horseman, a first-class shot and a keen and skilled fisherman. He died on 26 February 1952.

At a time when so much has been said and written about the reorganization of the legal profession, Hastings' career probably has a message to convey. The bar constantly asserts that special educational qualifications and training are essential for the making of an advocate, and especially an outstanding one. Yet here was a man who rose to the very pinnacle in that field, with little or no education worth the name, penniless when he began, and without influence or patronage.

He was probably the finest cross-examiner of his time; certainly his equal has not been seen since. He modelled his technique, a process of direct and simple questions, on Edward Carson. From Horace Avory he learned never to rely on notes, but to trust his memory to carry the case in his mind. Another lesson might be learned from that. Such has been the decline in the standards of advocacy in our courts that nowadays cases are uniformly opened by counsel reading the whole of their speech and, too often, virtually doing the same in their final address. Avory and Hastings would not have approved.

MGM retained to represent them Sir William Jowitt, KC, a politically controversial figure. He was born in 1885 at Stevenage rectory, the only son of the Reverend William Jowitt, and was educated at Marlborough and New College, Oxford, where he read jurisprudence. He was called to the bar in the Middle Temple in 1909, at the age of twenty-four, and became a King's Counsel in 1922. He built up a busy and lucrative practice in commercial matters, and was regarded as one of the outstanding men at the common law bar.

He was acutely intelligent and had an impressive bearing. He had steely blue eyes, was described as tall and gracefully athletic and carried himself with great dignity. He had great charm and wit combined with an easy nonchalant manner which, at times, disarmed his most scathing critics. That was probably as well, since he had a plethora of those because of his evident lack of settled convictions on almost everything, a maverick approach to politics and a highly developed degree of opportunism.

He entered Parliament as a Liberal in 1922. In the Campbell case, which so affected Hastings, he voted with the Labour Party. In the ensuing general election he lost his seat. When, in 1929, the Labour Government were returned to power and there were no Labour lawyers of any merit available, MacDonald offered the Attorney-General's office to Jowitt. He abandoned Liberal affiliations to accept the appointment and became Labour, accepting the knighthood which customarily went with the office. He was found a seat at Preston. Great public controversy resulted. Letters flowed into *The Times*, the legal fraternity were appalled, and all but one of the members of his chambers quit in disgust. When the 1931 crisis brought about a National Government and his position became precarious, he became a National Labour candidate. He stood for the seat of the Combined English Universities, having previously advocated the abolition of the university franchise. He was defeated and, as a consequence, resigned as Attorney-General.

Seven years later, having been absent from the political scene for all that time, he was readmitted to the Labour Party, and when Churchill led the coalition he became Solicitor-General, serving under his former pupil, Sir Donald Somerville, who became Attorney. In 1945 a further general election resulted in his appointment, under the third Labour Government, to the prestigious office of Lord Chancellor. When Lord Denning, as he has so often done, extols the virtues of the reeds at Runnymede, he might reflect that none of them could have swayed as flexibly with the winds of fortune as did Lord Jowitt of Stevenage.

The trial clearly displayed the essential difference between the styles of advocacy of the two principal contenders. All the obituaries speak of Jowitt as lucid, moderate, calm, frequently delivering his arguments with a stroke of brilliance. Even allowing for the principle of *de mortuis*, this is not, in the recollection of some, precisely the reputation which he had at the time. Indeed, as the course of the Youssoupoff case progressed, his manner seemed ponderous, lengthy and so bogged down in detail that it often looked as though the jury was losing its way. Perhaps that was part of the brilliance and exactly what he intended.

By comparison, Hastings' approach seemed cavalier in the extreme. He was often heard to say that in every case there was really only one point, and one should concentrate on that one essential to the exclusion of all others. This was, of course, an exaggeration, but it fairly exemplified his method, and it was never better illustrated or more brilliantly executed than in the Youssoupoff case. Jowitt's task was to show that no one in their right mind could possibly have thought that Prince Chegodieff and Natasha were the Prince and Princess Youssoupoff. Hastings clearly saw that the only point in the case was that, however many people might be called by Jowitt to say they did not believe the film portrayed the Youssoupoffs, if only some of those who knew them genuinely thought it did, that was sufficient for him. His adducing of the evidence and his cross-examination of Jowitt's witnesses were so concise and compact that many advocates would have thought he was neglecting to cover vital aspects and that he would lose the case as a consequence.

MGM, having starred the three Barrymores in the film, evidently thought they should have an extra star at the trial. In addition to Jowitt, they briefed Hubert Wallington, KC, as well as two juniors.

Wallington, who, in the event, played little part in the trial, other than to grace the court with his presence, was born in 1875. He was educated privately, which means that he lacked the advantage of public school and university, and was admitted as a solicitor in 1899. Eleven years later, he decided to go to the bar and was called by Gray's Inn in 1910. Into which chambers did he go? None other than those of Sir Patrick Hastings, so that when, in 1919, Hastings took silk and became a KC, Wallington succeeded to much of Hastings' junior work. That is the indispensable advantage of a barrister finding a seat in the right set of chambers. He developed a large and lucrative general practice, became Recorder of Birmingham and, following a pledge by Lord Simon, the Lord Chancellor, to strengthen the judiciary, especially in its divorce jurisdiction, he was appointed a High Court judge at the same time as Lord Denning. It was said that as a judge he was conscientious and took immense pains to get at the truth. The trouble was that, in the process, he never stopped talking. He presided over a case in 1922, as a result of which the Court of Appeal was constrained to order a retrial. His interruptions and questions ran into so many thousands that the court thought it appropriate to warn the judiciary of the danger of descending into the arena and getting mixed up in the dust of the conflict.

Just as MGM had procured a director for the film with, as all believed, a Russian name, although he proved to be a Pole, and just as one critic had thought that the director's presence was to demonstrate that there was, at least, something really Russian about the film, they brought in for the trial, as one of the juniors, Vladimir Robert Idelson. This time, however, they were spot on. He was, in truth, born in Rostov in 1881 and studied law at the University of Kharkov before going to the University of Berlin, where he obtained a doctorate in philosophy. He was called to the Russian bar in 1906. He then turned to banking, eventually securing a post in the Russian Treasury, but fled Russia at the Revolution and came to London to practise as an expert on Russian and international law. He was called to the bar by Gray's Inn in 1926, became a King's Counsel in 1943 and died in 1954 at the age of seventy-three.

The fourth representative for MGM, apart from the solicitors, was a junior member of the bar, Sylvester Gates.

The gladiators having assembled, the battle was ready to begin.

Chapter **Eleven**

Tuesday 27 February 1934 was, for most people in London, little different from the days which had preceded it. The Prime Minister, Ramsay MacDonald, was under attack for having refused to speak to the unemployed who had descended on London as part of an organized march; there was a report of some boisterous activity by a collection of hooligans, led by Oswald Mosley, called the British Union of Fascists; the nippies, in the excellent teashops run by the Joe Lyons Company, were busy taking orders and attending to their customers; Bemax was offering 'new hope for the constipated'; and the secret of 'youthful middle age' was within the grasp of everyone who would start taking Phyllosan tablets that very day.

Money went a great deal further than it would today. A pair of ladies' shoes cost twenty-one shillings; those for a man cost twenty-three shillings. A freehold property with entrance hall, living room, dining room, kitchenette, fitted larder, three bedrooms, bath, separate WC, large garden and garage, and all spanking new, cost £395. A staff maid earned fifteen shillings a week, a cook general a pound a week, and Sainsburys were starting trainee salesmen at twenty-five shillings a week at sixteen, rising to thirty shillings after six months, or when they reached twenty-one.

It was no ordinary day, however, for the Youssoupoffs, since this was the day on which their claim for libel was to commence in the Royal Courts of Justice in the Strand.

The Royal Courts of Justice had been opened in the Strand in 1883, when the judges moved from Westminster Hall, where for generations they had sat in far from comfortable circumstances. The vast new building had been built out of money locked in Chancery, the money of people whose estates had been the subject of dispute, where it was impossible to determine to whom it belonged. Over a hundred years later, the building is little changed. Designed in 'monastic Gothic', it is as wasteful of space as would be expected where something was being erected with some other unfortunate fellow's wealth. As one enters, there is a huge and exceedingly high hall with a fine mosaic floor, all of which in pragmatic terms is totally useless, occupying space which could have been better used as additional courts. From various points in the hall, winding staircases give access to the courts themselves.

Court Number 7, in which the trial would take place, is rather small, with, as they all have, a large bench for the judge. The walls are wood-panelled. On the walls to the left and right of the judge are rows of books, and facing him rows of wooden benches. The front row is for silks, the second row for junior counsel, and the next row for solicitors, who also have available a bench with tables in front of the silks. The public are admitted to the remaining benches and, in a case which excites interest, they stand in the well of the court on either side of the lawyers. There is a gallery for those members of the public without the influence to gain access to the floor of the court. On one side is the jury box, and the witness box is on the other side facing them.

As 10.30 a.m. approached, the court was crowded beyond its capacity. Every seat was occupied; the gallery was full, with people standing at every available point. Whenever there is a *cause célèbre*, there is always a clamour amongst those with the slightest influence for places at the hearing. The most privileged of all, the plaintiffs and the representatives of MGM, sat in the very front, ten feet or so from the judge's seat, on the solicitors' bench. The Princess, who was dressed in black, with a single string of pearls at her throat, so many rings on her fingers that they were clearly visible, and two pearls hanging from each ear, looked regal and dignified. She was wearing a spot veil which shaded her eyes, and a bunch of violets pinned to the fur collar of her coat. Those who had secured special places included Lady Diana Cooper, Lady Oxford, Lady Jowitt and the wife of Mr St John Hutchinson, KC, together with many other well-known people whose identities were not recorded.

There was a flurry as Sir Patrick Hastings and Sir William Jowitt fought their way into court. Hastings, carrying his brief marked with a fee of 1,000 guineas, plus a refresher for each day that the case lasted of 150 guineas a day. MGM, with greater resources at their disposal, had marked Jowitt's brief 2,500 guineas plus refreshers, which, by the monetary standards of the time, was a very large sum.

The usher pulled back the curtain covering the door at the back of the bench through which the judge would emerge, and the judge,

Mr Justice Avory, entered the court, moved to his place, bowed to those facing him and took his seat.

A layman might have been forgiven for thinking that it was exceedingly fortunate for the Youssoupoffs that the judge to whom it had fallen to try their case was none other than the lawyer who had given Pat Hastings his chance at the bar and had been his benefactor, his mentor and his friend. Such a thought, however, would not have entered the head of anyone who knew Sir Horace Avory, who was as incorruptible as any who had ever graced the bench whose incorruptibility is unrivalled in the world.

Horace Edmund Avory was born on 31 August 1851. His father had been the clerk in charge of the Central Criminal Court, better known as the Old Bailey. He went to Kings College, Cambridge, where he became captain of the Boat Club. He was called to the bar by the Inner Temple in 1875 and went into chambers which were predominantly engaged in criminal work, the head of the chambers being E.T.E. Besley, one of the leaders of the criminal bar. Not surprisingly, his early work was almost exclusively criminal, on the South Eastern Circuit, mixed, as often occurs, with liquor licensing work.

He was an excellent lawyer and rose to be one of the outstanding criminal lawyers of his day; indeed, it is arguable whether a better one has emerged since. He was not eloquent, but had a special ability to express himself clearly and in simple terms, never using two words where one would suffice. He became Junior Treasury Counsel at the Old Bailey in 1889 and was promoted to Senior ten years later. Treasury Counsel prosecute for the Crown at that court and are always juniors, not being permitted whilst holding that office to take silk. Virtually their whole time is spent pursuing that task, and those who see virtue in advocates both prosecuting and defending, and thus securing a more balanced view of the legal processes, believe the Treasury junior system to be unsatisfactory and anachronistic. One of his colleagues said of him, 'The prosecution was conducted by an advocate whom I have always regarded, from his strength, lucidity and fairness as the most deadly antagonist I ever met – Horace Avory.'

He prosecuted in innumerable famous trials, including those of Oscar Wilde, Jameson and his associates in the Transvaal raid, Jabez Balfour and Whitaker Wright, being led by Rufus Isaacs, Adolf Beck and many others too numerous to list.

In 1901 he took silk, which necessitated his relinquishing his role as Treasury Counsel, but he continued to be greatly in demand, and in

1910 he was made a judge of the Supreme Court. He quickly overcame his limitation of having been almost, although by no means totally, engaged in criminal law, and although he tried with great skill many non-criminal cases, it was in that field that he continued to excel.

He earned the reputation of being a hard – some called him a 'hanging' – judge. This was, in some respects, undeserved since he was more than capable of being merciful, but he had a stern, forbidding countenance, and this became more pronounced as he grew older. His less unkind critics would say they would not wish to be tried by him if they were guilty, but there was no judge by whom they would sooner be tried if they were innocent. One member of the Old Bailey bar, who always had trouble with his aspirates, said of him, ''Orace Havory was a 'ard and harbitrary advocate and 'e'll make a good 'anging judge.' In fact, he was a popular figure amongst lawyers, was chairman of the Old Bailey bar mess and a most popular figure at the Garrick Club.

The trials over which he presided were no less famous than those in which he prosecuted. They included those of Vacquier, the poisoner; Mahon, the Eastbourne murderer; Browne and Kennedy, who murdered a policeman in bizarre circumstances; and Hatry, the city financier, whom he sent to prison for the maximum available term of fourteen years, sending shocks through the City of London. He said to Hatry, after Norman Birkett, KC, had done his not inconsiderable best for him, and Sir William Jowitt had done his, as Attorney-General, for the Crown, '... I am asked to take into consideration that which is, in fact, the chief ground on which this plea has been put forward in mitigation of your sentence – namely ... that you were engaged in a large financial transaction from which you hoped to reap considerable profit. But what does that plea amount to when stripped of the rhetorical language in which it has been put toward? It is nothing more or less than the threadbare plea of every clerk or servant who robs his master and says that he hoped to repay the money before his crime was discovered, by backing a winner. Except that your crime was on a large scale, there is no difference between that excuse and the dishonest clerk or servant, and I can give no effect to that.'

He died, aged eighty-four the year after the Youssoupoff case, and was sitting, to the end, without the slightest impairment of any of his faculties. Indeed, I clearly recall seeing him try a case in the last year of his life as one of the judges in the Court of Criminal Appeal. When counsel appearing for the appellants got muddled with their names and their part in the crime, it was eighty-four-year-old Avory alone who was on to him like a hawk, which his face now resembled, correcting him.

Now, at the age of eighty-three he was to hear *Youssoupoff* v. *MGM*. The bewigged and gowned associate, who sat immediately beneath the judge, called and empanelled the jury and all was ready. The trial would normally have commenced with the plaintiff's junior counsel opening the proceedings, that is, telling the judge and jury, in brief terms, what the pleadings contained and the nature of the claim. However, it was Jowitt who at once came to his feet to make an application that the judge and jury might be allowed to see the film before anything else occurred at all. He was anxious, he said, that when the jury went to see the film for the first time, and he thought it inevitable that they should see it twice, they should have their minds completely open, uninfluenced by anything one side or the other may say.

'What do you say, Sir Patrick?' asked the judge.

'I have only received notice this application was going to be made two minutes ago,' he replied. 'It is, in my submission, not only a most unreasonable but an impossible suggestion. Your Lordship has not been told yet the nature of the case. It is a form of libel.'

'I have seen the pleadings,' said Avory.

Hastings pointed out that the test for libel was based upon a publication to persons who know the parties. 'No one', he said, 'would see anything defamatory in a film if they knew nothing about the individuals or the story ... Until the jury are in the position of knowing the parties and the stories they cannot form a judgement at all.'

Hastings thought the application should be renewed after the plaintiff had given evidence.

Jowitt clung on. He reiterated what he had said before, adding that arrangements had already been made for the viewing.

'In my view,' Hastings said, 'it will be quite unnecessary for the jury to see it at all, but Sir William thinks they should see it and I raise no objection. I am sure they will not want to see it twice after they have seen it once' – which was, curiously enough, the view the critics had taken.

Jowitt was becoming agitated. 'My friend is going to do his best,' he said. 'I know him well enough to inject, what I call from my point of view ...'

Hastings was back on his feet. 'Do not take an opportunity to say something which either of us will regret,' he told Jowitt.

'I am not going to say anything I shall regret,' Jowitt replied.

The argument, however, was brought to a conclusion. The judge ruled that no useful purpose would be served by the jury having a view of the film until they knew some of the details of the claim and the manner in which the plaintiff said she had been injured. Fifteen love to Hastings.

This done, and the pleadings having been opened, Hastings rose to address the jury.

'As you have heard,' he said, 'this is an action for libel and it is a very unusual case. I think it is probably the first case of its sort that has ever been tried. One thing I am sure you will have no doubt about, and that is that if the plaintiff is right in the view which I shall put before you, she has been defamed by what the defendants have done and the case is a very serious one.'

He told the jury that although they would take all matters of law from the judge, since it was so unusual a case he thought it would help them if he told them about the law.

'This libel', he continued, 'is contained in a film, one of the modern films, in which there are both pictures and speaking.' He told them that the defendants would argue 'that the person represented on the film as Princess Natasha, which is not the plaintiff's name, is merely a creature of fiction, not a real person at all, and therefore, they say the plaintiff is not entitled to recover damages at your hands'.

Clearly, he explained, it is libellous to say of Mr Jones that he is a thief, 'but you can equally libel the same person by not mentioning his name at all, but by describing him in caricature or picture or explanatory statement or otherwise so that people who know him will at once recognize the person portrayed as Mr Jones'.

'There is a further branch of our law,' he went on, 'which to some people may seem rather peculiar, but if one examines it, it is not only good law but very good sense. That is this: even if a person is fictitious; in an action for defamation (even though the person who publishes it did not know of the real plaintiff) it is sufficient if, in fact, the character portrayed is so much resembling the plaintiff that people reasonably understand the plaintiff to be the person aimed at, although he was not named.'

Hastings went on to tell the jury of the famous case concerning Artemus Jones, although he did not tell them that Artemus Jones was a barrister who some people thought had his eye very much to the main chance, although this did not prevent him later in life becoming a County Court judge.

The case of *Hulton* v. *Jones* has become part of legal history. Hastings described it thus: 'Somebody wrote an article in a newspaper and it purported to be an article about one of the perhaps more vulgar watering places. In the course of the article, the writer said this: "I saw today Mr Artemus Jones; he was staying at Deauville with a lady who was not his wife, and it is all the more remarkable because he is a church warden and lives at Peckham." Whereupon, a Mr Thomas Artemus Jones issued a writ claiming damages for libel. It was proved, and indeed admitted, that the author of the libel never intended to portray Mr Artemus Jones; that it was purely a fictitious person in his imagination.

'It was further proved, as a matter of interest, that the real Mr Artemus Jones did not live at Peckham and was not a church warden. Notwithstanding that, the jury, under the direction of the court, held that reasonable people would think it was the real Mr Artemus Jones and he was awarded heavy damages. The case went finally to the House of Lords and every court has decided that is the law. When I told you, therefore, that the defendants in this case are saying that the Princess Natasha is a creature of fiction I want to make two observations upon it. One is that I am going to show you, beyond all question, it is admitted by them that is not true. She is not a creature of fiction; they meant the Princess Youssoupoff, but even if they did not, it is still actionable, if you come to the conclusion that every person reasonably thinking, who knew the Princess and the facts, must think it was her.'

Sir Patrick went on to explain who his client, the plaintiff, was, telling the jury that her mother, the Grand Duchess Xenia, was still alive, and was the Tsar's sister, whilst her father was his cousin. He told the jury about MGM: that they had made a film about Rasputin, 'who is generally supposed to have been the evil influence of Russia during the early years of the war', and that Prince Youssoupoff, 'in pursuance of what he thought to be his duty to his country and his only way of performing it, assassinated Rasputin in order to bring an end to his evil influence'.

'It is a sad story, no doubt,' he continued. 'The film itself must have given immeasurable pain to a large number of people who are still alive because the chief characters portrayed in the film, and some of them, as I shall have to tell you, died in most tragic circumstances, are the Tsar, the Tsarina, the little Tsarevich and others whom I shall have to explain to you.'

Hastings told the jury his speech to them would consist of three parts.

The Imperial Family: Tsar Nicholas II and the Tsarina with their children

Rasputin and the German Empress were seen as evil forces leading the weak Nicholas and his country to destruction

Rasputin at a tea party surrounded by his court of female followers

Prince and Princess Youssoupoff – the early days

John Barrymore in profile with 'Princess Natasha' in *Rasputin the Mad Monk*

The 'other' royal family: the Barrymores with the boy from Iowa

Sir William Jowitt

Sir Patrick Hastings

Justice Avory

Fanny Holtzmann

FRIDAY. THE DAILY EXPRESS. MARCH 2. 1934.

PRINCE GIVES TERRIBLE DETAILS OF RASPUTIN'S MURDER

'ROOTED WITH FEAR' BEFORE MONK'S BODY

"I AM NOT A PROFESSIONAL MURDERER."—*Retort to Counsel*

NEW and terrible details of the killing of Rasputin, evil genius of the Romanoffs, were told by Prince Felix Youssoupoff in the King's Bench Division yesterday.

Once the prince was asked if, as Rasputin's body lay before him, he was so overwrought that he did not know what he was doing. He replied quietly: "It is natural. I am not a professional murderer."

This was the third day of Princess Irina Alexandrovna Youssoupoff's action against the Metro-Goldwyn-Mayer Film Co.

Irina from a film, "Rasputin, the Mad Monk," which portrays a character called Princess Natasha as being in love with Rasputin and as Rasputin's lover, and that he "gave" him back her.

HYPNOTISED BY THE MONK

Prince and Princess Youssoupoff photographed yesterday.

turned on a gramophone in an upstairs room.

Rasputin asked what the noise was, and he told him that his wife was entertaining friends.

That was to keep up the pretence that Rasputin was to meet his wife.

Sir William asked the prince if the nervous strain he was then undergoing was such that he hardly knew what he was doing.

"I am reply in quiet, level tones, was: "It is natural. I am not a professional murderer."

Again Sir William read from the prince's book, describing how Rasputin took doctored wines and cakes, the prince really unharmed and concluding with the passage:—

"All of a sudden his expression changed into one of fiendish hatred ... Never before had he inspired me with such horror.

"A mute and deadly contest argued to be taking place between us, I saw ... Another moment and I should ... had Another moment and I felt that, outfronted by those Satanic eyes, I was beginning to lose my self-control."

Then, added Sir William, you regained your presence of mind and offered him one last ...

HEAD SUNKEN TO

CLUTCH OF IRON

Prince Youssoupoff : My memory is a good one. If I could sing to him for half an hour or more, it shows I can keep my nerves under control. I was not, at the time, so nervous that I could not understand.

Sir William (continuing from the book).

I tried to tear myself away but his iron clutch held me with incredible strength and a terrible struggle ensued.

This dying, poisoned and shudden creature, raised by the powers of darkness to avenge his destruction, inspired me with a feeling so terrifying, so ghastly, that the memory lays with me to this day ...

The Prince assented.

Sir William asked the prince if it was not true that his nerves then completely broke down.

"Why?" asked the prince.

Sir William replied that Putiskevitch's diary had since been published.

WENT FOR LOADED STICK

"That," said the prince, "is the reason I quarrelled with Putiskevitch. I did not agree with his diary."

The prince agreed that he went to his room, where he had a loaded stick.

"Rasputin, on all fours, was rapidly making his way up the staircase, bellowing and snorting like a wounded animal."—Yes.

You say :

Suddenly he gathered himself up and made one final leap towards the wicket door. In the full certainty that the door was locked and that the key was in the possession of those who had left us, I stood on the landing above, grasping the loaded stick, but the wicket door opened and Rasputin vanished into the darkness.

So, though here were there, firmly grasping the loaded stick, you had not hit him with the stick as he was not foaming at the mouth, coming upstairs at all?—No.

You say, ... Then Putiskevitch runs after him ?—Yes, he did.

PEOPLE IN THE CASE

PRINCESS IRINA ALEXANDROVNA, a niece of the murdered Czar who brings the action. She is the wife of

PRINCE YOUSSOUPOFF, the man who says he killed

RASPUTIN, the peasant monk whose influence with the Czar and Czarina caused world-wide talk

METRO - GOLDWYN - MAYER Pictures, Ltd., producers of the film of which complaint is made.

SIR PATRICK HASTINGS, K.C., and MR. ST. JOHN FIELD, counsel for the princess

SIR WILLIAM JOWITT, K.C., and MR. H. J. WALLINGTON, K.C., counsel for the film company.

MR. JUSTICE AVORY, the judge

"And Puriskevitch fires four shots."—Yes, in the dark.

"The first two ... and the third and fourth hit him ?—Yes.

"Rasputin stumbled."—Yes, running then ?—Yes.

"Rasputin stumbled and fell near a snow heap. Puriskevitch ran up to him, stood still for a few seconds, and, having decided everything was now over and that Rasputin was killed, he rapidly strode returned to the house"?—Yes.

Then the servants bring the body back to the house ?—Yes.

Sir William continued reading: taking the story to the time when the prince was alone with the body. Of this, the book said :

Blood was flowing freely from his many wounds. I closed my eyes ... I waded to get away from this revolting scene, but an irresistible impulse holding me back ... My head was bursting ... I was thought were confused ... I was beside myself with rage and hate ... I rushed at the prostrate body ... I pushed at the body ... battering it with the loaded stick, in my frenzy I hit anywhere. ... At ...

'ENGLISH M.P. INVITED TO 'KILL RASPUTIN'

TELLS OF A PLOT TO SAVE THE CZAR

COMMANDER LOCKER-LAMPSON'S STARTLING EVIDENCE

ONE of the most startling statements made in a British court in recent years came from the lips of Commander O. Locker-Lampson, M.P., in the King's Bench Division yesterday.

Smiling slightly, he said : "I was invited by Puriskevitch to murder Rasputin."

The stunned silence that greeted this statement was but ... shattered by laughter when Sir ... Patrick Hastings, K.C., re- ...

COMMANDER O. LOCKER-LAMPSON during the war, when he stated in court yesterday, he was invited to murder Rasputin.

... not in any way taking sides in this case.

Asked if he knew a Miss Burhanan, Colonel Thornhill replied that she was now married. She was the daughter of his chief in Petrograd.

Sir Patrick : Has Miss Burhanan been engaged for months in trying to assist a Wright solicitor for the defence in the conduct of this case ?—I don't know.

She asked you to go to the private office of the film ?—Her husband asked...

... do you know that, in this action, Burhanan was going to be a witness for ...

... she was going to prove—that Princess Natasha was not Princess ...—Yes.

VISIT TO FILM

... illar evidence was given by ... Tchapline, of Colet-gardens, ... Court, W. He said that he ... retired captain of the Imperial ... Russian Navy and a son of a ... Russian Postmaster-General. ... oss-examination he said that he ... ifies the film with Colonel Thornhill had met Miss Burhanan that ... the first time.

Meriel Knowling, actress, ... W., was the next witness.

... did she was the daughter of the ... George Buchanan, British Ambassador, in St. Petersburg at the time ... She frequently met the ... Czarina, the Czar's daughters, ... Witch, and the Grand Duke.

Princess Irina arrest times.—Yes.

ADMIRATION FOR HER

... With reference to Princess Youssoupoff she said, "I never associated her with Natasha at all. I had, and have, with Natasha admiration for her, and the greatest admiration for her, and I knew she would never be connected with Rasputin or with any scandal."

Mr. Henry Herbert Sidney Wright, a member of the firm of Wright and Webb, the defendants' solicitors, said that he was chairman of the Metro-Goldwyn-Mayer subsidiary company in this country.

When complaint was made by the princess "cuts" were made in the film, and everything done to satisfy her.

Sir Patrick cross-examined, you, in this court, and who can show any question whether or not service this film—of Princess Youssoupoff—I had... made her way in July 1932 and June... criticised the film... papers throughout... that was first exhibited... sometime in 1932... ..... —It was produced...

CLUTCH (cont.)

The Secret Of Rasputin's Deadly Eyes

"Daily Express" Medical Correspondent

RASPUTIN'S eyes show a marked squint. This may have had much to do with the hypnotic effect he is reputed to have produced on many people.

It is a help to the hypnotiser if he has a cast in his eye. It aids the nature to the gaze of the person to be hypnotised, for he, or she, is caught by the unusual quality of the squinting eye and stares at it with

RASPUTIN'S EYES

the pertinacity necessary to produce the hypnotic state.

Men who hypnotise and who are not gifted with a cast in the eye have to use other measures to produce that fixity of gaze which comes easily to the subject of the squinting eye.

Somehow or other the "victim's" gaze must be kept steadily concentrated, and this is most readily achieved by the hypnotiser when there is some peculiar feature about his face on which the subject's gaze is easily riveted. Such was Rasputin's cast.

'A SOLDIER AND A DILETTANTE

WHEN RASPUTIN MESMERISED AND TRIED TO CURE HIM

THE SPHERE

With which is incorporated THE GRAPHIC

The Empire's
Illustrated Weekly

London, March 10, 1934

Prince and Princess Youssoupoff examine the offending film and, at the time of the trial

The first covered that part of history which the film intended to convey; the second, the story as portrayed by the film; and 'then I am going to tell you the part of the film which is introduced in a most dreadful manner, if my view of the case is right, in order to accentuate what they call the love interest, that part of the film which cast these aspersions upon the Princess'. Hastings paused and added, 'I may tell you at once that what we complain of is that this film attacks her chastity and depicts her as a woman who in her own words is not fit to be the wife of the man she loves.'

As he had promised, Sir Patrick proceeded first to tell the jury his version of the true and relevant history of Russia. Whether Russian historians would have agreed with all he said, may be beside the point. He spoke of the celebrations marking three hundred years of Romanov rule, and of the marriage in 1914 of the Prince and Princess, which he described with some exaggeration as 'one of the great episodes' of Russia. He told them of Rasputin, 'a person with some more or less unjustified claims to religion ... some sort of a monk ... with extra-ordinary hypnotic power, or was said to be'. He described him as 'utterly unscrupulous. His object in life was solely his own advantage ... a man of great coarseness who ... used his position solely or mainly for the purpose of obtaining advantages in money or otherwise for himself.' Whilst, in retrospect, Rasputin was a singularly unattractive figure, some of the things which Hastings said about him might have been difficult to prove beyond reasonable doubt, had that burden rested upon him, which, of course, it did not.

He described Rasputin's hold over the Court as a result of the Tsarevich's haemophilia. He told the jury how Rasputin was evidently able to cure the condition when it struck and commented, 'It was the more remarkable, and you will hear how it was explained in a moment, but when, at any time, his influence seemed to wane and there was a suggestion that his favour at Court had diminished, immediately the poor little Tsarevich became immeasurably worse. As such he obtained a position in Court' (he meant 'at Court'). 'He could do anything he liked and in the early years of the war his position in Russia was generally understood to be an absolute menace.'

Just as it was, of course, Hastings' purpose to present Rasputin to the jury in as ugly a guise as possible, so it was his task to present the Prince and the Princess in the best possible light. Thus, he described how the situation in which Rasputin had placed himself 'came to the knowl-edge of Prince Youssoupoff, who after the war had started, was undergoing a course of military training outside St Petersburg, where Rasputin was the subject of general and universal discussion'. Whatever training the Prince was undergoing, it was certainly not for active service in the front line, as the jury may have been led to infer; moreover, the war had been raging for over two years, so the Prince had been in no hurry.

When the Prince obtained his leave, said Sir Patrick, he put himself out and got to know Rasputin, doing it so well that Rasputin thought he had the Prince under his influence. At this point, Hastings was in danger of doing almost as much damage to Russian history as MGM had done in the film. He said that Rasputin told the Prince of 'the whole of his ambition'; 'the secret of his hold over the Tsarevich', which was because 'he had obtained assistance given to him by some of those curious people who live in Monasteries in Tibet, who had presented him with some remarkable healing herbs. Rasputin said the Tsarina could never get rid of him because he could cure the Tsarevich and he could kill him by giving or withholding the drugs of which nobody else in Europe knew but himself.' According to Hastings, Rasputin 'told Prince Youssoupoff that he was determined to become the ruler of the whole of Russia, a position to which he appeared to be rapidly approaching'. He had also told him that he was in the pay and employment of the German Emperor and that the plan which he was engaged upon with others was to persuade the Tsar to sign his abdication and to appoint the Tsarina as Regent, when, Rasputin boasted, he himself would be supreme and the complete ruler of Russia. It was then that Youssoupoff determined to kill him.

Thus, Hastings was presenting to the jury as facts much that has remained conjecture. Certainly, although the Prince's account of the part he played was never wholly consistent each time he told the story, he never overstated his role as much as Hastings was prepared to do when addressing the jury.

'It is a terrible story', said Sir Patrick, 'for anyone to have to tell. I do not know whether in those countries they regard things a little differently to what we do, but Prince Youssoupoff was quite determined to take all the blame, to take all the consequences on himself in regard to these matters.'

Some may have thought that in so overstating his case the great advocate was offering a hostage to fortune. It was most unlikely that anyone on the jury would have known about this episode of Russian history. If, however, Jowitt knew his history, he could cross-examine the Prince, in due course, to show him to be someone prone to exaggeration and who was endeavouring to present himself in a better light than he deserved. Time would tell.

'Prince Youssoupoff and three friends – ' said Hastings, 'I need not trouble with their names because Prince Youssoupoff has taken all the blame for this matter – determined to kill Rasputin.'

Having described the Prince's home in St Petersburg – the Moika Palace – and how a secret passage led to the cellar, he continued with the account of the poisoning of the wine and the cakes, 'although', he said, 'it is a tragic thing to have to tell, that the food, cakes – and I particularly ask you to remember that, cakes – ' (why, did not emerge!) 'and wine should be poisoned with enough poison to kill twenty men'. He told how the poison seemed to have no effect on Rasputin and asserted that the Prince thereupon shot him twice, when he fell as though dead. 'Some time afterwards, he apparently regained life and had to be shot again. Finally, he was taken and thrown into the river. The Prince was held by the police for questioning; he made no secret of the fact of what he had done.'

The main issue in the case was whether the fictitious Natasha and Chegodieff were really the Prince and Princess Youssoupoff. It might have been thought important that Hastings should only be allowed to tell the jury the provable truth about the Prince. There was certainly no word of protest from Jowitt, although it was not the Prince who had finally dispatched Rasputin but Pourichkevich, and it was Dimitri, the doctor and Soukhotin who threw the body into the river. Moreover, far from having 'made no secret of his part in it', the Prince denied any knowledge of the crime when questioned by the police; he spent time cleaning up his house in the hope that he would not be implicated, shot one of his dogs to corroborate his lying story, and generally did everything he could to conceal his involvement in the murder. It was only much later, when the story was fully known, that there was no point in further denial, and when he was safely away from Russia he spent his time writing in glowing terms of his part in the murder of Rasputin.

To conclude this part of his address, Sir Patrick told how the Prince had been exiled from Russia. In fact, he was never banished from Russia by the Tsar; he left voluntarily to escape the effects of the Revolution. 'You can well understand', Sir Patrick said, 'they have now left Russia penniless' (this was untrue); 'their whole estate and fortune gone' (untrue) 'and they now live with merely a memory of those days, which the film has brought back to them' – also untrue, since the Prince spent much time reviving, and glorying in, the murder, in the books he wrote.

In approaching the second part of his address, which was to describe the film, Hastings told the jury about Prince Chegodieff and Princess Natasha as played by the Barrymores.

The Prince Chegodieff of the film, he pointed out, had a palace at St Petersburg known as the Moika Palace on the banks of the Moika River. 'No other Prince had such a palace,' he told the jury. 'The Moika Palace was the palace of Prince Youssoupoff and of nobody else.'

'In the film,' he stressed, 'Prince Chegodieff determines that Rasputin shall die in the Moika Palace, and he is finally killed in the cellar of the Moika Palace and thrown into the river. In the film, Prince Chegodieff is brought before the Tsar, he is sent away by the Tsar out of Russia and he leaves to marry the only lady that we know he has married, Princess Natasha, or the lady whom I represent, and it will be of interest to know at some time whether anyone is going to suggest that Prince Chegodieff, who lives in the Moika Palace by the Moika River and who kills Rasputin in the cellar of that Palace, is a different person from Prince Youssoupoff.'

'The answer is "yes", Sir Patrick,' interposed Jowitt.

'It is even more interesting', replied Hastings, 'to be told that the answer is "yes". I can now see, possibly, why they are going to say the same thing about Princess Natasha. If they did not say that, it would be a little difficult, because there is no other royal princess who married Prince Youssoupoff.'

Hastings then read out to the jury the names of the characters portrayed in the film and those of the actors and actresses who portrayed them. He explained that the first four, the Imperial family and Rasputin, met their deaths by violence. Of the other four, he continued, Prince Chegodieff and Princess Natasha are said to be imaginary characters and the Grand Duke Igor (also listed) and Dr Ramezov do not really matter.

'These characters are described in the film opening shots, and I want you to listen to these words and see whether you think the defence are a little hopeful in stating that Princess Natasha and Prince Chegodieff are fictitious, because the Princess Irina, Prince Youssoupoff and one of the other two are alive. This is what appears after the cast: "This concerns the destruction of an empire, brought about by the mad ambition of one man. A few of the characters are still alive, the rest met death by violence." We know that the Tsar, the

Tsarina, the Tsarevich and Rasputin met their death by violence. If the Grand Duke Igor is the Grand Duke Paul, he met death by violence; he was assassinated. The three who remain are the Prince Chegodieff, Princess Natasha and the Court physician. I cannot tell you whether he is alive or dead; we do not know. If he is dead, the only two who are still alive are the Prince Chegodieff and the Princess Natasha.' He turned towards his clients in the front and pointing to them said: 'They are alive and they are here.'

The folly of Bernie Hyman, MGM's supervisor, in prefacing the film with those words was now becoming only too apparent. Hastings reminded the jury again of the case of Artemus Jones. 'The court said' he explained, 'you cannot, by putting in things which are not real' (in this case that he was a church warden, who lived at Peckham), 'say that means the person aimed at is not the person who complained. If people try to make a love story out of history, they always take liberties with it, and the liberties they took with this film are these: they wanted two things, apparently. A gentleman I do not know, but I should imagine he came first in the list, he is a person who commands a large salary, Mr John Barrymore – I do not know whether any of you, ladies and gentlemen, have heard of him, but I should imagine that as his name is put first on the film, you have – is playing Prince Chegodieff, and it may be that these theatrical gentlemen like to make themselves as romantic as possible. So it may be that, if they are members of that profession, they find they are more attractive to their audiences unmarried than married, and therefore the marriage with the Princess was destined to take place after the audience had left the theatre. That was one of the poetic licences they took with the story.'

He suggested the other poetic licence they took was for English audiences, who might prefer some greater motive for killing than 'a deep and almost religious duty'. Why precisely he thought that, was not explained.

He referred to 'a most unpleasant scene in which they made Rasputin go to the Princess Natasha and say, "You and I are going to punish Paul", under circumstances which leave no doubt in your mind that she is then going to become his mistress. I use the word "mistress" in a non-committal sense, because something has been said in the course of this case as to whether the action of Rasputin is that of a seducer, or violator of, the Princess, or, whether or not on more occasions, she submits to his advances and is therefore technically his mistress. Also that it is not a libel to say of a woman that she has been raped, because that may show she did not consent.

'These technicalities I will leave to the Metro-Goldwyn-Mayer Film Company, who no doubt are expert in these refinements. This film shows this lady, if it is her, a woman who has been sleeping with a man so utterly degraded as Rasputin, and ... when her lover comes to her and begs her to marry him, she turns round and says, "I thought this man came from God, but I know now he was only a man and I am not fit to be your wife." What does that mean – and all these books' – pointing to the bound synopsis of the film, in front of Jowitt – 'are here apparently produced to show you they do not mean it.'

'This is perfectly untrue,' interjected Jowitt, 'your last observation about Metro-Goldwyn-Mayer was totally uncalled for in this class of case. These books are not here to prove any particular fact; they are a record of the whole film. I do ask my friend not to assume what is in the books without having looked at them.'

'I assumed they were relevant, Members of the Jury,' rejoined Hastings, 'otherwise they would not be here.'

He continued by pointing out a number of things that were inaccurate from an historical point of view. The Grand Duke was not assassinated in 1913, as the film suggested, but many years before: Princess Natasha, if she were Princess Irina as he alleged was the case, was never a lady-in-waiting to the Tsarina, she was a friend or more correctly an intimate associate of the Imperial family. Hastings pointed out to the jury that such errors were no more decisive than was the fact that Mr Artemus Jones was not a church warden.

'For the purpose of the film,' he continued, 'they make the Princess the person who introduced Rasputin to the Tsarina. That is quite inaccurate. He was introduced to the Tsarina some years before and not by the Princess at all, who never saw Rasputin. Of course, you realize, Members of the Jury, in a story of this sort it is not a libel to anybody who does not know the facts. It is to people who know the story of both of them; who go and see the film and know perfectly well that Prince Youssoupoff is the man who killed Rasputin and know perfectly well that this lady is his wife.'

Since the question for the jury was whether the so-called fictitious Natasha was really Irina, it would be for Jowitt to list all the differences to show it was not she. Why, then, was Hastings doing Jowitt's task for him? In fact, it was better for Hastings to face these differences before Jowitt had the chance and to put them within the perspective of the law and his own case.

He read to the jury the letter before action which the Prince's solicitors had written in October 1933, asking that the picture be withdrawn from display, failing which they intended to issue a writ and seek an injunction to restrain further publication of the libel. The reply from MGM's solicitors listed all the events which must have come to the notice of the plaintiff well before October (the film had been at the Empire in June), as indicating that the sudden burst of indignation was hardly sincere. They added that since then they had entered into many commitments with cinemas: if it was now withdrawn it would cost them £40,000. As a result, the writ was issued, but instead of an injunction, which was refused, the judge ordered a speedy trial. The courts are most reluctant to grant such injunctions where it would seem that money would be an adequate remedy for any wrong done and there is no reason to believe that the defendants lack the means to pay it. They were even more reluctant in 1934, perhaps, than they are today.

Hastings was reaching the end of his address. 'Was there', he invited the jury to ask themselves, 'any other princess in Russia of the age of this lady so related to the Tsar, because she was in fact both his niece and his cousin ... is there any other lady in Russia who, in fact, could so approach her? You will hear the answer is "No".

'We say there is another Princess,' rather improperly interjected Jowitt.

'I always welcome my friend's interruptions,' said Sir Patrick, 'but he may say, if the jury hear "Yes" from him, they will hear "No" from me, and since he has already told me that what I have said is untrue, I hope he will not interrupt me again.' He told them it was a simple case which was capable of being made complicated. He correctly foresaw that, whether by accident or design, Jowitt would make his simple case an extremely complicated one. Hastings' final gesture was to stress again that MGM had admitted in the introduction of the film that some of those portrayed were still alive, and his client and her husband were certainly that.

The time was about 11.30 a.m. Hastings had opened the case for little more than an hour and the jury could now go and see the film for themselves. The court adjourned for that purpose and for luncheon until 2.30 p.m. The audience surged into the corridor, the Prince and Princess following with their friends.

Chapter Twelve

Immediately after the adjournment, when the jury had viewed the film, Sir Patrick Hastings called Princess Irina to the witness box. She walked slowly, it might almost be said majestically, across the court and into the witness box, where she took the oath.

She said she was the wife of Prince Youssoupoff and lived with him at 37 Rue Gothenburg, Boulogne-sur-Seine, France. She was temporarily staying with her mother at Windsor. She described her relationship to the Tsar and said that from 1913 to 1916 he had no other living niece. Hastings reminded her that in the film there is a person described as the Grand Duke Sergei. She said that at the date Hastings mentioned, the only Grand Duke alive was Paul; Sergei had been assassinated in 1905, and Paul met his death at the hands of the Bolsheviks in 1919.

The Princess, who said she had known the Tsar, the Tsarina and their son intimately, recalled an important state function in 1913, to celebrate three hundred years of Romanov rule in Russia. She had attended the celebrations and there was no other royal princess there other than herself. She said that in 1914 Rasputin was prominent in Russian life.

'Had you yourself ever met him?' asking Hastings.

'I never met him,' the Princess replied.

She said Rasputin's influence in Court circles was very great. Her husband, she said, had owned vast estates in Russia, but they had been stripped of everything they possessed. One of her husband's homes was the Moika Palace.

'Was there any other palace known in St Petersburg as the Moika Palace?' asked Hastings.

'There was my mother's palace, but it had a different name.'

'Is the street called the Moika?'

'Yes.'

'... But the Moika Palace was that of your husband?'

'Yes.'

'I think at the date of the assassination of this man Rasputin, you were not in St Petersburg at all?' asked Hastings.

'No, I was not,' was the reply.

The Princess confirmed that the murder of Rasputin had been the subject of discussion all over the world, and many books had been written about it.

'Whether it be right or not, and that we will hear from the evidence, who was the person who was popularly supposed to have been the cause of Rasputin's death?'

'It was my husband,' she said at once.

She said they had lived in various countries since the murder, and Hastings then asked, 'Did you next hear, or hear first, that the film *Rasputin* was exhibited in England, somewhere about August of last year?'

'Yes, that is right, about the end of August.'

'Who do you think is represented by the Princess Natasha of the film?'

'I think it represents me.'

Hastings then listed eight different characters portrayed in the film, and asked, 'So that out of the eight, five of them met their deaths by violence?'

'Yes.'

'There remains therefore Prince Chegodieff . . .'

At this point Mr Justice Avory interrupted. 'You are assuming, are you not, without asking the witness, whom the Grand Duke Igor represents?'

'The witness has told us', replied Hastings, 'that the only living brother of the Grand Duke Sergei in 1914 was Paul. He was the only living brother.'

The judge was not satisfied. 'I know, but is not the question, the witness having seen the film, whether she suggests that the Grand Duke Igor in the film represents any particular person?'

Hastings agreed and, turning back to the Princess, asked, 'Who do you think the Grand Duke Igor of the film represents?'

'He represented the Tsar's uncle, the Grand Duke Paul, the only one that remained alive.'

There then followed a discussion between the witness and counsel as to whom Dr Ramezov, in the film, was intended to portray. The Princess said the real Court physician was Dr Derevenko. She assumed this was the doctor they had in mind, but she did not know whether he was alive or dead. She also said that she had never been a lady-in-waiting, and neither had any other royal princess. With regard to the scenes in the film where Princess Natasha was dressed as a nurse, she said she herself attended the hospital at St Petersburg, as well as others elsewhere, and that she then wore a sort of white overall.

'Nurse's clothes?' asked the judge.

'Yes.'

In reading the transcript, it seems increasingly likely that none of those appearing for the plaintiff had sufficiently applied their minds to how they might argue that the film more strongly suggested seduction than rape. Certainly, to suggest that the Princess had been a willing and consenting party to sexual intercourse would have attracted far greater damages than suggesting that she had been raped. For some reason, Hastings throughout made little of this, until forced later to face it when the pleadings had to be amended.

'Do you remember', he asked the witness, 'the scene after Prince Chegodieff has shot at and failed to kill Rasputin, a scene between Princess Natasha and Rasputin, when he goes into the room?'

'Yes.'

'These are the words which he says; I can repeat them to you because they come from the script. Natasha says, "I heard a shot," Rasputin says, "Yes, my daughter," Natasha says, "It was Paul," Rasputin says, "Yes, my daughter, we are going to punish Paul, you and I," and then there is a scene in which he goes towards her, I think, after the door is locked. Had you any doubt in your mind what that scene was intended to portray?'

'No, I had not.'

'What did it to your mind indicate?'

Unhappily, as too often occurs, the judge then interrupted again and the witness lost the question. 'Where is the scene?' asked the judge.

'The scene is laid in a room in Rasputin's house,' Hastings told the judge.

Then, turning to the witness, he said, 'I do not know that it is necessary that I should press you about it, but what does that scene indicate to you; what is taking place between that woman and Rasputin in the scene? Is there any doubt about it?' Here was a muddled question; an example of examination in chief at its worst, but then even Homer nodded.

'No, no doubt at all,' came the inevitable inadequate response.

'Very well,' said Hastings, 'as the jury have seen it, I need not ask you any more about it.' This seems odd, since it would surely have been relevant and interesting to know whether the plaintiff's outrage stemmed from her belief that she was shown as having been a consenting or non-consenting party to intercourse with Rasputin.

Sir Patrick then referred to a scene in which, as Princess Youssoupoff said she inferred, Rasputin was seen threatening Princess Natasha that if she told the Imperial family what had occurred between them, he would be sent away and the Tsarevich would die.

Finally he said, 'Then do you remember the scene at the end, in the hospital, where Chegodieff tries to make Natasha come with him and Natasha says, "I have not the right to be your wife"?'

'Yes,' said the Princess, 'I remember it.'

'And Natasha says, "You told me what he – that is Rasputin – was. I should have known. I thought you were persecuting a man of God. Well, I have found out." Have you any doubt at all what that indicates?'

'No, no doubt at all.'

'What do you think that scene meant? What was she saying to her lover then?'

'That she had not the right to marry him after what happened between her and Rasputin.'

'I think', said Hastings, 'those are all the matters I need ask you about the film.' Precisely what the Princess thought was the allegation conveyed by the film, the jury were never told.

As Hastings sat down, Jowitt rose to ask, as it would make a difference to his cross-examination of the Princess, whether Hastings intended to call the Prince as a witness. Hastings replied that he was calling him.

It will be seen that Sir Patrick Hastings' examination of his client had, in accordance with his usual approach, been reduced to the minimum. He asked – with, perhaps, the one omission already noted – no more than he believed was essential and thus kept the issues for the jury simple and concise.

Jowitt began his cross-examination of the Princess with the question, 'Madame, do you think that anybody knowing the real circumstances could suppose for one moment that you were portrayed by Natasha?'

'Yes,' she replied, 'people might think that, of course.'

'My question was, people knowing the real circumstances?'

'Yes, they might, all the same.'

'Because I suggest to you that one of the real circumstances which must be known by anybody in regard to this matter of Rasputin is that you never met him?'

'I never met him,' replied the witness with commendable brevity.

'And you know it was the fact that you had never met him, that was the excuse for his being brought round to the house that night in order that he might make your acquaintance?'

'Yes.'

'And in every book, and there was a great number of them, which deals with this tragedy, is it not made quite plain that you never, in fact, had met him?'

'I never met him.'

The Princess was displaying the qualities of the perfect witness, concise and to the point.

Jowitt turned to fresh fields. 'Is it then, do I understand, to vindicate your character that you are bringing this action?'

'Yes.'

'Is that the sole reason?'

'Yes.'

'Because I am sure you will agree, Princess, if the truth were that you were trying to make money out of rather a far-fetched identification, if that were the truth, it would be beneath your dignity?'

'Of course.'

'And may I take it that all the advisers who have assisted you in regard to this litigation would be instructed by you to take that line?'

Understandably, the Princess could not follow the question. 'What did you say?' she asked.

'Would all the advisers who have been instructed by you in regard to this litigation have been instructed that your desire was merely to clear your character and not to make money?'

'Yes.'

So far the cross-examiner had made no progress. Jowitt moved on, and in the process demonstrated how pointless cross-examination can be unless the ground is properly prepared.

'Now let me ask you a question or two about dates,' he said. 'I think you said it was the autumn of 1932 that you first heard the film had appeared in America?'

'Yes.'

'That is the American film. Did you hear that you were represented in a bad light?'

'I did.'

'And was it your husband – I am asking these questions from the affidavit that you made [for the purpose of securing the injunction] – who gave you that information while you were staying in Menton?'

'Yes, that is right.'

'So that it is plain, of course, from that, he would know just as much about it as you did, because he was the source of your information?'

'Yes, that is right.'

'And, naturally, I suppose, you would trust him to do whatever was necessary in regard to the matter?'

'Of course.'

Jowitt then read to her a letter written by American lawyers on behalf of the Prince alone, complaining of misrepresentation in regard to his killing of Rasputin and asserting that it libelled him.

He then continued, 'Now, do you observe that having heard, as you told us, at the end of autumn of 1932 that the film represents you in a bad light, your husband writes and makes a claim in respect of the libel on him, and does not mention you at all. Why was that?'

Without a pause, the Princess replied, 'My husband was told he was represented in a bad light too. He was told he was libelled in the film, not only myself, but he too.'

Jowitt put the same point to her again, and elicited the answer, 'I was not there at the time he wrote that. He was probably told that he was libelled by the film.'

Sir William's point could, of course, have been a good one, showing that at first they never contended the Princess had been libelled. Unfortunately, he had unwisely assumed, and based his questions entirely upon the assumption, that the Prince and Princess had been together throughout. The judge burst the bubble.

'Sir William,' he said, 'would you ask where was the Prince at the time the letter was written?' Jowitt did so.

'Yes,' was the reply, 'in the beginning of January 1933, he must have been in Paris, I think.'

Jowitt endeavoured to recover his position, but now the effectiveness of his questions gradually petered out.

'Can you tell me when you came back from Menton?' he asked.

'Yes, I came back in August 1933.'

'Were you at Menton for a whole year?'

'Yes.'

'Then your husband was in Paris going, no doubt, backwards and forwards to see you at Menton. His headquarters were in Paris and I have no doubt he went to see you?'

'Yes, once or twice he came to see me.'

'He came to see you from time to time,' said Jowitt, somewhat dispirited. 'There, at any rate, the matter is.'

What could have been an important piece of cross-examination had fallen to the ground because Jowitt had failed to establish at the outset that the Prince and Princess had been together when he threatened his claim for libel.

Sir William endeavoured to get the Princess to agree that her friends must have written to her if they believed she had been libelled by the film.

'Nobody ever writes to me,' said the Princess plaintively, 'and I never answer letters.'

Next Jowitt turned his attention to Fanny Holtzmann, asking, 'On the 30th August did you give instructions to Fanny Holtz-mann?'

'Yes.'

'Is Fanny Holtzmann in court?' he asked, knowing full well she was not.

'No, she is not,' was the reply.

'She's in America,' interposed Hastings, thinking, no doubt, 'and a good job, too'.

Sir William now endeavoured to find out how Miss Holtzmann had got into contact with the Princess. The Princess said she was introduced to her by friends in Menton, but did not speak to her concerning the case there; she did that in Paris. She was also emphatic that she did not know of that lady's visit to the rep-resentatives of MGM and that she had never instructed her to tell them that money could settle the matter.

'On the 13th September, to be precise about the date, I am suggesting to you that Miss Holtzmann said to Mr Eckmann [the managing director of MGM in England], "Cable for authority to settle the case, it is only a question of money." I want to know whether, if that be correct, she made that statement with your authority.'

'No, I cannot remember.'

'Did you say "Yes" or "No"?'

'I do not think so.'

'You do not think so?'

'No, because I cannot remember it at all.'

Jowitt persisted still further. 'Let me ask you this then; would you have been prepared to settle for money?'

'No.'

It has always been a common ploy for advocates in defamation cases, and indeed for solicitors in negotiation of such claims, to present those who claim damages as being beyond the pale. It is just as difficult to understand why so many who receive damages are persuaded to give them away to charity. There is, of course, nothing at all to be said against donations to charity, if given in the proper spirit, but as a face-saving exercise it seems strange. The law rightly gives those who are defamed a right to damages, just as it gives a similar right to those who are injured by accident. Why, therefore, it should be suggested that there is something wrong in claiming and retaining that which the law rightly afforded for defamation is really beyond sensible comprehension. It would be salutary if the judges, when such cross-examination is pursued, intervened to point out precisely that.

Sir William Jowitt referred to the writ which had been issued in the proceedings which had been brought by the Princess in America. He told her she would not know the date it would have been served, but that it was 14 September. This upset Hastings.

'I do not know what you are putting in,' he commented. 'I have a document which has quite a different date on it.'

'Quite right,' said Jowitt. 'It is dated the 11th August, but not served until the 14th September.'

Hastings made it seem that all this was of vital importance, and went on for some time expressing the hope that the document would be properly proved, as it was all a question of a date which had some special significance. In fact it did not, but his intervention no doubt created the illusion in the mind of the jury that he was stopping Jowitt from taking an unfair advantage of the witness.

It transpired that all Jowitt desired to do was put to the Princess a long and rambling extract from the American statement of claim which, with the customary American prolixity, set out the events in the American version of the film which her attorneys contended showed her to have been raped. Jowitt read it out to her.

Having done so, he said, 'It is obvious to you, I think, if this is a fair representation of the American film, that it differs very much indeed from the English film?'

'Yes, a little,' said the Princess.

'The bedroom scene and the screams and so on, we have not any of at all, but allowing for those differences, do you or do you not say that the inference you ask the jury to draw from this film, from her being locked in the room and so on was' – and he quoted from the American statement of claim – 'that he, that is Rasputin, did in fact commit upon Natasha the crime of rape?'

'Yes,' she replied.

'Did you ever see the American version?' asked the judge.

'I never saw it,' she replied.

'You are only judging by this description?' asked the judge.

'I saw the English version, but I never saw the American,' said the Princess.

'You understood me?' added Jowitt. 'Your answer applied, of course, to the English version, which was the only one you had seen?'

'Yes, the only one I saw.'

Why Jowitt had relied on the American document, instead of the English one, where the allegation was the same, is difficult to understand. It did, however, light up the difference between the two advocates: Hastings introducing nothing which was not essential, and Jowitt ponderously wandering up roads and byways which seemed to lead nowhere.

He next again endeavoured to persuade the Princess to accept that she had instructed Fanny Holtzmann to obtain money to settle her claim.

'On the 9th October,' he put to her, 'and evidence of it will be given, Miss Holtzmann called to see Mr Wright, the solicitor instructing me, and said that the film company would get a pain in the neck, but they could still settle by a money payment. Now if she made that statement would it be made with your approval?'

'No,' said the Princess emphatically.

'Did you tell her anything of the sort?'

'No, I do not remember telling her anything.'

'It is not a question of remembering. I do not think there can be much doubt about it. The distinction between a desire to get your honour cleared, with which I entirely and completely sympathize – and nothing I will say will cast the smallest shadow upon it, if indeed there ever has been – and the desire to make money out of what I am going to submit is a fantastic identification, are two wholly such different things, are they not?'

'Yes.'

'You surely cannot have forgotten whether you told Miss Holtz-mann that all you wanted was payment of money?'

'No, of course not,' was the reply.

'Did you tell her or did you not?'

'No.'

'What did you tell her?'

'I told her I wanted the film stopped.'

Sir William had not really moved the witness at all. The original hesitancy and uncertainty, depending on an assertion that she could not remember, probably indicated that she had known and approved, albeit tacitly, of Fanny Holtzmann's tactics. By his subsequent pressure, all Jowitt had achieved was a more emphatic rebuttal of his suggestions.

It is interesting to speculate how his opponent, Sir Patrick, would have gone about this. Probably he would have followed the line of asking the Princess whether, if MGM had been prepared to pay a substantial sum to her without withdrawing the film, she would have accepted it, as Jowitt had done. The witness should then have been on the horns of a dilemma. If she said 'Yes', he would have made his point, but if she said 'No', as she did, he would have asked whether Miss Holtzmann must, therefore, have been talking sheer nonsense had she said what he would prove she said. Jowitt fell short of this and the point lost some cogency as a consequence.

Jowitt put it to the Princess that the fact that she had started so many actions, including those against 288 picture houses 'up and down the country', showed her desire to secure the maximum financial return.

Her answer destroyed even that suggestion. 'I wanted to stop the film, as I told you,' she said. Clearly, suing the picture houses would have been the most effective way of doing so.

The next series of questions which were put in cross-examination were, presumably, designed to mark for the jury the essential differen-ces between the events displayed in the film and the true historical facts, and to show that no one could have thought they had depicted Princess Youssoupoff. In that respect, the questions hardly succeeded.

'The Grand Duke Sergei as you have told us,' said Jowitt, after questioning her about her relationship to him, 'was assassinated in February 1905.'

'Yes.'

'You would then have been a child of nine years?'

It needs to be remembered that juries possess the faculties of ordi-nary people, chosen at random, and there is, perhaps, nothing which causes more confusion in the minds of such ordinary people than trying to work out family relationships outside the immediate circle. How much the jury were able to follow of what now transpired is difficult to assess.

'It is perfectly well known, is it not, that the Grand Duke Sergei had no children?'

'No children.'

'But he had two, may I call them for a moment, foster-children?'

'Yes.'

'Let me just make plain what I mean. The Grand Duke Paul married without the Emperor's approval?'

'Yes, the second time.'

'And, consequently, in accordance with the Emperor's directions, he had to leave Russia?'

'Yes.'

'And the Grand Duke Paul was out of Russia, I think – perhaps you can tell me if I am right – from 1902 to 1914? He returned to Russia in June 1914? I am not quite certain I am right as to 1902, but it was about then?'

'I am very sorry, I do not remember that at all. It must be about that time, but I do not remember.'

'At any rate, the Grand Duke Paul, having previously married, his wife died when she gave birth to the Grand Duke Dimitri?'

'Yes.'

'So the Grand Duke had two children, the Grand Duchess Marie and the Grand Duke Dimitri?'

'Yes.'

'And those two children were very small when the Grand Duke Paul was banished from Russia?'

'Yes.'

And so it went on. Jowitt established that the foster-daughter of the Grand Duke Sergei would have been six years older than the Princess Irina; that Irina became engaged at about eighteen in 1912: that she was formally betrothed in the summer of 1913 after the great Romanov celebrations, at which she was present; that her husband was, irregularly, called Youssoupoff at that time, although he would not strictly be eligible for the title until his father died; that they were married in February 1914 and, at the time of the assassination of Archduke Ferdinand of Austria on 29 June 1914, she was in London. He asked her about her escape to Germany, and if the jury had followed all these family gyrations and were wondering where it was all leading, the next question made that clear.

'So that it is perfectly impossible to imagine that you can have been present at a dance in St Petersburg during the course of which the assassination of the Archduke Ferdinand was announced?' Jowitt asked.

'Yes.'

Later he explained further, 'It is only that your husband has written a book and I am asking questions with regard to matters that he deals with. Now can you tell me this: When was it, having left Russia in February 1914, on your honeymoon, that you in fact got back and stood once more on Russian soil?'

'It was a few days after the beginning of the war.'

The atmosphere inside the court had become heavy; the jury, possibly the judge, and certainly the public in the court, looked rather bemused. Then the judge glanced at the court and came to his feet saying, '10.30 a.m. tomorrow.' The first day was at an end.

Chapter **Thirteen**

Before the start of the second day of the hearing, there were long queues of people waiting at the entrance to the court, hoping to gain admission to the public gallery. In the corridor outside Court 7, there was an unseemly struggle by those who hoped to sit in the back of the court itself. Indeed, so intense was the pressure at the doors that the usher had them closed and only admitted the would-be observers one by one until all available space was occupied. A number of young barristers donned their white wigs and gowns in the hope that this might secure them the access which they would otherwise be denied.

When the Princess had resumed her place in the witness box, Jowitt rose to tell her he intended to go back to the questions he had put when he began to cross-examine the previous day.

He reminded her that she had said none of her friends had written to her about the film, during or after it completed its run at the Dominion Theatre. She reaffirmed this.

'Now I see in the papers, the *Evening News* of the 18th October, the *Daily Telegraph* of the 18th October, and I think there is one other but I am not sure, this advertisement appears: "Rasputin. To those who have seen the film at the Empire, the Dominion Theatre or the Metropole Theatre, please write G. 19101." Can you help me at all about that? Do you know who G. 19101 was?'

'What was it − -G?' she asked.

'G is the box number: you can write to the paper anonymously in that way.'

'No,' said the Princess, 'I do not know.'

'You do not know whether it was Miss Fanny Holtzmann or Mr Barney Hollander or Mr Serge Shiskin [the American lawyers] or Messrs Langton & Passmore, who are your solicitors. At any rate, it was not yourself?'

'It was not myself,' said the Princess, adding that she knew nothing of it. Jowitt next asked her if she knew that after she had complained, and before the showing at the 288 picture palaces, cuts had been made in the film. The parts about 'punishing Paul' and 'I have not the right to be your wife' were deleted.

'Did you know that all those scenes had been cut out of the film?'

'But the harm was done already; it had been shown before,' she replied.

'The point I put to you is this,' persisted Jowitt, 'in spite of that fact, you are still threatening the 288 picture houses up and down the country with proceedings in respect of that truncated version of the film?'

'That is entirely in the hands of my lawyers,' came the quiet response.

'You must know that the lawyers do not act except on your instructions. Can you conceive that the film with such cuts can be a matter which you have the right or interest to stop?'

'Yes, it can.'

'Why?'

'Because they cut out some parts, but other parts remained.'

'What remains, in those circumstances, that is offensive or possibly offensive to you?'

'The part of the scene with Rasputin remains.'

'Do you mean when he comes down afterwards and says, "We are going to punish Paul"?'

'Yes.'

'That is cut out,' Jowitt commented sharply.

'Does she know that?' asked Sir Patrick, which, in turn, brought in the judge.

'You are assuming that the witness knows that these have been cut out,' he said and, turning to her, asked, 'Do you know exactly what has been cut out and what is left?'

'I know that some parts were cut out; I am not sure what.'

Sir William left it there, with the observation that as she 'did not know what part was cut, there was no point in pursuing it'. This whole aspect must have been something of a headache for MGM. I suspect they found themselves in a dilemma. If they cut parts of the film, as they did, this would be seen by the jury as something in the nature of an admission that those parts were accepted as offending, and thus, to some extent, conceding the merit of the plaintiff's claim. If they made no cuts, the probability must have been that the cinemas would not take the risk of exhibiting the film and they would incur heavy losses. Evidently they decided in favour of making cuts.

Jowitt referred the Princess to the letters which the Tsarina had been in the habit of writing and which had been preserved. With the aid of them, he secured her agreement that she had seen the Tsarina on an occasion in 1914, two occasions in 1915 and once in 1916, presumably designed to show that, unlike the Princess Natasha of the film, Princess Irina saw little of the Tsarina, and that her husband saw even less.

'My friend, Sir Patrick,' said Jowitt, 'used, by mistake, an unfortunate phrase: he said in opening his case to the jury your husband was exiled out of Russia.' (That was the fate of Prince Chegodieff in the film.) 'That is quite wrong; he was sent to his estate at Rakitnoe?'

'Yes.'

'Where is Rakitnoe?'

'In the middle of Russia.'

'I think', continued Jowitt, 'you left from the Crimea to join him there?'

'Yes, I joined him there.'

'And that is recorded in nearly all these books?'

'Yes, it must be.'

'So that, to anybody knowing the circumstances, it would be ridiculous, because you remember in the film how, after Rasputin was murdered, Chegodieff comes round to the Palace and, whilst he is waiting for his audience with the Tsar, in the film, he goes into a kind of secretary's office, where he sees Natasha?'

'Yes, I remember that.'

'So that it is quite obvious that the character Natasha, whoever she may be, is not only in St Petersburg but in the Royal Palace and still acting as a cross between a lady-in-waiting and a secretary?'

'Yes.'

The Princess, however, did not wholly accept that she was only infrequently in St Petersburg. Jowitt did not handle this very well; she was adamant that when she was there she always went to the hospital and, when there, wore a white uniform.

Having established from the witness that she never qualified as a nurse; that all the royal princesses assisted at the hospital and that Madame Vyroubova also did so, Sir William asked, 'She was the Empress's secretary and lady-in-waiting, was she not?'

'She was not a lady-in-waiting,' he was told. 'She was a friend.'

'She was a secretary.'

'Yes, she was.'

'She was an extreme intimate of the Empress, was she not?'

'Yes, she was.'

The witness was emphatic in refuting Sir William's suggestion that the Moika Palace was shut up at the relevant time, and that neither her husband's parents nor she and her husband lived there. Her husband's parents lived there all the time, she insisted, and she and the Prince lived there too.

'What was the palace called?' was the next question. 'I am afraid I must ask you for the Russian word because we are going to have a discussion as to whether you are right in calling it "the Palace". Would it be called the Dom Dvoretz?'

'The Dom Dvoretz.'

'The word "dom" is the word I want.'

'That is "house" and then there is "palace".'

'What is the word for "palace"?'

'Dvoretz.'

'What was the house known as, what was the Russian title of it?'

'Dom Dvoretz.'

'That is to say, the Dvoretz, Palace?'

'Dvoretz means palace.'

This was typical of the ponderous approach of this highly experienced advocate. Doubtless he had got from the Russian Idelson, trying desperately to earn his keep, this point, which seems to have been thoroughly bad. Even had it been good, it is highly unlikely that Hastings would have wasted the time of the court in establishing that the Prince lived in a vast house, which was not called a palace, in order to say that the scene in the film took place in a palace.

Jowitt then embarked on what may be thought an equally pointless pursuit, and, in terms of inflaming damages, perhaps a dangerous one.

'Now I want to try, it is very difficult but I hope not too difficult or painful for you, to get a little pen picture of your husband as he was then. Your husband has been to Oxford?'

'Yes.'

'He had come down, I think, from Oxford and returned to Russia in the year 1912?'

'I think so.'

'He suffered, did he not, from poor physique, from ill health?'

'Yes, sometimes he did.'

'In particular, he suffered from that very distressing complaint, asthma?'

'My husband? ... No.'

'I am only asking you about what is recorded in some of the books, one of which is apparently recommended as a book to which students may refer, in your husband's book, but you say that is not so?'

'That my husband suffered from asthma? Never.'

'What had he suffered from?'

'He had something wrong with his liver, I think.'

'It is very difficult to see ourselves as others see us. I take it it is very difficult to see your husbands as others see them' (an unhappy phrase, since she had only had one). 'Let me ask you if you would think this is a fair description of the impression he would make? Did you know Monsieur Paleologue, the French Ambassador?'

'No, I never met him.'

'You did not meet him yourself? "Frail and effeminate". Do you think that is a fair description?' The witness and the jury could have been forgiven had they thought Jowitt was describing the French Ambassador, but the witness caught on that he meant her husband.

'I do not think he looked like that; not to me anyhow,' she said.

'He was certainly frail, was he not?'

'Yes.'

'Gifted with great intelligence?'

'Yes.'

'And aesthetic tastes?'

'Yes.'

'But a dilettante?'

'Yes.'

'There is a very celebrated picture of him as a young man by Seroff, is there not?'

'Yes.'

'Seroff was one of the great Russian artists?'

'Yes.'

Jowitt passed a picture to the Princess to examine. This was too much for Hastings.

'May I suggest, as the Prince is in court and is going into the witness box, what some Russian artist thought about it, seems a little far away?' he interjected.

'But, Sir Patrick,' said Jowitt, 'you forget the passage of time.'

'I do not forget', replied Hastings, 'that yesterday you asked me if the Prince was going to be called, as that would obviate the necessity of asking some questions of the Princess. I should have thought questions about her husband's appearance might properly be left to him.'

Once again, it was left to the redoubtable Avory to burst the bubble. 'At what date', he asked Jowitt, 'do you suggest this picture was painted?'

'I should have asked that,' acknowledged Jowitt, and then to the witness, 'What date was the Seroff picture?'

The Princess allowed herself a smile. 'I think he must have been about fifteen years old.'

'As young as that?' queried Jowitt, somewhat embarrassed.

'Yes.'

Jowitt quickly realized he had to abandon this unwise approach. 'I will not press it, if my friend does not like it,' he said.

'Do not say if I do not like it,' said Hastings, gruffly pressing home his advantage. 'If you think it helps at all, put it by all means.'

'Perhaps,' said Mr Justice Avory, 'I can get over the difficulty if I say I do not like it.'

'If Your Lordship pleases,' Jowitt contented himself with saying, before returning to the witness.

'He had not done any military service?' he asked.

'No, never, only during the war.'

'That was a matter of his health?'

'Yes.'

'And only during the war he joined the Corps des Pages, a military school for the sons of the aristocracy?'

'Yes.'

Jowitt went on to establish that the Prince probably spoke to the Tsarevich on only two or three occasions, and that it would give a completely wrong picture to present him as the Tsar's pet or the Court favourite.

'It is obvious, is it not,' Sir William suggested to the witness, 'to anybody with any knowledge of the subject at all, that the author of this film has played very lightly, I mean has done what he liked rather, with the history of the matter?'

'Yes, some matters.'

The Princess agreed that some of these were important matters, and also that the author had tried to show the Tsar and Tsarina in a fair and favourable light. Jowitt developed this theme at some length, despite her acceptance, before producing another picture.

'It is notorious, is it not,' he said, 'that the persons who introduced him, Rasputin, primarily to the Court were the Grand Duchess Militsa and the Grand Duchess Anastasia?'

'Yes, I think so,' replied the Princess, although history makes it rather more notorious and more certain that it was Anna Vyroubova who introduced him.

'Just look at this picture,' he continued, and then to the judge, 'I should like the jury to see that, M'Lud.'

Hastings feigned boredom, remarking, 'If it's still another picture, I should like to see it before it goes to the jury.'

The judge looked at the witness. 'Do you agree that those were the persons who introduced Rasputin to the Court?' he asked.

'Yes, I think they were.'

Hastings slowly came to his feet. 'Again, may I ask, what does this purport to show? Here are two ladies,' he said, waving the picture aloft. 'Why do the jury want to see a picture of two ladies?'

'I do not know,' said Avory.

'I must know,' said Hastings, 'before I know whether it is admissible or not, what it is. Here is a very nice picture of two ladies who introduced Rasputin to the Court. I do not know what ages they were at the time we are discussing. Why is this being tendered?'

'I will answer my friend readily,' replied Jowitt, 'if he thinks I ought to explain every step.' He explained that in the film, which, he commented, the judge had not seen, the most striking characteristic of Natasha was that she introduced Rasputin to the Tsarina, although he had, in reality, been introduced years before, by the two ladies. Moreover, he pointed out, the picture he was producing (which was an illustration in a book) had a caption that they had so introduced them, and, what was to be considered was the state of knowledge of the reasonable man.

'That depends, of course,' said the judge, 'upon whether you assume that every reasonable man has read that book.'

Jowitt disputed that, adding, rather illogically, that he could duplicate it in other books, which presumably the reasonable man might or might not also have read.

Hastings said he would not object to the picture going in, if Jowitt would ask the witness how old these two duchesses were in 1914.

'I am not going to do that, My Lord,' insisted Sir William. 'My friend can do that in re-examination.'

'Then I object,' said Hastings.

'I am going to conduct my cross-examination in the way I want to,' said Jowitt testily, before the judge said he could see no harm in the jury looking 'at those two ladies'.

The judge pointed out that the date of the introduction had still not been fixed, to which Jowitt responded with an entry from the Tsar's diary, which read: '1st/14th November, 1905: We met the man of God, Grigory, from the Tobolsk Government.'

'That would be him, wouldn't it?' inquired Jowitt of the witness.

'Yes, it must be him,' she replied, accepting in answer to further questions that it would be a distortion of history, in the film, to put the date at 1913, and that the same applied to the onset of the haemophilia of the Tsarevich, which began in 1907. She also agreed that the scene in July 1914, when Prince Chegodieff is shown shooting Rasputin, whose life is saved by a steel breastplate, had no historical parallel.

Jowitt's next question misfired, or so it would seem. He was putting to the witness the incidents in the film which lacked historical accuracy. He asked, 'Then, incidentally, Rasputin's attitude with regard to the declaration of war. The story, you know, is that Rasputin used his entire influence to prevent Russia declaring war.'

'Yes, I think he did,' was the reply, which presumably was not expected. The Princess accepted the error in the film when the Tsar accused Rasputin of betrayal, and that in regard to the Tsarina asking Paul to kill him.

'So it is obvious ... that the author of the film has been playing fast and loose with history, has he not?'

'Yes,' said the Princess, 'but they generally do in films.'

'Perhaps they do, but do you not think it is rather far-fetched and ridiculous to try and assign an historical counterpart to every character in the film?'

'I did not quite catch that.'

Jowitt repeated the question.

'Well,' she commented, 'they are historical characters in the film.'

'You heard in the opening of this case nothing at all about the Grand Duke Dimitri?' was his next venture.

'No.'

'My suggestion is that any reasonable person, knowing the circumstances, would take Chegodieff to be a character of fiction. Do you follow that?'

'Yes,' she said, 'I follow that.'

'But that if you feel yourself, by reason of that little, may I call it journalistic flourish at the beginning, committed to say "Well, I must assume that everybody in this film represents somebody," my suggestion to you is that Chegodieff of the film is far more like the Grand Duke Dimitri than your husband.'

'Do you agree?' asked the judge.

'No, I do not,' was the answer. 'I find it much more like my husband.'

'Then I will go through it with you. Of course, you would agree that if a reasonable person comes away with the idea "Well, probably Chegodieff is Dimitri and is not Youssoupoff at all", it would be wholly unreasonable then to assume that Natasha is yourself.'

'Yes, but I saw him as my husband,' she insisted.

Sir William Jowitt then put to the Princess the facets of the film character which he suggested were more consistent with Dimitri. First his position and bearing as a soldier, second his extreme intimacy with the royal family, particularly the children, and third his 'iron nerve'. The fact that these were the characteristics of the film Chegodieff did not dissuade Jowitt from taking some time to put all the details of the characterization, rather as if the witness had disputed the matter with him.

Jowitt then turned to the characteristics of the Prince himself, in order to better make the comparison. The Princess accepted that her husband never entered anything until military school in 1916, never received any military decoration, was never ADC to the Emperor, was out of Russia at the declaration of war, and even if he had not been, 'it would be quite ridiculous imagining him expressing his views as to the comparative merits of German and Russian armaments; he was not exiled from Russia and he never obtained a commission in the English army'.

'So far as these aspects of Chegodieff are concerned, your husband doesn't fit the least bit in the world, does he?' asked Jowitt.

The witness was alive to the implication. 'From the other side, he does,' she said.

'What do you mean by "the other side"?' asked counsel.

'He was responsible for something,' she said meaningfully.

'Believe me, I'm coming to that,' said Jowitt, 'but I can only do it by stages.'

The Princess was willing to agree that Dimitri, as ADC, wore the white uniform, except that the buttons were gold instead of silver.

Jowitt then returned yet again to list Dimitri's military achievements, including the award of the St George's Cross, equivalent, he said, to the Victoria Cross. In his own ponderous and rather heavy way, he returned to his central theme: '... do you agree with me that if you are going to assume any real person for Chegodieff it is very much closer to the Grand Duke than to your husband, as a soldier?'

'As a soldier, yes,' was the uncompromising reply.

Jowitt now had another picture for the jury, which, he explained to the judge, illustrated the great intimacy between Dimitri and the royal children. This was something which the witness had already previously admitted and with which she again agreed. Jowitt, undeterred, highlighted the incidents in the film which showed that Chegodieff had an 'iron nerve'.

'Did you hear my friend say in opening this case that Prince Youssoupoff at once took all the blame [for the assassination] on himself?' asked Jowitt.

'Yes,' replied the Princess.

'... Did you know what he meant by saying that?'

'I really think you are pressing the witness too far,' said the judge.

'That is the last thing I want to do, M'Lord,' he said, then, to the witness, 'I will ask you this: it would not be right to say, would it, that Prince Youssoupoff confessed what he had done; it would be true to say, would it not, that he took every possible step to conceal what he had done?'

'They all did,' she said.

Hastings was back on his feet. 'I am sorry to interpose. My friend, Sir William, calls attention to what I said. May I ask him, as this lady has not got it before her, just to give it accurately. He said I suggested I said he at once took all the blame upon himself. If he can find such a passage, of course, he will, but what I said was that the Prince took the blame upon himself. That is quite a different thing; he did take the blame upon himself, and that appears from everything, I think, in the case.' Hastings was wrong about this; what he had said was nearer to Jowitt's version.

Momentarily, Jowitt ignored the interruption. 'Then, perhaps, you can tell me this,' he went on. 'I am not going to ask you what Sir Patrick Hastings means. Can you tell me when first Prince Youssoupoff took all the blame upon himself, because I really do not know what you mean?'

'No,' was the reply, 'I do not know when it was.'

'Neither do I.'

By this time, his junior had found the passage in their shorthand notes. 'I am very sorry, My Lord,' said Jowitt, 'if I misquoted my friend.

I had better read it. He is dealing with matters before the attempt was made ... I do not know whether in those countries they regard these things a little differently to what we do, but Prince Youssoupoff was quite determined to take all the blame, to take the consequences on himself in regard to these matters.' Jowitt spared himself further comment and continued his cross-examination.

'Do you agree with me here that if you have got to find any historical counterpart for Prince Chegodieff down to the incident of the actual murder in the film, you find a much closer parallel in the Grand Duke Dimitri than you do in Prince Youssoupoff?'

Mr Justice Avory was clearly tired of the repetition. 'I think you have already asked her that question,' he observed.

'Have I, My Lord?' said Jowitt, desperately trying to hide his exasperation.

'The witness's answer', said the judge, was '"I think that it was more like my husband".'

'I think, My Lord, with great respect, that was with regard to the totality of the thing; I am now dividing it into compartments. I do not think I have got this yet.'

He turned back to the witness. 'Down to this point, I want you to agree with me, if you will, the incident of the murder, the whole character is very much more like Grand Duke Dimitri than your husband.'

'I have a note,' persisted the judge, 'you can check it if you like by the shorthand note, of the witness's answer.' He read from his note: '"I do not agree that Chegodieff in the film is more like the Grand Duke Dimitri than my husband."'

'I know she gave that answer,' argued Jowitt, 'that is regarding the thing as a whole. I am trying to cross-examine her and deal with the thing in stages, and down to a particular stage I now ask her whether she does not agree ...'

'Down to which stage?' interposed the judge.

'Down to the date prior to the murder. It is difficult to make it quite plain to Your Lordship because Your Lordship has not seen the film. Down to the murder many incidents, Your Lordship will follow, took place.'

With this, he turned back to the Princess. 'All I am upon for the moment is this: down to that point of time you would agree, would you not, that it is very much more like Dimitri, if it is like anybody at all, than it is Prince Youssoupoff? Down to this point is there any incident (and believe me I am going on) which you would like the jury to understand, in your view, is more like Prince Youssoupoff than the Grand Duke Dimitri?'

'No,' said the Princess, 'I do not think so.'

'Very well,' was the response, 'I will pass on.'

Jowitt, who clearly had a penchant for pictures, now produced another. This time it was one of the Palace, as depicted in the film.

'It is plain, is it not, that there is no sort of similarity between the film Palace and the real thing?' he asked the Princess.

'My friend really need not trouble about that,' interposed Hastings. 'I am not suggesting that in Hollywood they erected a replica of the Moika Palace. If my friend wants the jury to see the Hollywood palace, I do not object to that.'

'I am perfectly content with that,' said Jowitt.

There can, of course, be two views as to the merit in Jowitt's attention to what some might regard as the minutiae of the differences between what was shown in the film and what was the historical reality. In the end, the jury would have to decide whether those witnesses, knowing the circumstances, who thought the character of Chegodieff was really Youssoupoff and that the Princess was, therefore, his wife, were honest and reasonable people. Whether the mantelpiece of the room in the Palace where the killing occurred was higher or lower than the real one seemed remote from the real issue, and had the advocate concerned been of lesser repute, it would be justly said that this was a waste of court time and likely to prove counter-productive. However, Jowitt produced photographs of the room in the film and in the Palace.

'I want you to notice the mantelpiece in the photograph. Do you see that?' he asked the witness.

'Yes,' she answered.

'And you see it is obvious, from the photograph you have there, that the mantelpiece in the film – one does not see the room as a whole in the film – but the mantelpiece, at any rate, is completely different?'

'Yes,' said the Princess. 'It is higher.'

'And it bears no resemblance at all, so far as one can see,' said Jowitt, trying to register his point, for what it was worth.

'There is something about it,' said the Princess. 'It is much higher.'

A discussion then ensued between Jowitt, Hastings and the judge. The plaintiff had given particulars in writing, in the course of the preparations for the trial, in which it was alleged that the two rooms were similar. Hastings explained that what they particularly had in mind was that both rooms displayed unusual columns, which gave weight to the argument that this was Youssoupoff's home which was depicted.

Jowitt said he would look at the columns when he had time, but abandoned his cross-examination on this aspect.

He secured the Princess's acknowledgement of further differences between the film version and the truth. In the film, Chegodieff was a bachelor, engaged to Natasha but not yet married to her; in reality, at the outbreak of war, the Prince and Princess were married, and had a daughter. In the film, Chegodieff detests Rasputin and can hardly bring himself to speak to him, whereas Prince Youssoupoff saw a great deal of Rasputin. The details of the fight and the killing were different in the film from the reality, and whilst Chegodieff, in the film, is seen disposing of the body through the ice, the Prince did not do this.

Hastings suffered this for some time before he came once again to his feet.

'I am most anxious not to intervene in any way,' he said, whilst effectively doing so, 'but I frankly confess that I do not follow this cross-examination. My learned friend asked me if I was going to call the Prince, in order to avoid asking this lady questions. My friend is now asking questions of which this lady knows nothing at all, of course, except that which was told her by her husband. It seems to me undesirable ... I should submit that technically it is not admissible. If I were not calling other evidence, it would not matter; but I submit this is not evidence at all.' The point seemed to be a good one, although if the evidence was inadmissible because it was hearsay, it would not have become admissible if Hastings was not calling other evidence.

Jowitt half-heartedly disputed this, but said that although he regarded his line of questioning as admissible, he would not pursue it. However, he immediately asked the witness again, 'I suggest to you, and I will leave it, that the method of killing in the film is wholly, absolutely and completely different from the facts as they have been recounted in innumerable books.'

'Again, with respect,' said Hastings, 'is that quite a proper question? I do not know what it means and I have been waiting to hear. If my friend is suggesting that Prince Youssoupoff did not kill Rasputin, of course, that is one thing ...'

'I am suggesting that, respectfully,' said Jowitt.

'That he did not kill Rasputin?' asked Hastings incredulously.

'That he did not kill Rasputin,' reiterated Jowitt. However, he added, he would pass from that matter 'if my friend thinks it better, and leave it to the Prince'. That statement notwithstanding, he once again returned to questions concerning the facts of the killing. This time the judge intervened to ask the witness if she knew anything about this and when she replied in the negative, Jowitt abandoned his question once again. It was noticeable that Hastings stymied Jowitt repeatedly, although Sir William may have thought that his questions, even when relating to inadmissible matters, would have some effect on the jury. Others may have agreed, but in a way which would be adverse to his case.

He returned yet again to the unmarried state of Natasha, and pointed out, correctly, that the film showed Natasha as having no mother, whilst the Princess's mother was still alive. He secured her agreement that the Natasha of the film was manifestly a mature woman, at a time when she herself was a mere girl, and that there was no point of resemblance between the Grand Duke Igor in the film and the real Grand Duke Paul.

'It would be quite ridiculous,' he said, 'to apply the film character of Grand Duke Igor to the Grand Duke Paul, would it not?'

'I do not know,' said the Princess. 'He was not Governor-General of Moscow, but he was there as the only one that may be.' This prompted a discussion as to the qualities of the Grand Duke Paul.

Jowitt next proceeded to read an extract from a book concerning someone 'exceptionally pure-minded, good-natured, responsive and unusually impressionable, whose spiritual impulses predominated over her reasoning and for whom religion played the chief part in her life'.

He asked the Princess if that fairly described Natasha in the film. She said she did not think it did.

'Why not?' asked Jowitt.

'She did not strike me like this in the film,' was the reply.

'In the film she is obviously pure-minded, is she not?'

'Yes.'

'She certainly has a certain mysticism about her?'

'Yes, she was very religious.'

'It is obvious, is it not, that spiritual impulses predominated over reason?'

'Perhaps, sometimes. I do not know.'

'You have seen the film and the jury have seen it. They can judge whether it is a fair description of the character they saw. That description is a description, is it not, of Munia Golovina?'

'Yes.'

'I have read from your husband's book, you know?'

'Yes.'

The Princess also agreed that, as stated in her husband's book, Madame Vyroubova's influence was a prime factor in Rasputin's power over the Imperial family. Inevitably, Jowitt produced a picture of that lady.

'Was she a single woman?' asked the judge.

Jowitt said she was married but had separated from her husband. He then mentioned what he described as a number of royal princesses and listed them as the Princesses Marina, Anastasia, Tatiana and Helene of Leuchtenberg. It seemed an odd point, since none of them had any association with anyone involved in the killing of Rasputin. He suggested to the Princess that everybody with an elementary knowledge of the history must have known she herself had never met Rasputin.

'I do not see how the witness can answer that question,' said Avory. 'How can she say what must have been known to everybody?'

'Because she must have read the books, I presume,' replied Sir William.

Sir Patrick Hastings languidly stood up. He told the judge he thought Sir William's questions were based on a misapprehension of a fundamental principle of law. The test, he said was 'Are the words, which do not name the plaintiff, such as reasonably, in the circumstances, would lead persons acquainted with the plaintiff to believe that he, or she, was the person referred to? That does not assume', he added, 'that those persons who read the words know all the circumstances or all the relevant facts.'

Jowitt, in turn, quoted the Lord Chancellor's words in the case of Artemus Jones: 'Libel consists of using language which others, knowing the circumstances, would reasonably think to be defamatory of the persons complaining and injured by it.'

'That is not the whole of it, though,' observed the judge.

Jowitt said he knew that, but the knowledge did not have to derive from having seen an incident, it could come from what the person had read.

'Sir William,' said Avory, 'I think the real objection to your question is that it serves no useful purpose to ask the witness what she thinks other people might think.'

'May I put this question in my way? I will put it to Your Lordship and you will rule on it. Is it not the fact,' he asked the Princess, 'that every work, or almost every work, dealing with this matter, states that you had never met Rasputin, and that the excuse by which Rasputin was got to the house this night was in order that he might make your acquaintance?'

'As a foundation for that question,' said the judge, 'you must ask the witness whether she read all these books to which you are referring.'

'I thought she had said that she had read a very large number of them.'

Here the witness spoke out herself: 'I did not read a large number. I read a very few, but I read some.'

'I will not press the question,' said Jowitt, and after one further question, which the judge also overruled, he concluded his cross-examination and sat down. What he had done hardly stands as a model for what outstanding cross-examinations ought to be about.

Hastings' re-examination, by comparison, was typically short, sharp, pithy and to the point.

'In the film, the Tsar is depicted as having a son, the Tsarevich?' he asked.

'Yes,' said his client.

'In real life he had a son?'

'Yes.'

'In the film, the Tsar is depicted as having a niece, Natasha?'

'Yes.'

'In real life he had a niece?'

'Yes.'

'Who was that?'

'I was the niece.'

'Was there any other niece?'

'No.'

'A number of names of princesses were mentioned,' he continued. '... As far as you know, were any of them engaged to any of the four people who were concerned in the assassination of Rasputin?'

'None of them.'

'Will you tell me about the Grand Duke Dimitri, was he ever engaged to you?'

'No.'

'Or to anyone?'

'No.'

As the questions proceeded, the Princess said that Dimitri was only married a few years before the trial, that she did not know if he entered the British army and that he had never lived in the Moika Palace. She said that, as far as she was concerned, it was only her husband who took the real part in the assassination and that the Grand Duchesses Militsa and Anastasia were over forty in 1914.

Hastings then turned to the question which had been put to the Princess as to her having continued to pursue the cinemas after cuts had been made in the film. She made it clear that she had little knowledge of that, which she had left to her lawyers. He then dealt with Sir William's long question in which he read an extract from documents filed in the action in America.

'You were asked this question,' he said to the Princess. 'Do you say or not say that the inference you ask the jury to draw from this film, from her being locked in the room, and so on, was that he,' that is Rasputin, '"did in fact commit upon Natasha the crime of rape". Do you know what "rape" is?'

'I am not quite sure.'

'What did you understand had happened to Natasha when you saw the film?'

'I thought she was seduced by him.'

'Whatever word is used, did you form a strong opinion as to what had happened between them?'

'Yes.'

Finally he put to her letters written by her legal advisers to show that her primary motive was to stop the showing of the film. He sat down. The Princess's ordeal in the witness box was over. She waited, looked round the court, then left the witness box.

Chapter **Fourteen**

Into the witness box strode Eugen Sabline, who told the court, in answer to Sir Patrick's questions, that he had been a member of the Imperial Russian diplomatic service until the Revolution. He had a number of Russian decorations, was a Commander of the Legion of Honour of France, had Belgian and Dutch decorations, and had been the First Secretary of the Russian Embassy in Great Britain during the war. He was personally acquainted with the Imperial family, had a special interest in Russian history and knew the Prince and Princess Youssoupoff personally. The Princess Irina, he said, was the only niece of Emperor Nicholas ii. Although he was in England from 1914, until and including 1916, he knew of the Prince's engagement and of the death of Rasputin.

'Who is the person, from general repute, who is generally, and I may say universally, known as the author of Rasputin's death?' asked Sir Patrick.

'Prince Felix Youssoupoff,' he answered.

Mr Sabline first saw the film at the Dominion Theatre in London and later saw it at a private showing. He agreed that there were many incidents in the film which were historically inaccurate, and he had seen the caption, at the beginning of the film, which stated that some of the characters were still alive.

'Who, in your mind, was the person indicated by Prince Chegodieff?'

'Prince Youssoupoff.'

'In your mind, had you any doubt of it?'

'I had not the slightest doubt.'

'Did you know the Youssoupoff Palace on the Moika?'

'I saw it many times in my life.'

'Do you know of any prince who had a palace on the Moika except the Youssoupoff family?'

'Not to my knowledge.'

The witness said he had been in court during the Princess's cross-examination and it certainly never entered his head, as suggested to the Princess, that the person indicated by the character Chegodieff was more like the Grand Duke Dimitri. He assented to the proposition that the Princess Irina was both a niece and a cousin of the Tsar.

'Having seen the film,' continued Hastings, 'and the character of Princess Natasha, had you any doubt, in your mind, as to who that character was?'

'No, I had not,' was the reply.

'Who do you think it was intended to convey?'

'Princess Youssoupoff.'

'I need hardly ask that you did not believe that this lady had, in fact, been either seduced or raped by or was the mistress of Rasputin?'

'Certainly not.'

In summary, the evidence of Mr Sabline raised an interesting point. To describe, or depict, someone as a fornicator, an adulterer or a thief is clearly defamatory. But is it so if the person to whom it is thus communicated does not for one moment believe it? The answer in law is 'yes', because, although it might affect the measure of damages, the question is not whether what is said or depicted is believed by the listener or observer, but whether or not it is true, and whether what is depicted would lower him in the estimation of right-thinking members of the public.

Jowitt commenced his cross-examination strongly and effectively.

'You are a friend of the Princess of many years' standing?' was his first question.

'Yes, I am a friend.'

'And when you went to the Dominion Theatre in October, did you go at her request or at the request of her solicitors?'

'At the request of her solicitors.'

'You knew when you went there that she was minded to bring an action ... in regard to this film?'

'Well, I was not exactly aware of it, but I knew there was something of that sort.'

'You would not claim to have any more knowledge than the ordinary well-educated man?'

'Yes, I agree with that.'

'When you went to see that film, did you or did you not believe, as a result of seeing that film, that the plaintiff had ever had any kind of intimacy with Rasputin?'

'I knew she never had any kind of intimacy with Rasputin.'

'And certainly nothing which you saw in the film, and it is for you to speak about your own state of mind, not about the minds of others, led you to have any sort of adverse opinion of the Princess?'

'No.'

Mr Sabline agreed that he was aware of this through the ordinary sources available to the man in the street, including books, some of which he had read. However, he added, he had conversations and correspondence with his friends in Russia.

'Do not all the books', pressed Jowitt, 'make it plain that one of the conspirators who was concerned in the death of Rasputin was the Grand Duke Dimitri?'

'He was ... he was aware of the project of Prince Youssoupoff.'

'Please do not hesitate to tell me because you know ...'

'It is quite clear what he says,' interposed Hastings.

The witness said he thought what Sir William had said was so: that the Prince had nothing to do with throwing Rasputin's body into the river, and though he fired the first shot, the second and third shots which dispatched Rasputin (Jowitt added if, indeed, he was then dead) were fired by Porichkevich. He also conceded that down to the time of the killing, the character of Chegodieff in the film fitted the Grand Duke Dimitri better than the Prince. Having got the answer he wanted, which would have satisfied most experienced cross-examiners, Jowitt plunged in again by repeating the question. This produced a less attractive response, since the witness now said, 'In my opinion, Prince Youssoupoff was always more hostile to Rasputin than Dimitri was.'

Jowitt asked him to repeat what he had said, and when he did so had to be content with asking, 'But you do not doubt that the Grand Duke Dimitri also was very hostile?'

The witness remained adamant. 'I do not doubt that, but still I maintain what I have just said, that Prince Youssoupoff was really ill with this question, because he believed that Rasputin was the great evil of his country.'

There followed a series of inelegantly phrased questions which confused the witness, who clearly could not understand them, and frustrated the point which Jowitt sought to establish. He had referred to the killing in the film, when Chegodieff had got into a fight with Rasputin and hit him about the head with a poker.

Jowitt sought to ascertain why, in connection with the killing, Sabline identified Chegodieff as Youssoupoff, who fired the first shot in the actual assassination, rather than Dimitri, who in reality helped put

Rasputin in the ice-bound river. His question, however, was, 'Why should you relate that incident more to the man who fired the first of three shots than to the man who assisted in disposing of the body in the ice?'

'Well, I knew that,' said the witness and then stopped, adding, 'Will you please repeat that because I am not sure of your question.'

Jowitt tried again: 'I ask you, having regard to the facts I have just put to you, why you should relate this man Chegodieff in the film more to the man who in real life fired the first of the three shots, Prince Youssoupoff, rather than to the man who, in real life, disposed of, or assisted in disposing of, the body in the river.'

'Well, I suppose', was the answer, 'that is the fiction part of the film.'

Jowitt repeated the question still again, achieving only the same answer. He gave up.

He asked the witness about Madame Vyroubova, but he said he had never seen her, then about Munia Golovina, whom the witness said he had never met, but he added, in disagreement, that from the books, whilst he agreed Vyroubova had an entree to the Court, Golovina did not.

'Knowing what you knew, did you believe for one moment that the character of Natasha was the Princess Irina?' the witness was asked.

'I did,' was his answer, and when the question was put three or four times, he still gave the same reply. 'The conclusion I drew was that the person called, in the film, Princess Natasha was the Princess Youssoupoff.'

'... I am only asking,' persisted Jowitt, 'do you suggest that you yourself believed that the character of Natasha, who had some kind of intimacy with Rasputin, was Princess Irina?'

'No, I certainly never thought such a thing.'

This was better, thought Jowitt. 'You never thought such a thing?'

'No.'

'Of course,' said the judge, 'that is a different question. I am not sure you are not at cross purposes.'

Jowitt tried again, but the witness insisted that he at once thought that Natasha was meant to be Irina and he never believed the latter had intercourse with Rasputin.

What he did say, when Jowitt asked, 'And seeing the film did not in any way alter your opinion?' was, 'Well, I was disgusted, if I may say so in court, with the film altogether.'

'I am sorry to hear that,' said Jowitt, 'I rather hoped you would take a different view of it.'

Sir William got nowhere with his questions, and the judge intervened again: 'May I put it another way to get an answer? After seeing the film, did you hold any different view with regard to the Princess and Rasputin?'

'I did not, My Lord.'

'Natasha, in the film,' resumed Jowitt, 'is represented as being the daughter of the Tsar's uncle; that's right, is it not?'

'That is so,' said the witness.

'And normally speaking, you know the daughter of your uncle is your cousin, not your niece?'

'That is so.'

'But there is this peculiarity, if you go to the particular case of Grand Duke Sergei, is there not, that the Grand Duke and His Majesty, the Tsar, Nicholas II, had married two sisters?'

'That is so.'

'But to anybody not knowing about the Grand Duke Sergei, but simply seeing that Natasha is the daughter of the Tsar's uncle, the natural, obvious inference is that she is a first cousin, is it not?'

'That is so.'

'So far as the Tsar's brothers are concerned, it is plain, is it not, that everyone knows none of the Tsar's brothers had any children at all?'

'No.'

'So the Tsar could not have had a niece by his brother?'

'No.'

Jowitt sat down.

'I do not know your view about these matters,' said Hastings to the witness, 'but if your wife has a sister who has children, do you generally regard them as your nephews and nieces? I do not know what you do in Russia?'

'Yes,' said Mr Sabline, 'we would do so in Russia.'

'So would we, I think,' commented Hastings wryly.

He elicited, for emphasis, that Dimitri never had a palace on the Moika, as Chegodieff has in the film, and then asked, 'I do not know what Sir William Jowitt meant by suggesting to you "the educated man in the street", but did he [the man in the street] get any of the information which came through to your Embassy in London, or was it a matter which came through from Russia to your Embassy?'

'It came through our Embassy,' the witness replied.

'So I should have thought,' said Hastings.

The witness said he had read Prince Youssoupoff's book and confirmed that it set down how Rasputin came to die: that poison was put in cakes and wine; that the doctor supplied him with the poison and that the first stage of the death took place in the cellar of the Moika Palace; that Rasputin was attacked with a stick, and that the assailant was, in fact, Prince Youssoupoff. The implication was that all these things were consistent with what was shown in the film.

'When you saw the film,' asked the judge, 'did it at any time occur to you that the character of Chegodieff really meant the Grand Duke Dimitri?'

'No,' said Mr Sabline. He then left the witness box.

When the Prince entered the witness box, he was seen to be a tall, slim and aesthetic-looking man, dressed in conventional English morning clothes, who spoke evenly, betraying no emotion as Hastings took him through his evidence-in-chief, describing quite shortly the events of the actual killing of Rasputin.

In getting the Prince to tell the story, Hastings emphasized those aspects of the killing which were specially evident in the film. Again, so typically of Hastings' concise style, the whole of his questioning occupied little more than ten minutes and concluded with him asking the Prince, 'You have seen this film?'

'Yes.'

'Who, in your opinion, is the character portrayed by Prince Chegodieff?'

'Myself.'

'Has it ever entered your mind that the person whom Sir William Jowitt's clients intended to portray was the Grand Duke Dimitri?'

'Never.'

Jowitt rose to cross-examine, pushing forward his wig towards the front of his head with a nervous, unconscious, habitual gesture.

'And you,' he said, 'at any rate, have followed this case, I hope with sufficient interest to know that what I am suggesting is that we did not intend to portray anybody, have you?'

'I do not understand your question quite well,' said the Prince.

'I hope you have followed the case with sufficient interest', repeated Jowitt, 'to understand that my case is we did not intend to portray anybody in Chegodieff.'

'I had quite a different impression,' came the answer.

As with the Princess, Jowitt's cross-examination of the Prince was exceedingly long, detailed and, in some respects, tedious – not least, as time passed, to the judge.

Jowitt told the witness he did not propose in his questioning to deal with the ethics of killing. His purpose was to make it apparent that the Prince and his character together were fundamentally different from anything in the film which the fictitious character, as he contended, did.

Hastings interposed to point out that the witness's command of English was in no way comparable to that of his wife, and if Sir William found it necessary to give such explanations it would be necessary to have an interpreter.

The Prince said his book, for a time, had a very large sale in England, America, France, Germany, Italy, the Scandinavian countries and Holland, and that it gave the authentic account of the death of Rasputin.

He also agreed that he used the pretext that Rasputin would meet his wife, whom he had been anxious to meet, to induce him to go with him to his palace. He took him through the meeting with Munia Golovina, and his long acquaintanceship with her; that she was pure-minded, good-natured and unusually impressionable; that it was through her that he came to meet Rasputin; and that during alterations to his house, he moved into Grand Duke Alexander Mikhailovich's palace on the Moika, all of which he described in his book.

'I had understood,' said Jowitt, 'I was no doubt wrong, we had been told there were no other palaces on the Moika.' He was referring here to what Hastings had said, and not the evidence of the witnesses.

'No, there was the palace of my mother and father-in-law on the Moika.'

'As a matter of fact, there are a very large number of others, are there not?'

'No,' said the Prince, 'only those two, our palace and the Duchess's palace, my wife's mother.'

'Surely there was the Orloff Palace which was a great centre of entertaining?'

'Entertaining yes, but it was not an important palace. It was not a palace, it was a private house.'

'Was it not called the Orloff Palace?'

'No, never.'

The Prince agreed with Jowitt that the Natasha of the film could be a kind of composite character of Golovina and Vyroubova.

This led Hastings to endeavour to object to this line of cross-examination, on the grounds that there could not be a questioning of each witness to discover whether or not they thought that someone in the film might be thought to be somebody else. It was not relevant to the inquiry.

It was a bad objection, as the judge ruled, without calling on Sir William. He said he could not exclude cross-examination which suggested that the character in the film did not represent the plaintiff, but represented some other person named in the Prince's book.

Jowitt put it to the Prince, as he had put it to the Princess – and she had agreed – that, unlike the character in the film, he had not at once gone to the Tsar and owned up. He laboured the point so much that Avory asked him if it was not sufficient for his purpose 'that the witness says he did not confess at once'. Even then, Jowitt insisted that the witness should agree that he told all sorts of stories about a dog and a drunken party.

'You have seen the film,' he told the Prince. 'I suggest to you that that sort of attitude is entirely and absolutely incongruous with the Chegodieff which you and the jury have seen on the film.' The Prince at first said he did not understand, but when the question was repeated he said, 'Yes, quite.'

Having previously extracted from the Prince his acceptance that Natasha was a composite of Golovina and Vyroubova, Sir William nevertheless spent what remained of the afternoon reading to the witness extracts from his own book. At the conclusion, he suggested 'that any reasonable person having to assume that Natasha had some flesh and blood counterpart, must say to themselves: "Well, there are very close points of similarity between Munia Golovina in real life and Natasha of the film." That is so, is it not?'

The answer which he got, however, was the opposite of the one he had previously elicited: 'No, I do not agree with that.'

It is, of course, true that the process of putting matters to a witness has the advantage that the members of the jury hear the questions and can form their own view, without regard to the witness's answer. Many advocates, however, in pursuing this course and constantly getting negative answers, might have deemed it wiser to omit the concluding question in summary, and leave that aspect for the ultimate address to the jury. At this point, Jowitt, whose wicket was showing signs of wear, said it might be a convenient moment to adjourn for the day and the judge agreed.

When the hearing was resumed the following morning, the court was even more crowded than hitherto. The newspapers were making much of the story of the trial, and this attracted so many additional members of the public, struggling for admission, that even those connected with the proceedings found it difficult to gain access.

Jowitt continued with his reading of passages from the Prince's book, pausing repeatedly to ask the Prince whether what he had written was accurate. Not surprisingly, he asserted that it was. There was thus little disagreement between them. Jowitt recounted how the Prince lay on Rasputin's couch to receive treatment; how he was asked and agreed to play the guitar; of Rasputin's invitation to visit the gypsies, although the Prince never went there with him; how the details of the plot were hatched with the help of others, including Dimitri. Laboriously, he trundled through the events in detail. He covered the insertion of the poison into the cakes and wine, and the collection of Rasputin at his house, then moved on to the details of the murder itself.

Jowitt read from the book how at one point the Prince offered Rasputin some of the cakes which had not been poisoned, concerning which the Prince had written, 'Why I offered him the biscuits which were not poisoned I cannot explain.'

Jowitt observed, 'I think the explanation is not difficult; the explanation is this, is it not, that the nervous strain, which I can well understand, to which you were being subjected, was such that you really hardly knew what you were doing?'

'It is quite natural,' responded the Prince, 'I am not a professional murderer.'

To the public in court, hitherto uninformed about the details of the assassination, this was gripping and fascinating stuff. To the press itself, it provided a surfeit of copy which was to them like manna from Heaven.

A journalist writing for the *Daily Express* described the cross-examination in this fashion: 'Blond, thin and flushed, wearing a collar that shone conspicuously whiter than any in Court, Prince Youssoupoff was made to relive the death-throes of Imperial Russia, by confirming, step by step, the story of his many efforts to murder Rasputin. No such detailed description of a murder has ever been given from a witness box. The Prince's reiterated dry-voiced "Yes, I dids" punctuated Sir William Jowitt's measured readings of his own accounts of the Rasputin death struggle. Over and over again these made the Prince wince. He cast agonised glances at the back of the Court, where such women as Lady Diana Cooper and others stood, jammed for three hours to listen to his evidence. The janitor's remonstrances with those at the door, who were still trying to force a way in, twice interrupted both Counsel and witness. Princess Youssoupoff sat with head bowed throughout the cross-examination.'

One person who was not so intrigued with the performance as time ran on was the judge, Mr Justice Avory.

'Sir William,' he asked, 'where is all this detail leading to?'

'It is leading to this, My Lord,' Jowitt replied. 'I want the jury to understand the facts, and what has been published to the world, in order that they may see the killing scene in the film bears no sort of resemblance to this thing.'

'Very well', said Avory resignedly, and Jowitt continued.

Some might have thought, however, that the crucial issue in the case was not the precise manner in which Rasputin was killed, but who was depicted doing it, and the effect on the jury of regurgitating all this detail could, in that regard, do Jowitt's clients more damage than good.

Jowitt went remorselessly on, reading page after page of the Prince's book to him, and getting his assent by no more than a 'yes' to what was being put to him. All he was really succeeding in doing was to further demonstrate that, despite the caption shown at the beginning, much of the film was historically inaccurate. In some ways, if people properly identified the assailant as the Prince, it made things worse rather than better.

Not content with reading extracts from the Prince's book, he began to read extracts from the published diary of Vyroubova. Hastings became concerned when the Prince said, 'It's all lies, the diary of Vyroubova.'

'If controversial matters are being introduced,' he said, 'I submit that my friend cannot read extracts from diaries as being evidence of fact at all. Of course, I could not use the Prince's book without calling the Prince. I would have been glad to do so; but I cannot. Equally, I submit that my friend is not entitled to read extracts from other people's diaries …'

'Unfortunately,' said Jowitt, 'it is impossible to call these people.'

'I have not intervened,' said the judge, 'because no objection was made; now that objection is made, I must rule that these extracts from diaries are not admissible.'

'Your Lordship rules that they cannot be put to the witness?' asked Jowitt, rather crestfallen.

'Yes,' said the judge.

That being the position, Jowitt returned to the Prince's book. Having by now covered the plot to kill, the murder itself, and the events which followed it, he had recourse again to the minutiae of the incidents.

'Did you observe', he asked, 'that whereas in your book and in the real facts the poisoned cakes were handed by you, in the film the poisoned cakes were handed by a waiter?'

'Yes.'

'In your book, the wine is poisoned?'

'Yes.'

'In the film, as I recollect, it is only the cakes?'

'Yes, I think it is.'

'If some persons went to the film and at the end of the ninth reel thought to themselves: "Why! Chegodieff must be the Grand Duke Dimitri," in the next two reels they would still see Chegodieff, in both characters, both as yourself and Dimitri?'

'I think in some parts of the film people admit it is the Grand Duke Dimitri, but in the part of killing Rasputin certainly not, because the public opinion all round the world is that Youssoupoff killed Rasputin and not the Grand Duke Dimitri.'

'The public opinion round the world has been instructed by your book?'

'Yes.'

'And you have agreed with me' (as earlier he had done) 'that the killing in the film, at any rate, represents a composite character. Do you know what I mean by that?'

'Yes.'

Then, having got the right answer twice, he fell again into the error not usually associated with advocates of his experience, and asked the question again: 'So far as the killing only is concerned, it is a composite character of the Grand Duke Dimitri and yourself?'

To which came the unwanted answer, 'That I did not understand.'

Having done the damage, Jowitt commented, 'I will not press it if you do not follow me.'

In the further questions on this, the witness was prepared to concede resemblances between Chegodieff and Dimitri but remained firm that people would see the killer of Rasputin as Youssoupoff.

He was also prepared to concede that the character of Natasha might be a composite picture in some respects of Golovina and Vyroubova; and agreed there were other historical inaccuracies in the picture painted of Natasha.

'The suggestion I make to you', said Jowitt in summary of this series of questions, 'is that no reasonable person, with any sort of knowledge of the facts as revealed in the book, for instance, could possibly think that the Natasha of the film was your wife.'

'He has already said the opposite to that,' said the judge.

'My Lord, he has,' responded Jowitt. 'I only wanted to put it to him definitely.'

Sir William next reminded Youssoupoff that he had written to his wife at the end of 1932 telling her a film had been produced which showed her in a bad light. The Prince assented.

'Yet the American proceedings are started ... by a letter of the 12th January 1933, on your behalf. Why is that?'

'That is quite easy to explain,' said the Prince. 'The first I heard about the film was from Mr Shiskin in Paris. He approached me several times and I did not see him. Then some American people came from New York. He brought them to me and he told me that the film in New York was going to be shown, and I ought to take some steps to stop that film ... we all went to the American Consul and I gave Mr Shiskin's son a power of attorney to deal with the matter. Then later, after I got some news from Mr Shiskin that my wife is in this film ... he advised me to tell my wife. I did, I wrote her a letter to Menton.'

'What were you complaining about?' asked counsel. 'Do you think there is anything in this film which is libellous on you?'

'No, but I did not see that film,' said the Prince. 'They asked me to give that power of attorney to them before that film was shown, I think.'

'Have you brought libel actions in respect of the other Rasputin films?'

'I did one where Conrad Veidt was playing in Germany.'

'Did you start proceedings there and then give them up?'

'Yes, but I want to explain the reason ... I signed papers and sent them to Berlin and I really did not interest myself very much about that because I had a lot of work to do at that moment. Then suddenly I read in a paper that the lawyer who was chosen in Berlin settled for me;

they were going to pay me quite a big sum of money, but they were not going to get out of the film the part which compromised me. So I cancelled the whole thing because I could not take the money because the film would not be cut. That is the whole story.'

'So you abandoned your action?'

'I gave up my action.'

'Do you tell me you refused to accept a sum of money?'

'Yes, I did.'

'Have you any letters about that?'

'Not with me,' said the Prince. 'Probably I have some at home.'

'Did you not give those letters to your wife's solicitors in this action? I should have thought they would have been interesting to see?'

'Why should I?' asked the Prince with justification.

'Well you did not then?'

'No.'

Here was another example of Jowitt's prolixity and heavy approach, which Hastings would never have emulated. Jowitt had a great reputation as an advocate, but he demonstrates that, on analysis, understanding of and adherence to the simple basic rules do not call for great mental equipment. He asked a series of questions without the slightest idea what he was likely to elicit, and the answers he got did far more good to the plaintiff's case than to that of his own client. Moreover, his questions about the letters relating to a claim brought by the Prince were singularly uninformed. They had no relevance to the instant proceedings, would not have had to be disclosed on discovery of documents, when the parties give their opponents access to their own relevant documents, and would not have been of the slightest interest to the Princess's solicitors.

Jowitt then asked the Prince about Mr Shiskin, who, he said, was a kind of agent.

'Does he work in connection with Miss Fanny Holtzmann?' asked Sir William.

'I do not think so,' was the reply.

'Did you get in touch with Miss Fanny Holtzmann?'

'No, it was my wife who did that.'

'Did you come over here with Miss Holtzmann?'

'Yes, I did,' said the Prince.

'Did you stay at an hotel with her?'

'Yes, I did.'

'Did she pay for you and make you her guest?'

'No, the first time I stayed by myself, and the second time we stayed with my wife at an hotel.'

'My question was, did Miss Fanny Holtzmann pay your expenses, treat you there?'

'I do not think so, because all the bills were paid by me.'

'For the apartments?'

'Yes.'

'At the Hotel Splendide?'

'No, not there; we were the guests of Miss Fanny Holtzmann.'

'So the American lawyer brings you over to London and you stay as her guests at the hotel. My suggestion is that Miss Fanny Holtzmann has been exploiting your wife.'

This was beyond the understanding or command of the language of the Prince. 'She has been what?' he echoed, his voice rising.

'I do not know of a simple word for that; I had better leave it.'

'Well!' expostulated Sir Patrick. 'I do not know what you intend to imply but it can be put into English. Merely because this gentleman does not understand, I do not like to have unpleasant suggestions on the record and then have them dropped.'

Jowitt was forced into a corner. 'I am suggesting', he said, 'that Miss Fanny Holtzmann has been taking advantage of this situation to influence your wife, to persuade your wife and yourself to bring these proceedings?'

'Ought not that suggestion', said Sir Patrick, without rising from his place, 'to have been put to my client? The Princess has been in the box and it is now for the first time suggested that in some way or another someone has influenced my client.'

'It was put as plainly as it could be, when I dealt with Miss Fanny Holtzmann and her statement about "It is only a matter of money", and so on.' Then, turning to the witness: 'However, she came with you here. I will leave it at that.' But he was not to be allowed to do so.

'No, she came back by herself and I came by myself,' said the Prince.

'You came by yourself and met her here?' asked Jowitt as he resumed his seat.

'Yes,' said the Prince.

'As far as you know,' asked Sir Patrick, in re-examination, 'have you or your wife done anything dishonourable in bringing this action?'

'No,' answered the Prince.

'Has anyone ever suggested it until Sir William Jowitt suggested it at this moment?'

'Never.'

Sir Patrick asked about only one further matter, namely to establish that the Grand Duchess Marie, who it had been suggested might be Princess Natasha in the film, had a brother, who was, in fact, the Grand Duke Dimitri.

'So that if the suggestion of the defence is that Prince Chegodieff is Prince Dimitri and Princess Natasha is the Grand Duchess Marie, they are brother and sister?'

'Yes,' said the Prince. He then left the witness box.

Sir Patrick's plan was to call a number of witnesses – six, in fact – with knowledge of the circumstances, who had no doubt that the character of Natasha must have been portraying Princess Youssoupoff. The first of these was Sir John Hanbury-Williams, a white-mustachioed upright figure, who lived at Henry III Tower in Windsor Castle. A Major-General, he had been chief of the military mission with the Russian army in 1914. He said he knew the Tsar and Tsarina; was familiar with the death of Rasputin and, as a matter of history, knew that the Prince was the man believed to have killed him. He knew he lived in the palace on the Moika River and that the Prince and Princess were betrothed in 1913, subsequently marrying. He had seen the film at a private showing which had been specially arranged.

'In your mind,' asked Sir Patrick, 'had you the slightest doubt who was the person ...'

'Do not put to him the slightest doubt,' interposed Sir William Jowitt.

Hastings amended the question to 'Had you any doubt as to who was the person in fact depicted in the film Prince Chegodieff?'

'Not the faintest,' responded the General.

A special requirement for barristers is that they are supposed to be experts in the law of evidence and its application. Yet when Jowitt objected to a leading question (one suggesting to the witness the answer required), Hastings substituted another equally leading question, and nobody turned a hair or cared a hoot.

The witness, of course, added that he had not the slightest doubt that Prince Chegodieff in the film was meant to be Youssoupoff or that Natasha was Irina, his wife. Hastings was content.

Jowitt's cross-examination was commendably short. In answer, the General said he did not know that anyone else was engaged in the murder; knew nothing about Pourichkevich; knew nothing as to who disposed of the body in the ice and had never read the book *Rasputin*. That said, he left the witness box.

The next to enter the witness box was Admiral Sir Aubrey Smith. He was a retired admiral, and because he was hard of hearing everyone was exhorted to speak up, which meant they were well nigh shouting at him. He had been Naval Attaché in St Petersburg between 1908 and 1912. He, too, knew the Imperial family and had once said 'How do you do' to Princess Irina at her parents' house. He had maintained an interest in Russian affairs and understood that it was Prince Youssoupoff who had killed Rasputin. He had seen the film, he said, whereupon Sir Patrick propounded his usual leading question:

'Had you in your mind any doubt who the character, Prince Chegodieff, was intended to be?'

'Not the slightest,' was the not unexpected response, just as the Admiral had not the slightest doubt that Natasha was intended to portray the Princess Irina.

'You formed the conclusion at once, did you?' asked Jowitt in cross-examination.

'Yes, certainly.'

'I meant directly the thing started you said to yourself, Youssoupoff?'

'No,' said the Admiral, 'I cannot say that, but after I had witnessed the whole of the film, I came to the conclusion that the man represented therein was Prince Youssoupoff.'

Jowitt explained that the killing scene started in the film halfway through Reel 10.

'... at the end of Reel 9,' said Jowitt, 'the last words are that the Tsarina says, "Paul, we must find Paul." That is where the Emperor's letter has come in 1916. Do you remember the Emperor's letter?'

'No, I do not remember that,' said the witness. Asked again, he said he did not remember it at all. He did remember the scene of the party at Chegodieff's house.

'Do you agree with me down to this point,' asked Sir William, 'that so far as the first nine and a half reels are concerned, the character is much more like the Grand Duke Dimitri than it is Prince Youssoupoff?'

'I do not see why,' was the reply.

'You do not?'

'No.'

'You regard it as Prince Youssoupoff all the way through, do you?'

'I do not say that. I never connected the character depicted in the film with the Grand Duke Dimitri. I never did; and it does not enter my head now to do so.'

'The only thing you rely upon at all is the killing, is it?'

'What I rely upon', said the witness, 'is that the film depicted somebody who killed Rasputin. I have always understood that Prince Youssoupoff killed Rasputin, and there at the time that the film was completed, I thought I had witnessed a film showing Rasputin being killed by Prince Youssoupoff.'

In answer to further questions, the Admiral said he knew the Grand Duke Dimitri, as a gallant soldier, but when asked again whether he believed that Youssoupoff alone was concerned in the killing, he said, 'I cannot tell you that I ever thought much about it . . . Who took part in it in addition to the Prince or not, I did not know.' He said he was asked by solicitors to see the film; he answered no advertisement, and presumed they heard of him because several people knew he had been in St Petersburg. Hastings put three questions, in re-examination, to confirm that the witness knew the Moika Palace on the Moika River, and then called the next witness.

The first two independent witnesses had admitted being sought out and specially invited. It is inconceivable that they were not told – and if not told, did not inquire – exactly why they were being approached and what was hoped of them. Had it been elicited, it must, to a certain extent, have tainted their opinions, and it seems extremely strange that Jowitt never sufficiently probed this.

By contrast, the next witness, Alban Gordon, who lived at Hove in Sussex, said he had seen the film at the Regent picture house at Brighton, not far from his home. It neither emerged in examination-in-chief nor in cross-examination how he came to be a witness, although it seems certain he must have approached the plaintiff's solicitors and offered to give evidence.

He had no special qualifications, save that he said that he had read many books about Russia, as a matter of interest.

'And from your reading,' inquired Hastings, 'who do you understand to be generally supposed to be the person who killed Rasputin?'

'Prince Youssoupoff,' he replied.

'Did you form an opinion as to who was portrayed by the character of Chegodieff?'

'I did, very decidedly,' said Mr Gordon.

'And who did you think it was?' asked Hastings in copybook style, having abandoned leading questions.

'The Prince Youssoupoff,' replied the witness.

'And did you also form an opinion as to who was indicated by the Princess Natasha?'

'I did.'

'Who did you think it was?'

'Princess Irina.'

At this point, Hastings took a surprising, clearly unorthodox and mildly improper course. He had previously strenuously objected to Jowitt relying on books and diaries without calling the authors, basing his objection, rightly, on the fact that they were hearsay and, as such, inadmissible. The judge had ruled in his favour. Now Hastings proceeded to follow the very course to which he had objected. It is one of the peculiarities of the English system that this frequently happens, without the slightest intervention by the judge, presumably on the grounds that the duty to object is that of the advocate, and in the absence of objection it is not for the judge to interfere. It is one of those rules which sometimes make a trial at law seem more like a game than a serious protection of the rights of the citizen.

Hastings handed the witness the volume of the Tsarina's letters which had, as he pointed out, previously been referred to by Sir William.

'I dare say', he said, 'you have read in the papers the suggestion which is being made about Dimitri being a man of iron character?'

'Yes,' said the witness.

'Would you read what the Tsarina wrote to the Tsar at page 259 about him?'

The witness read: 'We spoke long about Dimitri ... he says he is a boy without any character and can be led by anybody. Three months he was under the influence of N.P. and held himself well at the Headquarters and when in town with him, kept himself like the other and did not go to the ladies' companies – but out of sight – gets into their hands. He finds the regiment perverts the boy as their coarse conversations and jokes are horrid and before ladies too and they draw him down. Now he is used as an aide-de-camp.'

'Is there something about his character?' asked Sir Patrick. '... I think it is September the 8th or 9th, 1915?'

'On September 8th, at page 150, there is this postscript to the letter: "Are you thinking of sending Dimitri back to the regiment? Don't let him dawdle about doing nothing, if his character does not get formed at the war – he was not out more than one or two months."'

'I think that is enough,' said Hastings. 'Is that the Tsarina's description of the man whom Sir William described as a man with an iron nerve?'

Mr Gordon's only knowledge of Russia was based, as he had said, on limited reading of Russian history. He had never met any of the characters, and if Jowitt's use of the books to ask whether witnesses held the same views was subject to objection, as the court had held, Hastings' use of them was an outrageous abuse. Nevertheless, it went unchecked.

As Hastings sat down, Jowitt rose to cross-examine. He elicited again that Dimitri had been given the cross which was said to be equivalent to the Victoria Cross, but the witness thought they came in different degrees. However, he agreed he had not the slightest wish to belittle the gallantry of a man like the Grand Duke Dimitri. Other books which Jowitt sought to refer to him, he had never read. Jowitt, therefore, returned to the letter which he had discussed with Hastings.

'The Tsar had assumed supreme command in June, had he not?'

'Yes,' said the witness.

'And at that time, Dimitri was acting as aide-de-camp?'

'That I cannot remember at the moment.'

'It did not occur to you, a very natural thing for a young man in his position, that regimental service would be much better for him than hanging about Headquarters?'

'Yes,' said the witness, doubtless understanding the purport of the question, which was rather clever of him.

'And that is the point of the Tsarina's letters?' suggested Jowitt.

'That may be the point of the complaint,' said the witness, in a complaisant mood.

Jowitt put to the witness the titles of a number of books which Jowitt said he had read, and all of which the witness, in turn, claimed also to have read.

'At any rate,' he then asked, 'from your reading, you would agree, that so far as the killing is concerned, there are four people concerned?'

'Five, I think,' said Mr Gordon. (Since his knowledge came only from reading, the cross-examination carried some of the aspects of the television programme *Mastermind*.)

'We will leave the doctor out; there are four besides him?'

'Yes.'

'And do you agree with me that the four people, all of whom play their parts, are in the killing, in the film, telescoped into one?'

'I would prefer the word "garbled" than "telescoped",' was the reply.

'If by "garbled"', said Jowitt, 'you mean they have departed from the facts, "garbled" is not a strong enough word. Every incident in the film is totally and fundamentally different from real life, is it not?'

'Nearly every incident,' said the witness.

'At any rate, what is left of real life is telescoped, these four characters?'

'I find it a little difficult to accept that,' said Mr Gordon.

'How would you put it?' asked Jowitt.

'I would have said it purports to be a description of Prince Youssoupoff's actions with embellishments.'

Pressed further, Mr Gordon said he had no recollection of seeing the burial in the ice depicted in the film.

'Perhaps you left and wanted to catch the bus home?' said Jowitt.

'No,' he replied, 'we stayed to the end, but I do not remember seeing the burial in the ice.' He would not have it that his belief that it was the Prince who was depicted, was based solely on the killing scene; he began to think that was so halfway through, and when asked which incident brought this about, he said, 'I think his connection with the Princess, his title of Prince, his hostility to Rasputin, and finally, when the first of those two receptions in the palace on the Moika took place.'

Jowitt commented in reply on Dimitri's known hostility to Rasputin, which, he said, Prince Youssoupoff's book records.

'Does it?' asked the witness. 'It is a long time since I read that book. I understood the Grand Duke Dimitri had never even met Rasputin.'

'People are often very hostile to people they have not met,' rejoined Sir William, 'but you may take it from me the book does record it. You have forgotten that, have you?'

'No; there were about two hundred million people in Russia, and I understand all but about two hundred of them were hostile to him.'

Mr Gordon thought that Dimitri's being on intimate terms with the Tsar's children, as shown in the film, could have applied to a good many people. Jowitt was not making the progress with the witness for which he hoped.

'You are not trying to argue this case, are you?' he asked. 'Do you not think that the charming actress who was playing the part of Natasha was obviously not portraying a girl of seventeen?'

'Yes.'

'Then I may take it, for that reason, you reject Natasha as being the plaintiff?'

'No, I am afraid I do not.'

Mr Gordon said his presence at the trial was not because he was one of the people who answered an advertisement, but try as he might Jowitt was unable to move him from the opinions he had throughout expressed which meant that he believed Natasha portrayed Princess Irina.

Hastings, as usual, asked very few questions in re-examination. He dealt with the difference in age between the actress and the Princess at the relevant time, pointing out that Sarah Bernhardt had, on one occasion, played Hamlet as a boy of nineteen. The witness had no personal recollection of that, however, so Hastings turned to his next witness.

This was Prince Nikita, the brother of Princess Irina. Due to the congestion in the court, he had difficulty in gaining access, although it is questionable whether it would have mattered much had he not suc-ceeded. His evidence was exceedingly short. He too, he said, took Natasha to be his sister, and he told the court that the Grand Duchess Marie, who was Dimitri's sister, married a Swedish prince in 1908. She lived in Sweden, but in 1914 she was divorced both there and in Russia, to which country she had returned. It is not easy to understand why Hastings went to the trouble of calling this witness, since little had been made in the case of the few matters to which he referred.

Hastings had only two more witnesses to call. The first was Elsie Marie Budd, a married woman, who, like Mr Gordon before her, came from Brighton. There, also at Brighton's Regent Theatre, she had seen the film; she too had been interested in modern Russian history and had read books on it; and she too thought that Natasha portrayed Princess Irina.

'To what do we owe the pleasure of meeting you today?' asked Jowitt, when he commenced his questioning.

'Well,' said Mrs Budd, 'I was rather disgusted with the film. I thought it was a misrepresentation of the facts and I volunteered my evidence.'

'Did you see the advertisements?' asked Jowitt.

'No, I had never heard of it until I read it in the paper last night,' she said.

'Then did you see Mr Gordon?' asked Jowitt, following the obvious hint of a connection.

'No,' she replied. 'I met him eleven years ago in Brighton and I have never seen him since, until today.' She said she had telephoned the Princess at the Ritz Hotel the previous night, offering to give evidence.

The last witness for the plaintiff was Frederick Theodore Gade, who, for seven years, from 1916 to 1923, had had business interests in Russia and Siberia. He was also the president of the international committee set up for the defence of foreigners in Russia. He understood that it was Prince Youssoupoff who killed Rasputin and that it was he whom Chegodieff portrayed in the film. Accordingly, he thought Natasha was meant to be the plaintiff.

Cross-examined by Jowitt, he said he did not answer an advertisement. He had gone casually to the Hippodrome, and when he could not get in had strolled to the New Palace cinema where he had seen the film. He said he was a friend of the Prince.

'And happening to see the film, did you happen to write a letter?' inquired Jowitt sarcastically.

'No,' said the witness, 'I had lunch, as a matter of fact, with Prince Youssoupoff in Paris a week or two afterwards. I told him I had seen the film and I was frightfully disgusted with it; he then told me of the proceedings and that was the first I heard of it.'

After Sir William canvassed a few more inconsequential matters, he sat down. Hastings did not re-examine but said to the judge, 'My Lord, that is the plaintiff's case,' and the matter passed into Jowitt's hands.

Chapter **Fifteen**

As Jowitt began his address to the jury, in opening the defendant's case, the Princess could hardly have realized the dangers she would face, as a result of the error on the part of the barristers acting for her – an error which might have marred Hastings' customary outstanding feats as an advocate.

Sir William first dealt with the law, which, as he outlined it, was necessarily no different from that which Hastings had already told the jury. In short, were the words or depictions used ones which would reasonably, in the circumstances, lead persons acquainted with the plaintiff to believe she was the person referred to in the film?

He then mentioned the case of Artemus Jones, saying it was a case where a man with a rather peculiar name was referred to by name. 'There was added in the libel,' he said, 'something about him being a church warden at Peckham.'

'That was not part of the libel,' the judge corrected him.

'No, My Lord,' agreed Jowitt. Then, turning to the jury, he said, 'It may well be, as the judge points out; one knows in one's professional life all sorts of things. Amongst many people I know – I know my learned friend Mr Wallington – but I have not the least idea whether he is a church warden of Peckham or anything else. Nothing would surprise me about him, but I do not know what he is.' His junior counsel, Wallington, looked at Jowitt in some surprise, as well he might, before it dawned on him that this was intended as a piece of light humour. Jowitt then told the jury it was not necessary for everyone to know to whom the article referred, it was sufficient 'if a substantial number did so'. Here Jowitt was not accurately describing the law. It is not necessary to have a substantial number of persons identifying the plaintiff. It is quite sufficient if 'a person' (not a great number) 'hearing or reading the alleged libel would reasonably believe the plaintiff was referred to'.

He spoke of the second peculiarity of this class of case: the distinction between libel and slander. Slander needed special damage, 'that is to say,' he said 'you had to prove you had lost this, that or the other and put your finger on the slander'. Whether the jury understood what he meant is not known; it seems unlikely, since others would find it difficult to fathom. He proceeded to develop the argument that a 'talking film' was a combination of both: 'what you see with your eyes ... is plainly ... libel; so far as concerns what you hear with your ears, I presume you are dealing with slander'.

The judge, he told the jury, would direct them as to the law on this, but he said he attached a great deal of importance to it because in the present case the plaintiff's claim was, and he read from the written statement of claim, that MGM 'caused to be exhibited photographic pictures and words which mean and were understood to mean that the Princess Natasha had been seduced by and was the mistress of Rasputin'.

'Would any reasonable person seeing that film', he inquired, 'draw the conclusion that Natasha, the film character, was seduced by, or became the mistress of, Rasputin? ... I understand the word "seduced" to mean, in the English language, a woman who gives herself – persuaded – she gives herself. I understand the word "mistress" to mean there is obviously a continuity of association. I suggest to you that it is a complete abuse of language to say that a woman was the mistress of a man if they had one isolated act of intercourse.'

Jowitt was clearly moving on to strong ground. The plaintiff's case – based on her written pleading, drawn up by St John Field and approved by Hastings – alleged that the film showed her to have been seduced or a mistress. Seduction, necessarily, involved an induced consent and did not include submission by force. If the jury believed – as well they might – that the effect of the film script was that Natasha was taken by force and had not been seduced, they could justly find for the defence. Anyone closely observing Hastings, and especially his junior, at this moment would have seen an element of restiveness and concern which they were desperately trying to disguise.

Sir William continued to develop his argument. 'Whether or not it is libellous to say of a woman that she was forced, that she was raped, is a matter which I should have very grave doubt about. The usual definition of libel is something which holds a person up to hatred, ridicule or contempt. I think of what I have always thought to be one of the greatest poems in our language, Shakespeare's "Rape of Lucrece". You remember how Lucrece, when her husband Collatine is away, is visited and forced by Tarquin; and you may remember how, after communing with herself, she at last decided that life has lost its savour for her and she kills herself. Whatever else anybody may feel in regard to that great poem, I cannot myself conceive the frame of mind of a man who could feel towards Lucrece either hatred, ridicule or contempt. But whether or not an accusation of rape would be a charge of a defamatory nature, against a woman, is not the matter with which we are here concerned. I speak to you subject to My Lord's direction, of course we are concerned here merely with dealing with this allegation which is made: do the words of this film mean that the Natasha of the film has been seduced by, or was mistress of, Rasputin?'

He then drew the jury's attention to various scenes and aspects of the film which he invited them to note, were they permitted, as he hoped they would be, to see the film again. These were all passages which he contended showed Natasha as 'obviously a girl of complete purity, innocence and sweetness of mind'. He said that, in the film, Natasha goes to see Rasputin to warn him of danger because she believes Chegodieff has it in mind to murder him. 'Rasputin', he said, 'is called out of the room, because at that very moment Chegodieff has come and the servant says, "Grischa, Prince Chegodieff"; Rasputin goes out and Dunia locks the girl Natasha in, leaving the key outside.' He described the incident upstairs which follows when the Prince tries to shoot Rasputin, but fails. When Rasputin returns to the room where the girl is waiting, 'she says to him, nervously, "I heard a shot." "Yes, my daughter." "It was Paul?" she asks. "Yes, my daughter. We're going to punish Paul, you and I." I submit it is perfectly plain, to an intelligent person, that there is no ground whatsoever for saying that Natasha has given herself or promised to give herself and her body to this man.'

He drew on further examples from the film, down to the moment at which Natasha says she no longer has the right to be Chegodieff's wife and he added, 'I ask you to say that those words are not capable, sensibly taken, of bearing either the one meaning or the other of these two allegations made.' At this point the judge decided to adjourn for a short recess.

When the court resumed, Jowitt reminded the jury that Sir Patrick Hastings had said that the scene in the film when Rasputin told Natasha 'You and I are going to punish Paul', was made 'under circumstances which leave no doubt in your mind that she is then going to become his mistress' [that is to say Rasputin's]. Jowitt continued: '. . . to use Hastings' opening words: "I use the word 'mistress' in a non-committal sense, because something has been said in the course of this case as to whether the action of Rasputin is that of the seducer of the Princess or a violator, or whether or not she, on more occasions, submits to his advances, and is, therefore, technically his mistress. I have heard observations made at some stages of this case throwing doubt upon whether or not it is a libel to say of a woman she has been raped, because that may show she did not consent. Those technicalities I will leave to the ingenuity of the Metro-Goldwyn Film Company who, no doubt, are experts in these refinements" . . . Members of the Jury,' Jowitt went on, 'I hope that I realize – at my age I ought to – what is meant by technicality . . . Anything less like a technicality than that, I can tell you, in a very long experience of these courts, I have never heard.'

Sir William told the jury that whilst he now agreed that the judge had been right to delay their viewing of the film until they learned what the case was about, 'I cannot help saying that I think, under the circumstances, it would have been better if you had had a survey made to you' (he was referring to Sir Patrick's opening address), 'less completely one-sided than the survey was.' He read Hastings' words and said that what he found most offensive was when Hastings had said of Chegodieff, 'In the end he was exiled out of Russia and not allowed to return.' This, of course, was a description by Hastings of Youssoupoff's fate and clearly was incorrect; moreover, in saying it, he wrongly equated it with the fate of Chegodieff as depicted in the film.

Still another cause for complaint in this regard, he contended, was that because Chegodieff, in the film, took the blame for the killing upon himself at once, Hastings had opened the case by saying Youssoupoff had decided 'to take all the blame', which was far from the truth.

He said he wanted to deal with other aspects of the film and, in doing so, commented, 'With regard to Natasha, you may say: Why did they want to show Natasha as a royal princess in the film at all?' This was, as the politicians say, a good question, but although he went on at some length, he does not appear to have answered it. He rambled rather over the need to bring out, in the film, the nobility of character of Chegodieff, but did not answer his own question.

He told the jury he did not intend to call the authors of the script or any other evidence to show what they had in mind. He did not tell them, as was doubtless the case, that he knew full well he dare not do so, but he conceded that to give verisimilitude to the historical slant they must have had real characters in mind. From this he argued, as he had implied during cross-examination, that two of the characters were composite portraits. Natasha was an amalgam of Munia Golovina and

Madame Vyroubova, and Chegodieff was partly an invention and partly the Grand Duke Dimitri. This too was rather improper, since he was, in fact, indirectly giving evidence of what the authors had in mind when he had no intention of calling them as witnesses.

He extended his heartfelt sympathy to the Princess and those like her who 'have lost the right to go back to their fatherland; who lost many of those who are near and dear to them and are penniless', but, he told the jury, 'I remember when I was a boy at school, in my classroom there used to be written up above the master's desk, above the fireplace, these words: "Money lost, little lost; honour lost, much lost; heart lost, all lost".' He did not go on to tell them whether there was written above the master's desk the consequence if the case was lost. 'There is', he submitted, 'no reasonable person, seeing this film, who could possibly suppose that the Princess had had any concern, of any sort or kind, with Rasputin.' Moreover, he stressed, 'You have heard some of the witnesses called. There was not one of those witnesses called who said that they thought any bit the less of the plaintiff; we have not heard anybody.'

He said, 'The only thing I regret in this case is that I have not had the opportunity of seeing Miss Fanny Holtzmann', and he put it to the jury, 'Do you not think a possible view of this case is that it was Miss Fanny Holtzmann, who pays the bill of the Prince Youssoupoff at the Hotel Splendide, who thought to herself: "Well, I will persuade these people to bring this action; it will be a very celebrated action and Miss Fanny Holtzmann will, perhaps, get some reputation out of it, and there is going to be litigation all over the world." So Miss Fanny Holtzmann comes over here, as you will hear from the evidence, and states that money will settle the action.'

'I cannot object, of course, to my friend opening anything, but I hope he will restrict himself to everything he can prove by admissible evidence,' interrupted Hastings.

'I can certainly prove that,' said Jowitt.

'I said "by admissible evidence",' said Hastings. 'Perhaps we will wait and see.'

Jowitt returned to the fact that the first claims had been made by the Prince and not by the plaintiff, and that the advertisement addressed to those who saw the film 'so far as we can see, does not seem to have brought forth any fruit'. He could not overlook Mrs Budd. He did not want to say anything disrespectful of her, 'but upon my word, if that is the sort of evidence which my friend is driven to call, it must show, must it not, how extraordinarily difficult it has been for him to get anybody to come and say that they understand this as referring to the plaintiff at all'.

On damages, if the jury thought MGM were wrong, they should again bear in mind that 'not one single, solitary soul has been called into the box to say that they thought she had any kind of intimacy with Rasputin'.

He alluded to the opening caption to the film and its unfortunate statement that 'A few of the characters are still alive'. Of this he said, 'Well, you know, Members of the Jury, you have friends sometimes who stand up in their seats and say: "Now I am going to tell you a perfectly true story", then you prepare yourself for something which is not quite the truth.' Jowitt must have been calling on his political experiences. From this, he argued, somewhat inconsequentially, that the audience would soon have forgotten the opening bars.

He concluded: 'First of all, looking at the film as a film, altogether apart from any identity at all, Natasha was never seduced by anybody or was the mistress of the Rasputin of the film. Next, I say Chegodieff of the film is quite plainly a character so wholly different from the Prince Youssoupoff that it is ridiculous to apply the argument which my friend is applying: because Chegodieff is Youssoupoff, therefore the girl to whom he is engaged is the lady to whom Prince Youssoupoff was married ... Then I ask you to say, with regard to the character of Natasha, that if you have to find an historial counterpart at all, you find her in the combination of Munia Golovina and Madame Vyroubova.' He told them of the witnesses he would be calling and his opening address was concluded.

There followed a discussion as to when the jury should again see the film, and the judge ruled that this should take place after all the evidence had been heard. It was then that Hastings came to his feet to endeavour to extricate the plaintiff from the considerable difficulties into which he and his junior had got her.

Hastings rose 'to bring something to Your Lordship's attention', as he put it, 'and, if necessary, to make an application'. His objective was to correct the manifest error in his junior's pleading and to try to frustrate Jowitt's attempt to get the jury to find, at least, that Natasha was raped, in which case, Hastings' statement of claim did not claim other than that she was seduced or a mistress.

He first sought to justify his position by what had been said in the preparations for trial when an application by MGM for further and better particulars of the statement of claim had found its way to the Court of Appeal. Hastings' arguments in this connection were singularly unconvincing and only appeared to show that he should have seen the danger earlier and corrected it.

He said both Jowitt and he had been at the hearing in the Court of Appeal, when the distinction between libel and slander had been canvassed. He summarized the main point as follows: 'Both Sir William Jowitt and I pointed out in the clearest possible terms, and I am glad to say there is a shorthand note of it which I can give to Your Lordship, that in the view of both of us and of every member of the Court of Appeal, the word "seduction" was used by the pleader to include both cases of intercourse with consent and intercourse without consent, and therefore, on my agreement or suggestion to the Court of Appeal, that we would give particulars of the identity, the Court of Appeal made no order.'

Passing a copy of the shorthand note to the judge, he commented, 'I assume Your Lordship would not allow a Court of Justice to be used merely as the place for a game,' implying that such would be the situation, because it was due to what Jowitt had then said that he did not apply to add the word 'ravish' to 'seduce'. It might have been pointed out that had proper steps been taken in the first place and the case correctly pleaded, the word would have been there in the first place.

Sir Patrick then read the words used by Jowitt in the higher court. In fact, what he read was no different from what Jowitt had recently told the jury. He had said that 'seduced' involved consent; that the film, if it showed anything, showed only violation, and the passage on which Hastings crucially relied – erroneously it might be thought – was where Jowitt had said to the Court of Appeal that the words used in the statement of claim 'incline me to believe that the learned pleader is using the word "seduced" to cover a state of facts in which the woman is not giving her consent to what is taking place'. Clearly, in saying this, he was implying that the junior counsel had been misguided. Hastings argued, however, 'He therefore expressed the view that, so far as the pleading is concerned, he [St John Field] intended to cover both cases.' Later Jowitt added, as Hastings read out, that whatever is the real meaning of the word 'seduction', that seemed to be giving a forced meaning to the word.

Hastings read from the transcript that he had indeed told the Court of Appeal that he did not, himself, draw any distinction between what the nature of the seduction or ravishment was. That may have been so for the purpose of his argument there, but it hardly seemed to alter what was in the document itself.

Hastings said, not very convincingly, 'We thought Sir William intended one thing; if he says that he intended another, I accept it at once, and I suggest the only possible thing to do in the circumstances is to add "ravishment" to the word "seduction".'

'My Lord,' interrupted Jowitt, 'I gather this is an application to amend.'

'I do not mind putting it that way,' replied Hastings, 'I was misled and I am astounded at having been misled. I do not believe I could have been misled in this way unintentionally, but, having been misled, I formally ask Your Lordship to allow me to put the matter right by adding the word "ravishment" to the word "seduction".'

'I gather', said Sir William, with both advocates on their feet at the same time, 'that my friend is making an application to amend. My friend says that he is astounded; I am bound to say I am astounded at the course he has taken. In the middle of this case I suggest he cannot possibly have this amendment.' He reiterated what he had said in the Court of Appeal, which had been read out by Hastings, adding, 'in spite of the fact that in the Court of Appeal I plainly, and in terms called his attention to the danger he was in, he had not thought fit at that stage to amend'.

That was really the measure of it. Hastings' admirable practice was to reduce everything to a minimum, and it frequently paid off, but there was another side to the coin. His technique of concentrating only on essentials resulted in his failing, on occasions, to concentrate on detail which he should have considered. This was a case in point. He should have realized the picture depicted rape as much as seduction, if not more so, and drawn the need for amendment to the notice of his junior. What St John Field had in mind when he drew the pleading is anyone's guess. Either he thought seduction included rape, which seems unlikely, or he had not taken the trouble to see the film first and, as a result, had failed to appreciate what it portrayed.

Jowitt repeatedly urged on Mr Justice Avory that it would be wrong to permit an amendment to the claim at such a late stage in the case, saying, 'I ask Your Lordship to say, more especially as the point was plainly brought before them in the Court of Appeal, that the question the jury ought to be asked, and the only question, is:

"Do these words and these pictures mean that Natasha was either seduced by, or was the mistress of, Rasputin?"'

'I do not agree with you there,' said the judge. 'I shall tell the jury, quite apart from any innuendo which appears on these pleadings, that they will have to say whether this picture coupled with the words was defamatory of the plaintiff, although they do not find the particular innuendo.'

That, for Jowitt, was that; although he made it clear that he was not to be taken as assenting to the course which the judge proposed to take.

What the judge was intending to do was most unfair to Sir William Jowitt and his client, and almost certainly wrong in law. He was clearly, it seems, misdirecting himself. It was quite true that it is always open to a jury, where no innuendo or indirect meaning is pleaded, to find what words or pictures are defamatory of the plaintiff. Thus, if in the film the murderer of Rasputin had been called Prince Youssoupoff and Rasputin was shown raping or seducing his wife, the jury, if they thought an allegation of rape was libellous, could obviously find this to be defamatory, quite apart from any construction the plaintiff, in her pleading, sought to put upon it. In this case, however, that was not the situation. To make it defamatory of the plaintiff, the observer would have needed to know that Chegodieff was a disguise for Youssoupoff; he would need more knowledge than the words or pictures of themselves conveyed. The judge, in fact, as will be seen, must have had second thoughts, or discussed it meanwhile with a brother judge, because later he changed his mind.

MGM's first witness was Sir Bernard Pares, a rather handsome man. He had written some excellent books on the history of Russia, but by the time he finished his evidence Sir William may well have wished he had limited himself to the written word. As a witness, he was everything which a witness should not be: loquacious, rambling, argumentative and, on the subject of Russia, rather intellectually arrogant. Some might think this surprising, since he went, as a Foundation Scholar, to read Classics at Trinity College, Cambridge, after leaving Harrow. He was reputed to be a very friendly man, with a great love of people, and to have an alertness of manner which was blessed with a saving humour. A photograph of him in a group hangs today in the Common Room of the Faculty of Arts of the University of Liverpool, where he was also Professor of Russian History.

Jowitt left it to his fellow KC, Wallington, to examine him in chief.

By his answers he said he was a Professor of Russian Language, Literature and History in the University of London, and Director of the School of Slavonic and East European Studies at the same university. He was in Russia throughout almost the whole of the war period, served as official British correspondent with the Russian army in 1914 and 1915, and worked for the War Office from 1915 to 1917. He described his regular and frequent visits to Russia. He had edited the Empress's letters to the Emperor but he did not know the plaintiff personally. He told the court he had seen the film three times.

'Now did you consider whether any of the characters in the film had any reference to actual people?'

'Yes,' said Pares, and off he went on a frolic of his own: 'May I say that I thought the film was a great improvement on the sort of publicity which has been given earlier to the characters of the Emperor and Empress. The Emperor's character was exceedingly well done, I think, except for one thing, the complete absence of what was his chief characteristic, a wonderful personal charm. I did not find that in the film.' Noticing the look of alarm and dismay on the faces of all the lawyers and the judge, he added, 'Shall I continue now or not?'

'Yes,' said Wallington, unwisely, 'if you will,' adding with emphasis, '*Very shortly.*'

'Did you consider', asked counsel, 'whether Chegodieff had any reference to any actual person?'

Off Pares went again at a canter. He said he first thought Chegodieff was the Grand Duke Dimitri, whose full family names he then gave; he referred to the scene where he pulled the little boy's hair, adding that the Emperor and the Empress had at one time contemplated Dimitri as a possible husband for one of their daughters (which was, of course, not in the film), but this showed, he said, his intimacy with the royal family. As the film progressed, he thought Chegodieff was more like Dimitri, 'which', he said, 'went on until quite a later part of the film, except for one thing. I must say just how it struck me. The first thing that ever suggested to me Princess Youssoupoff was the likeness between Natasha and Munia Golovina. That was the first thing that ever suggested to me Princess Youssoupoff.'

Wallington must have shared the general difficulty of following the logic of these last unsolicited views. He said, 'I will ask you about that later,' but Pares, always ready to oblige, took over and chose another subject.

'Then I will leave that,' he said. 'Then we get down to the

murder, shall I answer you at once about the murder, or leave it till afterwards?'

Wallington was in difficulties. He clearly thought he should try to get the answer to the question he had already asked. 'Will you tell My Lord and the jury', he repeated, as formally as he could, 'why you thought that Chegodieff was a fictional character and if he was not a fictional character, who he was most like?'

'He has already said that,' said the judge, who was certainly not enjoying Pares' evidence.

'That is down to the murder,' commented Wallington, only to find that Pares was off again.

'The murder is a very mixed affair,' he went on. 'There were several people who had tried to do this and had wanted to do it before; for instance the Minister of the Interior definitely tried to murder Rasputin; there were lots of people who wanted to do it, and the one thing that seems most intelligible is the motive that prompted Prince Youssoupoff in the matter. That is before. Now as to the actual plan or plot to murder Rasputin ...' and so he went on at very great length, delving into the various attempts on Rasputin's life. It was all too much for Sir Patrick. He rose.

'What are we doing now, My Lord?' he asked. 'This gentleman is telling us certain things about some gentleman's conversation as to what they were going to do. Does he know? Is he telling us what he knows? I only want to follow it.'

'Will you kindly answer the question' said Avory firmly to the witness. Jowitt stood up to try and defend him, looking far from happy.

'I was asking you', said Wallington, 'why you thought it was not Prince Youssoupoff or why you thought it was the Grand Duke Dimitri, when you saw the film depiction of the murder?'

Even the leading questions, predictable perhaps, in the circumstances, were of no avail. Pares had moved to the other side, although not quite.

'When it got to the murder,' he said, 'it seemed to me clear it was a mix-up and was mostly Prince Youssoupoff; but not entirely. For instance, there is one crucial fact: after Rasputin's death he was still alive because his lungs were full of water; and so it is hard to say what was the last act in killing Rasputin ... There are several people in it ... but the leading part to my mind is taken by Prince Youssoupoff.'

'That is of the murder?' asked Wallington, mystified.

'Yes, the murder.'

'In the film?'

'No, in fact.'

Wallington sighed audibly. 'Now will you deal with the film and tell My Lord and the jury what view you formed as to the film version of the murder.'

'It was totally different from the actual story,' said Pares.

'In what way?'

'To start with, it is Rasputin who does the shooting and not Prince Youssoupoff.'

'We know the film,' interposed Hastings impatiently, 'he need not tell us the story of the film again.'

'I think there are a number of differences which have already been pointed out,' said Pares, undeterred.

'If you know of any other differences will you state them; if not, I will leave it there,' said Wallington dispiritedly.

'I do not think I know of any other differences,' said the witness. He said he thought Natasha in the film was a fictional character; different people supplied elements, the first of these, he thought, was Anna Vyroubova.

'Did it strike you', asked Wallington, 'that looking at the film as a whole, Chegodieff was Prince Youssoupoff?'

'As a whole, certainly not; three-fourths not at least.'

'Looking at the film as a whole, did it strike you that the character of Natasha represented the plaintiff?'

'It never even distantly occurred to me that it could represent the plaintiff. Of course, I knew the fact best known about the plaintiff, that she had never met Rasputin at all.'

Wallington sat down and must have been pleased to do so.

Sir Patrick Hastings' cross-examination was predictably quite short, especially when compared with those of Jowitt, which had preceded it. He had formed a judgement concerning the witness and he was not going to allow him to wander on, if he could avoid it.

'The story of the murder of this man Rasputin is, of course, one that is of general world-wide interest? And that, of course, is really the central idea and incident of the film?'

'Yes, to my mind the central incident of the film . . .' Pares was about to embark on another bumbling discourse but he was pulled up sharply.

'It is so much shorter if you say "Yes",' said Hastings.

'Yes,' said Pares.

'Speaking not as a professor, but merely as a person who knows the world, for many, many years past the name always popularly associated with the assassination of Rasputin has been Prince Youssoupoff, has it not?' asked Hastings.

'Not so exclusively to me as to other people,' the witness replied, in a fashion difficult to follow.

'I did not say exclusively to you,' rapped Hastings. 'You will not answer my questions. Speaking generally – not of you as a professor, but of the world generally, who are interested in these things – the name popularly associated with the assassination of Rasputin is Prince Youssoupoff?'

'Yes, I would say that is the common view,' said Pares, who would never use one word where there was a chance to use a few more.

'Then the answer would be "Yes", would it not?'

'The common view', Pares replied.

Hastings would not wear this. 'Putting it concisely, the answer would be "Yes".'

'Yes,' the witness at last conceded.

'Therefore, if people, taking an interest in these matters, saw a representation of the assassination of the man Rasputin, the popular view would be "The man who does that is Prince Youssoupoff" ?'

'I think it might be popular and it might be erroneous,' parried the witness.

'Again, can you say "Yes" or "No"?'

'I cannot say "Yes" flatly to that because I think it would be erroneous.'

'It really follows from your last answer, doesn't it?' persisted Hastings.

'Popularly, yes,' Pares had to admit.

'Now, here you saw a film, the central interest of which was the murder or assassination or murder of Rasputin?'

'I thought not,' he parried again, 'I thought the central interest of it was the cure of the boy.'

'I asked you the same question before, and I thought it was one of the few questions to which you said "Yes", without any assistance, but apparently I was wrong. May I ask you to assume that some other person, not being a professor, saw the film of Rasputin about the mad ambition of one man, would he think that the central incident was the assassination of Rasputin? Some people might, might they not?'

'They might certainly think so,' said Pares.

'And if they did, as they were told it was a story of real people, they would think that the person primarily concerned in the assassination was the Prince Youssoupoff?'

'They might draw that conclusion.'

'Then the answer is "Yes", is it not?'

'Yes, they might draw that conclusion.'

'As a matter of historical interest, where did Prince Youssoupoff live when he was in St Petersburg?'

'Prince Youssoupoff lived in the house of the Youssoupoffs on the Moika.'

'Was that known as the Youssoupoff Palace on the Moika?'

'I could not tell you accurately; I should say it was known as the house,' said the witness, adding loftily, 'but I do not think it is material.'

'You have heard the Prince, who lived there, say it was known as the palace?'

'I am quite prepared to accept it.'

'As a matter of interest, was the gentleman in the film who was portrayed as the assassinator of Rasputin, a gentleman who lived in the Moika Palace?'

'That is one of the things which made me ...'

'Is the answer "Yes"?' asked Hastings sharply.

'Yes.'

'It is rather odd, is it not? He is also a Prince?'

'Yes.'

'He lives in the Moika Palace; you would expect him to be Prince Youssoupoff. He is a prince living in the Moika Palace?'

'I did not say I would expect him to be Prince Youssoupoff.'

'Will you assume that if I ask you any question about yourself the answer would be "No", that is why I am asking you about other people. The murder takes place in a cellar in the Moika Palace?'

'That is where it took place.'

'And this gentleman, whom the public might take to be Prince Youssoupoff, was, in 1913, engaged to be married?'

'Yes.'

'And he is engaged to be married to the lady who is sitting in front of me?'

'That is so.'

'At the end of the film, he goes off to be married to the Princess Natasha?'

'He goes off to be married ...'

'The answer is "Yes", is it not?'

'Yes.'

'And Prince Youssoupoff is married to the lady sitting in front of me?'

'Certainly.'

'Speaking now, not as a newspaper man, but as a professor, do you know the eight characters of this film?'

'Yes.'

'As to the Tsar, he met his death by violence?'

'The Tsarina, the Tsarevich and Rasputin, the same?'

'Yes.'

'The Grand Duke Igor, if he was the sole surviving brother of Grand Duke Sergei, also met his death by violence?'

'If so, yes.'

'There remain, therefore, Chegodieff, Natasha and the Court physician?'

'Yes.'

'Did you notice, thrown up on the screen: "A few of the characters are still alive"? You had just seen the characters, is that right?'

'Yes, I saw that.'

'"The rest have met their deaths by violence." Who were the few you thought were still alive?' asked Hastings seeking to drive Pares into a corner.

'I did not take it that had to be taken literally.'

'Is it as a newspaper man or as a professor, you took that view?'

'As a professor.'

'Then I may take it, you ignored this fact, as a professor would?'

'No, I read it carefully.'

'And then ignored it.'

'No.'

'But an ordinary person believes that the Metro-Goldwyn-Mayer Picture Corporation are people who truthfully represent facts to the people who pay for their tickets; if they told the truth, as the ordinary person would assume, who would be the few persons who were still alive?'

The witness glibly sidestepped the question.

'But I saw about twenty other characters in the film, who were not on this list as the characters who were being referred to.'

'I read exactly what you have read,' Pares insisted, 'and I did not draw exactly the same conclusion, that that is to be taken literally, as you take it.'

Hastings resumed his seat.

Jowitt in re-examination elicited that the witness was not a news-paper man.

'I thought he was a correspondent,' commented Hastings.

Pares said he was a correspondent to the British government.

Jowitt, no doubt, had decided to take the re-examination in the hope that he might succeed with their own witness where Wallington had failed; he was not to succeed.

'You were asked if the name popularly associated with the killing of Rasputin was Prince Youssoupoff. Do you think the Grand Duke Dimitri is known by the public too?'

'He is not known, for the best of reasons,' said Pares unhappily. 'He would never say a word about it.'

'Is he known by the people who have read Prince Youssoupoff's book?'

'Yes.'

'How can the witness tell us that; *they* can tell us that,' Hastings interposed wryly and accurately.

The judge commented that that was an observation Jowitt could better make to the jury, and after Jowitt finally got from the witness again that what was best known about the Princess Irina was that she had never met Rasputin, Pares was allowed to leave the witness box, his testimony finished, and, it seemed, with a sigh of relief on all sides.

With his departure the court adjourned for the day.

Chapter **Sixteen**

Friday 2 March 1934 was the fourth day of the trial and far from having diminished, interest had increased. True, it had moved from a major spread on the front of the *Daily Express* to page seven, where it shared the headlines with the denial, in the course of a trial, by a group of Fascists that one of their number, expelled from Mosley's British Union, had been attacked by a mob of them and compelled to swallow an exceedingly large quantity of castor oil.

Jowitt called to the witness box Colonel Cuthbert John Massy Thornhill, who told the court that, besides being a company director, he held the CMG, the DSO and Bar, the Legion of Honour, the Order of St Vladimir with Swords, the Order of Stanislaus with Swords, the Order of St Anne with Swords, the White Eagle of Serbia with Swords, the Rising Sun of Japan, 'and so on'. He retired as a Lieutenant-Colonel in 1920, and learned Russian in Moscow in 1910 and 1911. As a member of General Allenby's staff he went, in 1915, to Petrograd in charge of the British intelligence mission, where he was attached to the Russian headquarters staff. He knew the Tsar and his daughters, the Dowager Empress, the Tsarevich, the Grand Duchess Marie and the Grand Duke Michael. He had seen Dimitri but never met him. He knew Pourichkevich well and met Prince Youssoupoff once. He had read a number of books dealing with the matter under investigation, and he knew the Moika, which was on the banks of a canal. He said there was nothing like it in London, and he had always heard it called a house and not a palace.

In answer to Jowitt's further questions, he said he went to see a private showing of the film about two months previously, in company with Captain and Mrs Knowling.

'Did you – or did you not – come to any conclusion?' asked Sir William, '... as to the character of Princess Natasha?'

'Very definitely.'

'What conclusion did you draw?'

'That it was a fictional character.'

'Do you think it was drawn at all from anybody in real life?'

'It might be two or three people who were intimates of Rasputin.'

'What names occur to you?'

'Vyroubova, for one,' said the witness, 'and Golovina for another.'

He said the character of Chegodieff in the film he also considered 'decidedly fiction', and that, in real life, there was nothing like the scene where Chegodieff shoots at Rasputin and a breastplate saves him. He thought the character was much more like a Colonel Drentl, an intimate of the Tsar, who had been in the Chevalier Guards. Then he thought it was much more like Dimitri, particularly when he saw him in the uniform of an aide-de-camp. He said the killing scene in the film was quite different from real life, and, in answer to a most leading question, the Colonel said it never entered his head that Natasha was Princess Youssoupoff.

'Are you really trying to help the jury in this case?' asked Sir Patrick Hastings when he began his short cross-examination.

'Certainly,' said the witness.

'I mean, are you not in any way taking sides in the matter?'

'Not a bit.'

'Would you mind telling these ladies and gentlemen, what part the gentleman of whom we haven't heard before, took in the assassination of Rasputin?'

'None at all,' replied the Colonel, thereby exposing the inanity of his earlier answer.

'And yet you seriously tell the jury that that is the person you gave us first, as the one you thought the film assassinator of Rasputin represented?'

'Certainly, at the commencement of the film.'

On being questioned further, he said he had been asked to see the film by a Mrs Knowling and her husband, who were accompanied by Mr Wright, MGM's solicitor.

'Do you know Miss Buchanan?' asked Hastings.

'Yes, she is Mrs Knowling.'

'Do you happen to know, has Miss Buchanan been engaged for months trying to assist Mr Wright in the conduct of this case?'

'No.'

'Are you telling these ladies and gentlemen that when you went to see this private viewing, with Miss Buchanan, you did not know an action was pending?'

'I certainly did.'

'And did you know that the whole basis of the action was whether or not Princess Irina was represented on the film?'

'Yes.'

'And did you not know that Miss Buchanan was trying to prove that she was not?'

'I did not know anything about it.'

'Did you know that in this action Miss Buchanan was going to be a witness?'

'Yes, I did.'

'And what she was going to prove was that the Princess was not Princess Irina?'

'Yes.'

Sir Patrick was skilfully steering the witness towards the converse of what he had already said.

'You knew that before you went to the film?'

'Yes.'

'So that you are taken there by the daughter of your chief, to see the film, knowing that the lady who took you was going to prove that the Princess Irina was not the Princess Natasha?'

'Yes.'

'And knowing that, do you seriously say that it never entered your head that she was?'

'I said that I would give my opinion when I had seen the film.'

The witness said it was correct that he knew the lady who took him; he was prepared to swear on oath that it was not Princess Irina, but he did not know that Miss Buchanan had taken three people to view the film.

'Do you happen to know that she has taken a large number of people to see the film?' continued Hastings.

'No, I did not.'

'Do you know that she has taken several?'

'Yes, I do.'

'With what object – trying to see if she could get people to take their oath in the same way that she was going to do?'

'Exactly; give their opinions on the film' – but, the witness added, because she was going to swear something it did not mean he was going to swear the same thing.

'You knew the story was the murder of Rasputin?'

'Yes.'

'And you seriously tell these ladies and gentlemen,' asked Hastings, looking towards the jury, 'knowing that, and knowing Prince Youssou-poff is saying that he is the person represented in this film, you first of all came to the conclusion that the person intended was Colonel Drentl?'

'Quite definitely.'

As Jowitt stood up to re-examine, he gave his wig one of his custo-mary pushes towards his forehead. 'Do you think anything happened to prevent you making up your mind fairly and equitably on the matter?' he asked.

'I said I would not give evidence until I had satisfied myself after seeing the film,' said the witness, which might have caused the jury to consider it could hardly have been otherwise.

The Colonel's place in the witness box was taken by George Tchapline. He too described a veritable clutch of meritorious Russian medals which he held and said his father had been the Russian Postmaster-General. He knew the Mesdames Vyroubova, Golovina and other prominent Russians, but had never met Prince Youssoupoff, although he had seen him. He too had been taken to a private showing of the film. He also thought Prince Chegodieff was a fictional character but added that he first thought it was the Grand Duke Michael; later, when the character was 'kicked out of the army', he thought it was fiction, which was also the view he had formed concerning the charac-ter Princess Natasha. Into the same category of fiction he placed the scenes depicting the killing.

Cross-examined, he said he did not know Miss Buchanan until he arrived at court but had seen the film with Mr Wright, although he knew neither that he was the managing director of the English MGM company, nor that he was their solicitor in the action.

'And it was all fiction to you?' asked Hastings.

'Absolutely.'

'The killing was pure fiction,' commented Hastings, with another meaningful glance at the jury. 'Just tell me: was there a man in Russia called Rasputin?' His questions now assumed a touch of irony.

'Yes.'

'What happened to him?'

'He was killed.'

'Where?'

'On the Moika in the house of the Youssoupoffs.'

'And in what room?'

'He was killed in the yard.'

'First of all, was he given poison?'

'Yes.'

'Where was that done?'

'In the house of the Youssoupoffs.'

'In what room?'

'According to the books that I read, in the basement.'

'Did you happen to notice in the film a character called Rasputin?'

'Yes.'

'Was he fiction?'

'No.'

'Did he come to an untimely end?'

'Yes.'

'How?' This technique of asking very short questions, sometimes only one word, was in the style of the great advocate Carson, whom Hastings so much admired.

'He was killed,' said the witness.

'Where?'

'In the basement.'

'In whose house?'

'In the house of Prince Chegodieff.'

'And where did Prince Chegodieff live?'

'On the Moika.'

'And in what particular house, the Moika Palace?'

'Prince Chegodieff in the Moika Palace,' said the witness.

'Are you seriously telling us that you thought that was all pure fiction?'

'I did not say that the whole film was pure fiction,' said Mr Tchapline.

'You know you said the killing was pure fiction,' corrected Hastings. 'What you really meant was this, was it not? It purported to be an account of a real incident, but the details were not accurate?'

'Yes.'

'Is that your idea of fiction?'

'If I am not mistaken . . .' began the witness, but Hastings interrupted him.

'Is that your idea of fiction?' he repeated.

'No, it is not,' the witness admitted.

'Then what did you mean by saying the killing of Rasputin – because I wrote it down – was pure fiction?'

'I meant that the whole scene of the character was wrongly recon-structed.' The witness was obviously agitated.

'Exactly: it was a real incident inaccurately portrayed?'

'Yes.'

'Is that what you call fiction?' came the question again.

'I am not a perfect ...' the witness began.

'Is that what you call fiction?' asked Hastings, interrupting him again.

'Please let him answer,' said Jowitt.

'Did you mean to say you were not a perfect English scholar?'

'Yes.'

'I accept that at once,' replied Sir Patrick.

'Is that the same word which you used for the Prince and Princess?'

'Yes.'

'Did you mean the same thing?' was the last of Hastings' questions to him.

'Yes.'

Jowitt did not re-examine and the witness withdrew. Sir William called for Commander Oliver Locker Lampson and he entered the witness box. He said he had been a Member of Parliament for twenty-five years, was a Companion of the Order of St Michael and St George, held the DSO and the Imperial Russian Orders of St Vladimir and St Anne, also the Cross of the Order of St Leopold. He had raised a force of armoured cars which he had taken to Russia, where he saw service, and he described, by name, the prominent Russians known to him. He only knew the plaintiff and her husband by sight, however. He also knew Vyroubova by sight, but did not know Golovina at all.

Having read about the case in the newspapers, he had telephoned Mr Wright, the solicitor, and asked if he could see the film. He went to see it at a private showing only the previous evening and, he told Jowitt in answer to another leading question, he saw it with an open mind.

Asked to describe, in his own words, the conclusions he drew, he said, 'Well, first of all, as a monarchist and a lover of order, which we stood for in Russia, I felt this play was an ennobling play and not a degrading one.'

'That is not the cause at issue,' observed Avory dryly, as if thinking aloud and not addressing anyone in particular.

The MP said he did not connect Chegodieff in the film with Prince Youssoupoff, and, if it were anybody, he thought it was Dimitri.

'Now,' said Jowitt, 'with regard to the character, the Princess Natasha, what do you say about her?'

'Well, I say it would never occur to me that it was the Princess who was portrayed. The lady who acts in the play must be several years older than the Princess was at the time. She does not really look like her and the spirit of her relationship seems to me to be different from what one would have anticipated had it really been her. Indeed, I would have thought, if a real character was intended at all, it was Madame Vyroubova who was intended, as she was the historical link between Rasputin and the throne.'

His presence at the hearing, he asserted, was due to the fact that he knew all the parties and so many of the people concerned. 'Pourich-kevich,' he added, 'I knew intimately.'

'Of course, you're a busy man?' was Hastings' first question.

'Yes.'

'Did you take time to read details of this case in the papers?'

'Well, I don't abstain from reading the daily papers.'

'What had the case to do with you? Why did you want to waste your time by going to look at a film and communicating with Mr Wright?'

'Well, I served in Russia. I have an interest in fair play and right, and I was actually acquainted with not only Rasputin himself, whom I saw, but Pourichkevich and the other actors. I was actually invited by Pourichkevich to murder Rasputin.'

Stunned silence in the court greeted this statement.

'But you have not come here merely to tell us that, have you?'

'I thought that was what you wanted.'

'Did you really!' said Hastings sarcastically, and loud laughter ensued when he added, with implied suggestion as to the witness's real motivation for his presence, 'You will be in the papers even more prominently now than as a Member of Parliament. You will be the star line in the *Evening News* and all your constituents will read it. Do not go too far, will you! Let me ask you about the facts of this case ... In your detailed experience of life, do you realize that sometimes actresses are a little older than the people whom they endeavour to portray?'

'Yes.'

'Do you happen to know whether the people who produced this play happen to know the precise age of the Princess Irina?'

'No.'

'So they may have chosen an actress for her beauty or other reasons, who did not exactly correspond in age?'

'Yes,' said the MP, 'but, on the other hand, they may have done the reverse.'

He said he did not know the producers of the film or if any one of them was in court, although he agreed they would be the best people to tell the jury whom they intended to portray.

Reverting to the character of Natasha, Hastings asked, 'You said she was more like the lady Vyroubova?'

'Yes.'

'Was that lady in real life a stout lady of about thirty-five?'

'She became that, yes.'

'No, at that time when she was sixteen?'

'No, not at that time. I remember her as thinner.'

The cross-examination ended with renewed laughter in the court.

'How stout was she when you knew her?' asked Hastings.

'I cannot gauge her measurements in memory,' was Locker Lampson's reply.

When Mrs Meriel Knowling began her evidence, she said she was the wife of Captain Harold Knowling of the Welsh Guards and the daughter of the late Right Honourable Sir George Buchanan, who had been British Ambassador at St Petersburg during the war. She herself held the Order of the Russian Red Cross and the Order of St Anne. She had written six books on her Russian experiences and read a lot more. She had been in Russia from 1910 to 1918 and had met many prominent people at the Embassy who, at Jowitt's invitation, she listed. She had met the plaintiff several times but only knew the Prince slightly.

She had never seen Munia Golovina, but had seen Madame Vyroubova but never met her. As Jowitt put it, it went without saying that she had never met Rasputin.

She said she had seen the film at the Empire, Leicester Square, in June, before the action started and when she, therefore, knew nothing of it. She thought it was beautifully produced (which tends to show the critics may not always reflect public response), but thought it 'entirely incorrect'. She was, she said 'very puzzled' about Prince Chegodieff in the film. 'At one moment I thought it might be the Grand Duke Dimitri. It has a certain resemblance to Prince Youssoupoff but I thought it might have been a composite character of the two.'

The witness was manifestly seeking to give her evidence fairly, but it is interesting to note a hint of auto-suggestion in the evidence of all the defendant's witnesses. All of them conceived the idea that Chegodieff was a composite character. This may, of course, have been entirely their own idea, but it also raised the possibility that, when the solicitors to MGM were taking their statements, or proofs of evidence, they may well have asked, quite properly, whether they saw him, and indeed Natasha, as a composite of more than one person, and perhaps, suggested the names of whom these people might be.

Mrs Knowling, however, said she thought the character of Natasha was wholly fictitious, but in answer to Jowitt's question 'Insofar as she portrays a person in constant attendance on the Empress, who would that be?' she replied, 'Well, that might have been Madame Vyroubova.' She said it never occurred to her in the slightest to associate Natasha with Princess Irina.

She had been approached by Mr Wright through her publishing agents, she said, and had given him the impressions she had formed in June.

'I just want to make it plain,' said Hastings as he rose from his seat and was turning to the witness, 'are you merely here as a witness with no interest in this matter at all or not?'

'None at all,' she replied.

'Then I may take it that any suggestion that you are being remunerated for your work in this matter would be entirely unfounded?'

'Entirely unfounded,' the witness said with deliberation, not intending to be intimidated by the great Sir Patrick.

'Why have you been doing this then?'

'I did some of the historical research for Mr Wright. I did not know I was to give evidence; I have been subpoenaed to give evidence.' She said the only person she had taken to see the film was Colonel Thornhill, and she had seen it twice.

'How many times did you see Madame Vyroubova?'

'I saw her several times at Court ceremonies.'

'Was she a middle-aged, fat woman?'

'She was not very fat.'

'I do not know what "very fat" means. Was she fatter than Miss Diana Wynyard?'

'I do not think so, when I first saw her.'

'You do not call Miss Diana Wynyard fat do you?'

'No.'

'Then what do you mean by saying this other woman was not very fat?'

'She was not any fatter than Miss Wynyard when I first saw her.'

'I am talking about 1916. She walked on crutches, did she not, in 1916?'

'She had an accident, but recovered.'

'She was crippled in an accident, was she not?'

'I do not think she was crippled. She had a bad accident and she was ill for a long time.'

'You did not see much resemblance between a very fat woman who could not get about because of an accident and Princess Natasha?'

'There was not very much resemblance.' This response was the first answer which Hastings elicited from this witness which assisted him.

In answer to Jowitt, Mrs Knowling said that Madame Vyroubova had broken her leg in a railway accident but she did not hear of her being ill for longer than a few months.

Neither side seems to have been particularly diligent with their research, including the witness, who had agreed to pursue it for Mr Wright. As already seen, Anna Vyroubova's injuries in the railway accident were far more serious than a broken leg; she was on crutches for a long time and ever after walked with the aid of sticks, as Rasputin had allegedly foretold. This was not known to the jury, even if, and it requires a big 'if', this degree of detail was of real importance in the suit.

The daughter of a gentleman called Shaposhnikoff, who was thus of Russian birth, was called next. Her name was Mrs Lubov Hicks, and her uncle had been the Mayor of Moscow down to the Revolution. Jowitt, having suggested that she had met many members of Russian society when in Russia, was nonplussed when she denied this, on the grounds that, as she had already said, she lived in Moscow and not St Petersburg.

She was disarmingly frank, and when she said she had seen the film, having been asked whether she had tried to make up her mind fairly, she replied, 'Well, I felt somewhat biased, because I knew what the case was about.'

Jowitt looked nonplussed again. He was obviously wondering why on earth he had called her, and his last question did nothing to clarify it:

'Having had your mind directed to who's who, so to speak, what conclusion did you draw, with your knowledge, as to the character Chegodieff?'

'Chegodieff, I did not connect with anything until the end of the play. Then I thought, "Well, I suppose this man is supposed to be Prince Youssoupoff." About Princess Natasha, I could never have connected her with Princess Youssoupoff, for whose character I have the greatest admiration. I know she could never be connected with

Rasputin or do anything at all which would connect her with scandal of any sort.'

Jowitt's tactics sometimes seemed to be counter-productive. He was constantly stressing how far the storyline of the film deviated from the truth. The problem he faced was that once a person, knowing the true circumstances, reasonably identified Natasha as Irina, the introduction of fiction tended to make this position worse rather than better. Libels are fiction; if they are true they are not libels. The point of real importance was the identification.

'Of course,' asked Hastings in cross-examination, 'you thought it was Prince Youssoupoff because he was the man whom everyone knows; he is the person to whom is attributed the assassination of Rasputin?'

'Also because I know the case tended that way,' said the witness frankly.

'You thought it was not Princess Natasha because you knew her, and you knew that she was not a person who would allow herself to be seduced by Rasputin?'

'I did not say seduced,' was the reply, 'I said "be connected".'

'But if you had not known her well, let me ask you this. Who was the Prince Youssoupoff betrothed to, in the year 1913?'

'There was no common knowledge; I did not know anything about it. Princess Youssoupoff told us so. In 1913 nobody knew about her betrothal.'

'Not even the public betrothal?'

'That was not in 1913; that was later.

'When was it?'

'I suppose in 1914.'

Hastings changed his date to 1914, but the witness said she still did not know. She did, however, know that Irina married the Prince. Although she knew they married, she did not know the date of the betrothal.

'She was married in 1914?' asked Hastings.

'I dare say,' she replied, 'but I have looked at the film and in it that was the only date I could connect.'

'Forget the film for the moment,' Hastings entreated. 'You told us you thought, and presumably other people might think, that the Prince Chegodieff was this gentleman sitting in front of me?'

'I do not know what other people think.'

'Of course you do not,' agreed Sir Patrick, pointing to the Princess, 'but this is the lady whom he married?'

'Yes.'

'And you realized, at the end of the film, that he was going off with Princess Natasha to be married.'

'I also realized that in real life she was already married to him.'

'Of course, but you do know enough, do you not, about dramatic work to know that they try and keep their principal characters unmarried as long as possible?'

'Only in bad films and bad books.'

'Is this a bad film?'

'Apparently it is.'

'You think it is. Then let us assume that, this being one of the class you call bad films, they keep their chief characters unmarried as long as possible?'

'That's nothing to do with my opinion of the case.'

'Who else was Prince Youssoupoff betrothed to except Princess Youssoupoff?'

'I do not know anything about the private life of Prince Youssoupoff.'

The witness had contributed very little to the sum of knowledge involved in the case, and Hastings had made no progress with her at all. He sat down.

A company director who had spent twenty-two years in Russia gave evidence. He did not appear to have met anyone of any great note, although he knew the Russian Secretary of Police. He said he did not know of the legal action until after he had seen the film and formed his opinion, which seemed to be that it left him in a state of great confusion. He thought the whole film was a sort of fantasia, particularly because he understood that not more than four or five people were present when Rasputin was killed and in the film hundreds of people, or at least many tens, were present. He was further confused because it was said, in the film, that Natasha was the daughter of the Grand Duke Sergei and he had died in 1905, without children. If he formed any conclusion at all, beyond a merely made-up figure, it was that the woman was Madame Vyroubova.

Once again, it was difficult to see what the witness really contributed and that was clearly Hastings' view. He asked a few desultory questions as to how the witness had got into the act, as it were, in the course of which it emerged that he was a close friend of one of the junior counsel, Mr Idelson. At least the witness could claim he had contributed rather more to the proceedings than his worthy learned friend appeared to have been able to do.

Jowitt's last witness, according to the transcript of the trial, was

Henry Herbert Sydney Wright, the solicitor. This gives rise to something of a mystery. The transcript is an unedited document, yet I myself, who was present during much of the case, have the clearest recollection of another witness whose presence or testimony is unrecorded. Whilst the memory plays tricks, the circumstances were so unusual that it is inconceivable that it can be mere imagination.

I recall that Jowitt called a young Welsh woman, who was a domestic servant of some kind, who said that she had seen the film, knowing nothing about Russia, but she did not think whoever was being portrayed had been raped or seduced.

If this is so, it was in itself quite remarkable, since such evidence was not remotely admissible. Indeed, it was because of this that Hastings dealt with it in this unusual fashion to underline this point.

Having asked her name, which was distinctly Welsh, he cross-examined as follows:

'I see you come from Wales?'

'Yes,' said the girl.

'From a place well to the west of Wales?'

'Yes.'

'I imagine you like it there?'

'Yes, I do; very much.'

'And I imagine you are anxious to get back there, aren't you?'

'Yes I am.'

Hastings slowly sat down, saying to the witness, as he did so, 'Very well, run along then.'

The electric atmosphere of the court was broken as everyone present, including the judge, joined in the laughter, though Avory permitted himself only a smile. That recollection can hardly have been the product of an over-active imagination, although there is nothing of it in the transcript at all.

Mr Wright said he was a member of the firm of solicitors Wright & Webb; that he was instructing Jowitt in the case and was Chairman of MGM's English company. He said the policy of the company was dictated from America. Jowitt then endeavoured to refer to, and presumably intended, to read extracts from, an affidavit which the witness had made in the interlocutory proceedings. Hastings asked to what issue it was directed, to which Jowitt said it related to Miss Fanny Holtzmann. Having canvassed it, and without giving any information concerning it beyond that, Jowitt, who must have known he could not get away with it, abandoned it, saying he did not want to introduce anything which was the least bit questionable.

The remainder of Mr Wright's evidence in chief contributed no more than had the earlier part. He read the letter before action which had been received from the plaintiff's solicitors and the reply which he sent. He concluded by confirming that certain cuts had been made in the film, without specifying them, Jowitt saying he would leave it to Sir Patrick to ask further about them if he wished.

'I will ask you about those cuts in a moment,' said Hastings, beginning his cross-examination, 'but there are one or two matters first. Do you remember when an application was made to fix a very early date for the hearing of this case, that counsel on your behalf pointed out to the court that you would require considerable time to get evidence, particularly as you might have to get evidence from abroad?'

'Quite right.'

'Your company is very closely associated, is it not, with the American company which produced this film?'

'Yes.'

'They are the same thing, except that their legal entities are different. They are the same company, are they not; one controls the other? They are interested one in the other.'

'Yes.'

'Of course, you agree with me, do you not, that one of the things anyone might desire to know and might be vitally interested in, is what the gentlemen who produced this film intended by the character of Prince Chegodieff?'

'I should not have thought so,' said Wright.

'Do you not,' asked Hastings with an incredulous air, 'do you not think, if it were a fact, that the American producers always intended this gentleman and his wife to be the real characters on the stage, it might make a very great difference to the plaintiff?'

'I do not think so.'

'Do you not think it would be an important element in your case, if it were true, to be able to say that even if there was a misconception, the producers of this film never intended to portray Prince Chegodieff?'

'No,' persisted Wright, 'I do not think so.'

'Now think!' Hastings admonished him.

'No, I should not. I should not have advised sending the producers over here, even if I could have got them in the time. I accept responsibility.'

'I did not ask you that. Are you seriously suggesting that if you honestly believed that you could prove that no one intended to portray this lady and gentleman, you would not have given that evidence to the jury, if you could?'

'Quite right. I do not think I should, having regard to the authorities. The authorities say expressly ...'

'Never mind about the authorities,' said Hastings, rudely interrupting him.

'But you must allow the witness to answer,' protested Jowitt.

'Quite right,' said Hastings, adding with less than honesty, 'I was only trying to keep the matter short.'

'I submit, My Lord,' said Jowitt, appealing to Avory, 'that the witness must be fairly treated with regard to his answer.'

'I am sure Mr Wright knows I am trying to be perfectly fair to him,' said Hastings.

When Wright referred to 'the authorities', he was, of course, using the legal terminology for the decided cases on the subject which set precedents. Whether his answers were evidence of his failure to understand the full implications of Hastings' questions or whether he was deliberately fencing with him was not clear. The authorities which, doubtless, he had in mind did make it clear that if the jury thought the words were defamatory and referred to the plaintiff it was, truly, immaterial, as a matter of primary liability, whether those who perpetrated the libel or slander intended to refer to the plaintiff. The Artemus Jones case was a good example.

What, however, was highly relevant – and it is inconceivable that neither Wright nor those instructed by him did not, and could not, know this – is that the measure of damages which the jury were likely to award would be immeasurably greater if the defamation was deliberate than if it were unhappily accidental.

'Have you brought into court from America', continued Hastings, 'anyone who can throw any light on the question of whether or not the person who wrote this film, or produced it, deliberately intended to portray Prince Youssoupoff?'

'No, I have not.'

'As far as you know, are the producer and author both alive?'

'That I could not say.'

'As far as you know?'

'I have no knowledge.'

'You know nothing to the contrary?'

'Nothing to the contrary.'

Those answers must have left the jury wondering. If intentional or accidental conduct was not in Mr Wright's mind at any time, and if this did not give cause for interviewing the authors and producers, it was an odd way to prepare the case.

Hastings would not allow these answers to pass. 'No doubt you have been in communication with your principal company in America about this action?' he asked.

'Yes.'

'And, as far as you know, none of the persons of the class I have suggested, is here in court?'

'None is in court.'

'Is the view which you are putting forward that no reasonable person could have thought that this character was Prince Youssoupoff?'

'Yes.'

'And is the view you put forward that, as soon as the Prince and Princess complained that it was they, you did your utmost to stop it?'

'I took the precaution of having certain cuts made in the film.'

'Just let me see about that. You made an affidavit in the case, did you not?'

'Yes.'

'Was it brought to your knowledge, and did you so state in your affidavit, that immediately after this film was produced in London, the *Morning Post*, the *Star*, the *Evening Standard*, and the *Queen* all said that this film was a thinly disguised version of Prince Youssoupoff?'

'I do not recollect making a statement to that effect.'

Jowitt jumped to his feet. 'My Lord,' he said, 'that seems to me a most objectionable question, but the damage is done now. My friend must know that it is wholly irregular; he cannot put to this witness extracts from papers and thereby make the extracts evidence. I make my protest; I do not say anything further. The damage is done.'

This was a curious, indeed, some might say, singularly stupid objection by Jowitt. Either he lacked any real understanding of the rules of evidence, or he had not thought clearly what he was about. There was nothing objectionable about the questions, and neither their purpose nor effect was to make the contents of newspapers evidence. Hastings was questioning the witness about the contents of one of his own affidavits, in order either to test his veracity or to establish, through the mouth of the witness, that something to which he had sworn was believed by him to be true.

That was also the view taken by Mr Justice Avory, who said, 'I understood the question was whether the witness has made an affidavit?'

'That is so, My Lord,' said Hastings.

'Verifying those facts,' added the judge.

'I would be obliged,' said Hastings, 'if, when my friend is making a legal objection, he would not always say things are grossly improper; it is so unusual, to be done between us.'

He returned to the witness, who had been standing passively in the witness box whilst the wrangling proceeded.

'I am putting to you questions on your affidavit,' Hastings said.

'May I have a copy of my affidavit?' asked Wright. One was handed to him.

'Will you look at paragraph 23,' said Hastings. 'Of course you realize there was no necessity, in criticizing the excellence or otherwise of this film, to draw any parallel between real people and dead people, was there? The film was either good or bad, and that is what the critics come to see?'

'That is so.'

'But in fact did you say this: "Between July 1932 and July 1933, the said film was criticized in over one hundred newspapers throughout the country? When was it first produced in England?'

'Do you mean first exhibited in England?' corrected Wright.

'Yes – was it in 1932 or 1933?'

'In June of 1933. That was the first public exhibition.'

'When was the first time the critics were invited to see it? When was the time it was first criticized in England?'

'I think it is in this affidavit,' said Wright, looking down at it. 'It is quite impossible for me to give the date at this moment.'

'Just think,' admonished Hastings, 'don't trouble about your affidavit. This film was produced in America in 1932 wasn't it?'

'That is so.'

'You must know when it was produced in England, whether it was in 1932 or 1933.'

'In 1933; I think I am right.'

'Could the newspapers have criticized an English performance before June of 1933?'

'It is possible, yes.'

'Did they? Where did they do it?'

'They might have had a private view of the film in our theatre.'

'Without your consent?'

'Oh dear no.'

'Did you give your consent to it?'

'If such a view took place.'

'Did it take place?'

The witness looked singularly uncertain. 'I should say it did.'

'Would you tell me when it was, because I suggest no papers criticized this film, so far as I know, until June 1933.'

'I see what you are driving at.' Mr Wright looked at his affidavit in his hand. 'I think this may be an error.'

'What may be an error?' echoed Hastings.

'Between July 1932 and July 1933 the film was criticized in over one hundred papers,' the witness explained.

'I do not know what you are saying,' said Sir Patrick. 'Will you just answer my question? Was this film criticized in England, by reason of an English production, before June 1933?'

'May I look at the criticisms?' asked Wright, not unreasonably. 'We have them here.'

'As far as I am concerned, we can pass on,' said Hastings.

'No,' disagreed Wright, 'and I should say this is a typographical error in the affidavit.'

'Will you tell me where the error is, because I cannot see it. Let me read the first line to you again.' Hastings reread the sentence. 'Is there any error up to there?'

'Yes, "July 1932". I do not think the film was over here in 1932.'

'That is what you swore in answer to our application for an injunction. You were saying, amongst other things, that we were too late?'

'Yes, my ground for saying that is that the film was exhibited in America in 1932, it was exhibited again here in June 1933; you had a private view of the film in our theatre in 1933 and no steps were taken until October 1933.'

'I am asking you a question. If this affidavit is wrong, will you correct it; I cannot. How do you want me to read it?'

'May I see the criticisms?' Wright again requested.

'No, I cannot wait for that,' said Hastings. 'Do you not know how to correct it? If not, I will pass on.'

'It is quite impossible for me to carry a date in my mind that you put at a moment's notice,' Wright protested with justification.

'You have some clerks sitting in front of you,' was Hastings' response; 'just ask one of them to look and see what was the earliest date. Now let us go on. You say "the said film was criticized in over one hundred newspapers throughout this country, in none of which criticisms is there any suggestion or mention of the plaintiff in this action". I will just stop there. You have told me that in criticizing a film it is no part of the duty of the critic to draw attention to the similarity or otherwise between real people and the characters in the film. Is there?'

'No.'

'Now the next sentence is: "And in only five is it suggested that the character Prince Paul Chegodieff is that of Prince Youssoupoff." What I ask you is this: are those five, the *Morning Post*, of the 19th June 1933, the *Star*, of the 19th June 1933, the *Evening Standard* of the 17th June 1933 – I think those are the only daily papers – and in the *Queen* of the 28th June 1933? Are those the five papers?'

'That's only four,' said Jowitt.

'Then I am afraid I have not followed your five,' said Hastings.

'Shall I give them to you?' asked the witness.

'Will you give me one more?'

'The *Daily Mirror*.'

'Are there any others?'

'No – I think it is the *Daily Mirror*.'

'That is quite sufficient for my purpose. You see, therefore, that you knew as early as June, that the press, who I assume had no particular knowledge of Russia, were saying: "This man in this film is Prince Youssoupoff?"'

'Yes.'

'When you say that you wanted to cut out those parts which were undesirable, did you try and cut them out then, or put anything in the film, to show that it was not Prince Youssoupoff?'

'No.'

Hastings next made the point again that whilst it was no part of the critics' duty, several of them had noticed the resemblance.

'Now in America. Did you see the American criticisms?'

'No.'

'Do you happen to know, or were you told by your principals, that there were criticisms in the press of this film during production?'

'No.'

'Is there anyone in this court who can tell us what, if anything, actually happened to bring to their notice this gentleman who was being cartooned in this film, during production; is there anyone in this court who can throw any light on that?'

'No, I have no one here from America at all with regard to my company or the American company.'

'Have you asked your principals in America any questions as to intention in this matter?'

'No, I have not.'

'Is that because you thought it wiser not to do so?'

'Most decidedly not.'

'And there is no one here from America to say "If we have libelled this lady, we did it in the best of good faith and we never intended it for a moment"?'

'I have already said,' commented Herbert Wright, 'I have no one here from America, and I accept full responsibility for it.'

This concluded Hastings' cross-examination.

Jowitt, when he came to his feet, once again embarked on a fruitless pursuit. He asked Wright whether he had seen an American criticism of the Grand Duchess Marie. Hastings said he did not object to Jowitt putting the American criticisms, although he doubted whether they were admissible, but if Jowitt read from them, he would seek the opportunity to refer to others of them. Jowitt weakly protested that Hastings had concluded his cross-examination, but when the judge told him that if he did put them, he thought Jowitt ran a risk, he again abandoned the venture, and all other re-examination to boot, and the evidence in the case was concluded.

Arrangements were made for the jury to view the film again, it being agreed, on Jowitt's request, that it should be momentarily stopped at the end of each reel.

Jowitt suggested that it might be best to delay the resumed hearing until Monday as there would be little time left after the jury returned. 'I shall be very short,' he said of his address to the jury, as if he really believed that to be something of which he was capable, but then more guardedly he added, 'But still, I suppose I shall be some little time, and my friend will be, as he generally is, short, too and if Your Lordship is going to sum up at any length, there might not be time to finish today.'

Jowitt's prognosis was more accurate in relation to his amended estimate than his original one. He was not only to take 'some little time', but, as was doubtless inevitable, a very great deal of it; by comparison, Hastings would, indeed, be short.

Chapter **Seventeen**

There was renewed enthusiasm for gaining access to the court on Monday 5 March 1934, since it was expected that this would see the end of the case. Lady Diana Cooper had not missed a day of the trial. Lady Oxford and Asquith and two others were seated in a small balcony at the side of the court; the rest were packed like sardines into a courtroom designed for only a fraction of the number present. Princess Youssoupoff, it was reported, 'pale, drawn and nervously toying with a lace handkerchief', sat at the front of the court, between her husband and her solicitor, Mr Harold Brooks.

To the parties concerned and most of those present, the case was by far the most important event of the day. The fact that some hundreds of Nazis had invaded Holland – not at that time more than temporarily – was not in the forefront of their minds, any more than was the fact that a little man had caused consternation at the BBC by asserting over the air that they had outrageously censored a talk he had been scheduled to give as a British working man. The great anxiety for those in court was to see the end of the proceedings and whether the Princess would win or lose.

Before Jowitt began his final address to the jury, the judge told him that he had reconsidered the point which Jowitt had made as to the distinction between seduction and rape, explaining, 'I have come to the conclusion that I ought to allow the amendment in the innuendo by adding, after the word "seduced", the words "or ravished". I do not think this case ought to go off on a point like that.'

Jowitt accepted the decision with good grace – indeed, he could hardly have done otherwise – but he added, referring to his right if necessary to go, if he lost, to the Court of Appeal, 'All such rights as are open to me are open to Your Lordship.' A proposition from which it would have been difficult to dissent.

It was, however, questionable whether the case should have gone on, rather than off, as the judge said, on a point such as he made. He had manifestly realized his earlier decision was wrong; that the allegation by the plaintiff that she had been seduced or been a mistress was unlikely to cover a depiction of rape and that St John Field's pleading was inadequate. To have allowed such an amendment so late in the proceedings was a course which many judges would have refused to permit, particularly since, in 1934, written pleadings were given even greater importance than they are today.

Jowitt thanked the jury for their care and attention, and told them that he would first remind them of the matters of which the Princess complained. He read from the statement of claim that 'the photographic pictures and words meant, and were understood to mean, that the plaintiff therein [i.e. in the film] called the Princess Natasha, had been seduced by and was the mistress of the Russian known as Rasputin, and following what My Lord has said, we must now add "and/or ravished by".'

'Seduced or ravished,' interposed the judge.

It is perhaps to be noted, although it was not the subject of any comment during the proceedings, that an allegation that the plaintiff 'was seduced by *and* the mistress of Rasputin' is totally different from an allegation that she was 'seduced by *or* the mistress of Rasputin'.

Sir William's first point was that if the jury thought the film was libellous it was important to see 'whether the fictional character with whom the person is identified is a good character or a bad character'. He argued that Natasha, in the film, was portrayed as a person of noble character, with perhaps an excess of simplicity and purity.

He then reverted again to the distinction between slander and libel, confessing that he had no idea what was the law on this subject and 'My Lord will tell you, because, as you have heard, this is the first case of its kind'. He drew a distinction between what one hears and what one sees. Had it been a silent film, the words 'I am not fit to be your wife', he said 'would have been a passage where you heard nothing; you would not know what the characters were saying'. This was an odd argument; Sir William could not have seen many silent films or he would have known that in a silent film, these words would have appeared on the screen, whilst the pianist played an excerpt from 'Hearts and Flowers'. Moreover, that, if defamatory, would certainly have been libel.

'Therefore', he continued, 'I submit to you that so far as the reception through the eye is concerned there is plainly no libel at all, and really the libel, if libel there be, comes through the sound, and coming through the sound, it is slander and is not actionable without proof of special damage (and there is no proof of special damage) unless it attacks the chastity of a woman.'

He stressed that the burden of proving the case rested on the Princess, and said what Wright had equally mistakenly been trying to say earlier as to their failure to call the authors of the script, as witnesses, or the producer.

'I cannot help thinking that if they had come here and stood in that witness box, Sir Patrick Hastings would have been the first to read and stress this phrase, that it makes no difference whether they intended that, or whether they intended the other. At any rate, we have not brought them here, and I suggest rightly.' From his point of view, he may well have acted rightly, since their presence could have done his clients no good. It was a reasonable assumption that, at best, they would have had to admit they used their best endeavours to disguise the fact that the film portrayed Prince Youssoupoff, and, as Jowitt must well have known, if MGM lost, the damages would have been considerably inflated.

Sir William reiterated what he had sought to present in the course of the evidence, that the plaintiff had clearly to establish that Prince Chegodieff was, in reality, her husband, and he said that character was closer to Dimitri if anyone. He listed again the various factors the witnesses had mentioned which, he argued, made this assumption feasible. He read to the jury the answers which the Princess had given to him in cross-examination in which she conceded that down to the killing scene, Chegodieff displayed characteristics which better fitted Dimitri, and the respects in which the character differed from Prince Youssoupoff. He did likewise when he dealt with the answers given by the Prince in cross-examination.

He summed it up, perhaps a little over-enthusiastically: '... you get clearly this proposition, that, down to the killing, everybody in this case agrees that the character of Chegodieff is more like the Grand Duke Dimitri than the Prince Youssoupoff.' Hastings did not, as he must have wished to do, interpose *sotto voce*, 'I, at least, don't agree.'

Jowitt jettisoned that part of the evidence of his own witnesses who thought Chegodieff might have been either the mysterious Colonel Drentl or the equally mysterious Colonel Rodzianco. 'When you get to the killing,' he told the jury, 'you must eliminate them, because they had nothing to do with it; but the Grand Duke Dimitri did.' He stressed again the wide discrepancy between the killing scene in the film and what occurred in real life, and took them laboriously through the details which they had already heard over four days in evidence. He, by implication, upbraided Hastings for having suggested to a witness in re-examining him that, according to the book written by the Prince, Rasputin was finally struck down with a loaded stick, whereas the fact was, and the book did not suggest otherwise, that the Prince had struck Rasputin with a stick after he was lying prostrate on the ground, probably dead.

By now, it had become evident that despite what he had earlier told the judge, Jowitt was not going 'to be short'; he was not even going to take 'some little time'; he was going to take a lot of time, and he was in the process of doing so.

He declared that it was never his policy to ignore any good points which the other side had made. He conceded the film showed Chegodieff giving a dance in his home, which was the Moika Palace. 'For many years,' he said, 'people have been trying to get the gilt without the gingerbread as well, and if you want to stress that the dance took place in the Moika Palace, you must remember what it involved.' It was depicted as taking place on 28 June, but, he argued, almost everybody knew Youssoupoff was not in St Petersburg on that date, but was in the country. Jowitt must have thought the jury highly credulous to believe that almost everybody knew that.

The second concession he made was that, at the time, Dimitri was neither married nor engaged, which was not the case with Youssoupoff; but, he said archly, he had not married the daughter of the Grand Duke Sergei, as Chegodieff had done in the film, for one very good reason: there was no such person. At this point he again summarized and repeated the points he had already made, observing that he hoped he had not spent too long on it.

'The second fence,' Jowitt continued, 'which was the real difficulty in my friend's way ... is that it is really impossible for anyone to say that the character of Natasha in the film represents the Princess Irina. Natasha is shown as a lady-in-waiting; she introduces Rasputin to the Court; she is the cause of Rasputin meeting Chegodieff, whom she endeavours to persuade as to Rasputin's holiness; she is treated with familiarity by Rasputin; she visits him in his apartment and gratifies his whims and wishes. Is there one single feature', he asked rhetorically, 'which comes within one hundred miles of the plaintiff? I suggest there is not.'

He repeated the points developed throughout the hearing which suggested, so he claimed, that Natasha was Vyroubova or Golovina, if anyone at all. 'Do you think', he asked the jury, 'Miss Diana Wynyard was endeavouring to play the part of a child of seventeen who, so far as the world knew, was not engaged at all?'

He again developed the reasons already given in evidence for suggesting that Natasha was, if anyone, one of the other two ladies, and made the point, perhaps one of his strongest, 'that the fact best known about the Princess is that she never met Rasputin, because that was the pretext under which Rasputin was brought to the house'.

He read extracts from the evidence of witnesses called by the plaintiff, namely Sabline, and 'the gallant Sir Aubrey Smith', as well as his own witness, Pares, but he over-reached himself when he asked the jury to accept that before the case commenced a week before, 'if you did not know anything about the Princess Youssoupoff, the fact that you knew the commonest fact about her, the fact best known about her, was that she had never met Rasputin'.

In the more recent debate which has proceeded about the special qualities of the bar, and the vast experience and skill which barristers claim to possess in rendering matters plain to juries, this speech of Jowitt's does little to lend credence to that argument. Here was a silk of great experience assuming that a jury, albeit a 'special jury', chosen at random, knew something of this nature concerning a Russian princess. He would have been lucky if one of them knew anything about her, and, if that assumption were right, his argument, far from assisting him, would have caused the jury to believe that the rest of his arguments and assumptions were, in all probability, equally hair-brained.

He took the jury again through the evidence of the witnesses called by Hastings, with the exception of Prince Nikita. 'I have passed over Prince Nikita,' he said, 'because I want to say nothing against him; he was a brother of the Princess Irina and not in a position to form an impartial judgement.'

He referred to another of his better points: that although the Princess 'had hosts of friends and large numbers of acquaintances in this country, she was not aware of the fact that this film was shown in June until several months afterwards. Do you not think that fact speaks about as strongly as any other? Do you not think that if really her friends and acquaintances in this country had thought that this film referred to her, she would not have received letters or ... information? ...June passes, July passes, and this film is advertised in all these papers up and down the country – she hears nothing.'

He explained that the reason he objected to Hastings putting to

Wright the criticisms in the papers, which said that Chegodieff was a thinly disguised Youssoupoff, was that the witness box was the place to call the five editors, so that he too could have asked them a question or two. Jowitt must by then surely have realized that that was never the purpose of Hastings' questions. It was his instructing solicitor and the chairman of the defendant company who had mentioned this in an affidavit, and Hastings' point was that if he knew the press were saying that, why had not more been done sooner to eliminate the damage?

Undeterred, Jowitt returned again to a further analysis of the evidence of the various witnesses. When he reached Mr Hartley, he thought it necessary to say, oddly enough, 'Mr Hartley was the gentleman who had been introduced by my friend Mr Idelson, whom I am very proud to be associated with in this case. If you knew Mr Idelson, as I do, the fact that the introduction was made by him, is certainly nothing against Mr Hartley.' This piece of hyperbole was best calculated to put ideas in the jury's head which would otherwise not have got there; at least, he did not tell them, by analogy to what he assumed they knew about the Princess, that at the outset of the case they must have known what a splendid fellow Idelson was, as, no doubt, he was.

Jowitt said that Mrs Knowling, who, he added, was the daughter of Sir George Buchanan, had come to court as every good citizen should, and then he complained that Hastings had made an unfortunate error, 'as we know', in asking her whether or not she had been paid, and whether she was receiving money. He renewed again his description of the evidence before he further complained that Hastings had asked Commander Locker Lampson, 'How does this matter concern you?' commenting that 'it is not a matter for my friend to ask'.

'Members of the Jury,' he continued, 'it really comes to this: that on that very shadowy imperfect evidence which my friend has called, little more than the gallant Admiral Smith – if I may use a nautical phrase – his steering has rather got out, because his sense of gallantry has got the better of his sense of judgement – who is asked to go and see the film just before the action comes on, for a lady whose family he has known for many years, and Sir John Hanbury Williams, and really, if it had not been that Mrs Budd had rung up the Ritz Hotel we should have had hardly anybody at all, and there is not a letter.'

This part of his speech is difficult to follow, since he appears to have started off on one theme, left his phrase unfinished and his argument in the air; perhaps, his own steering had 'got out'.

He then said that the Princess had been over-persuaded into bringing the action. 'I am not attacking her character; I am not attacking her honour. I am attacking her judgement when I say, I think it is a very great pity that this lady should ever have allowed herself to be caught up in this whirlwind of litigation, in regard to this sort of case.' She would, at least have the satisfaction, he suggested, whatever the result of the case, 'that it would go forth to the whole world, from the way in which this case has been conducted, that there is nobody who can cast the slightest stone against the honour and integrity of Princess Irina'.

After a long time, in the process of which Sir William had hardly made what he would later regard as his best speech, he concluded; 'I ask you to say, Members of the Jury, that the plaintiff has not discharged the onus which is upon her: she has not made out to your satisfaction that reasonable people seeing this film would think that Natasha represented her. I ask you, therefore, to say that it is your duty in this case, on the evidence, to say that not having made out her case, a verdict should be returned for the defendants.'

The length and tediousness of Jowitt's speech had not been lost on the court, and least of all on Hastings. He made this quite clear when he began his speech: 'In the morning of Tuesday of last week, I, in accordance with my duty, had to open this case to you and I have had the curiosity to look and see how long I was talking. I find that I took up twenty pages of shorthand notes in what I said to you. I have tried to find, through the some three hundred pages which follow of shorthand notes, any part of the case where I appear to have taken any part at all. I have found some little difficulty in finding it. You have had two very long speeches, I do not mean too long by any means, of excellence both in length and substance. You have had some remarkable cross-examination. One of the witnesses I called was cross-examined for five hours, another for between three and four hours, and the others in diminishing proportions. The Princess, of course, is not of our nationality, and I am anxious that you and she should not think, merely because I did not cross-examine every witness for five hours, that it was not because I thought I would be assisting her case if I did, but because I knew I should *not* be really assisting her case if I did. I followed, with interest, but some amazement, a good deal of what has happened in this case.'

He told them his speech would last a very short time, adding, 'It is never my habit to read long extracts from the words of my opponent and to criticize them. After all, we are not here fighting each other; it is our clients we are concerned with, and, therefore, I do not propose to refer to any word which has been said on the other side, but merely to call your attention to certain principles with which I do not agree.' He did not, strictly speaking, keep this promise.

Sir Patrick said he could not remember a case in which there had been so many statements of principle and of issue which were so fundamentally and absolutely wrong. He reaffirmed his intention to be brief, but said he was anxious, 'as far as I can, to assist you to keep your minds clear on the matter and not be muddled'. He referred to the fact that they had 'had a long disquisition on the law of libel and slander, and about the chastity of women and things of that sort, which I am sure you paid great attention to, but they had no more to do with this case than if you were asked to consider the liability of a bus driver on the wrong side of the road, because there is no claim for slander at all ... It only looks as though they are there to make the case more difficult.'

'You cannot sue a cinematograph machine for speaking to you,' he argued. 'Sir William Jowitt seems to suggest that there is a slander if a mechanical machine, having something recorded on it, grinds it out and speaks it.' He urged them to dismiss all this from their minds.

This presented a very interesting analogy which Sir Patrick drew. He was really saying, with some force, that the difference was between the spoken and transient word, which is slander, and the recorded and permanent word, which would be libel.

He was on less solid ground when be moved to his point, which was the difference between seduction and ravishment.

He now introduced an additional word for it: 'This lady, if I am right, married, and with a daughter of eighteen, is depicted to the public as a defiled woman. I do not care what word you use. I am not here to go into long discussions about words which do not matter. If I am right, she is portrayed as a woman who has been defiled by a blackguard. Whether it be with her consent, I do not know, and probably you do not. What does a woman mean when she says to her prospective husband: "I am not fit to marry you. I thought this man was a man of God, but I found out he was not"? Which of us is going to say what happened between those two which made this lady say she was not fit to be the man's wife? ... I say those words meant she was either seduced or ravaged and was a defiled woman.'

An observer might have been wondering why they had not used the word 'defiled' in the pleading; it was of more general application, unless, perhaps, it related only to someone who previously had been a virgin, but that, of course, was not what St John Field had written down. Some judges might have interrupted Hastings to inquire whether he wanted to amend the pleading once again to add the word 'defiled'.

However, rather as if that was what he had already done, Hastings continued, 'If we are right that this lady is portrayed as a woman who had been defiled, I wonder who is going to ask an English jury to say that is not defamatory.'

The next point, he said, was one at which he was even more surprised. This was that the intention of the person perpetrating the alleged libel was irrelevant. He said it was accurate that it was not a defence to a person who libels to say he did not intend to do it, 'but it makes all the difference in the world, upon the question as to what the plaintiff is going to recover'. He pointed out that in the Artemus Jones case, Lord Justice Farwell had set out, in the clearest terms, that intention, on the question of damages, may be vital.

He reminded the jury of Wright's acknowledgement that no one was being called from America and asked whether, if they could really have said it was not intended as Prince Youssoupoff, they would not have been over here in a second. 'Just think for yourselves', he told the jury, 'how they may be, at this moment, sitting in America, chuckling to themselves at the thought of people in England seriously considering whether this was intended to be Prince Chegodieff and whether it is he ... These people sitting over in America and saying "Well, I wonder how Mr Wright is going to get over the trouble that we did not go there to say we did not mean it."'

Sir Patrick was making the most of this very strong point, which the defendants had either tried to evade or overlook, or, most improbably, misconceived.

He said he would satisfy the jury that they did, in fact, intend to represent the character as Prince Youssoupoff and that was the reason why they had not come to the court to say the contrary. Mr Wright dared not bring them over because they would have had to say, 'Of course we meant them; there was nobody else and we made this love story of these two, because the whole world knew Prince Youssoupoff; and in America and elsewhere, we have only to mention Prince Youssoupoff, and let people know it is a real story and they will flock in thousands to see it. They will not go to see a fictitious story; they get them every day.'

He said that when they were told the question of intention does not matter, it passed his comprehension how they could be told that. The question of whether or not it was a defence was another matter.

He then turned to still another matter which he said he found impossible to understand, namely the question of people knowing the plaintiff. No one had every suggested that the person responsible for the death of Rasputin was not Prince Youssoupoff. 'What does it matter', he asked, 'for the purpose of a dramatic story that he was thrown into the ice by somebody else or thrown in the ice by himself? Drama has to be adapted, I suppose, for the exigencies of the screen, but that is the man' (pointing to the Prince) 'who is known throughout the world as the man who assassinated Rasputin. Now where did he live? He lived in the Moika Palace, the Youssoupoff Palace. Where was Rasputin killed? He was killed in the Moika Palace. In what room did the Prince kill him? In a cellar underneath the drawing room. Where was he killed in the film? In the cellar underneath the drawing room. What is the good of saying, because somebody else wears a medal in that first act, that it is more like somebody else than it is this gentleman?'

Sir Patrick said he had been trying to think of an example to illustrate this point. He recalled the case of Crippen, who murdered his wife. He briefly detailed the essential facts and asked what use it would be if in a film giving those facts his name was changed to Smith and, although Crippen went to Canada, in the film the man is shown as going to Australia. What did it matter if Crippen had been a little man and the part in the film had been played by Godfrey Tearle, who is a big one? What if Crippen was a dentist and in the film the man was a doctor?

The conclusion of Sir Patrick's example brought smiles to the faces of many in court, when he said, 'Supposing they then said "in point of fact everybody who knew every detail of the trial would have known that a famous doctor was called to give evidence against Crippen, Sir Bernard Spilsbury, and although we do not say he was the person we intended, Mr Smith is more like him than Dr Crippen"!'

It was a skilful way of sending up the case which Jowitt had presented. Sir Patrick said if that sort of defence was going to succeed, it was really giving licence to the film companies to defame real characters by making slight changes in the story. He was now in full flow, and when that occurred, there were none better than Sir Patrick Hastings.

'Out of all the hours that this case has taken by the defence, and it has really taken hours – you have had two- or three-hour speeches alone – ten minutes have been taken up with the one thing, except for which, I submit, this case always was an undefended one. When you have got a point which you cannot get over in court it is not a bad thing, sometimes, to say that you want to take every point and to take the things you can get over, and pay very little attention to the ones you can't get over. Now there is one point in this case that, in my submission to you, is a thing that nobody can attempt to get over. These people who are not called, were not here because this branch of the American company, if that is the right word, know what they did and they published to the whole world that this was a true story, of real people, in real life with a real murder. That is how they got their money for it. This is what they said: "This picture concerns the destruction of an empire" – that is true – "brought about by the mad ambition of one man" – that is Rasputin – "A few of the characters are still alive, the rest met their deaths by violence." Members of the Jury, if that was not intended to be true why have they not come here to say so? Why did they leave it to my friend, Sir William Jowitt, in the course of his almost continuous speech for four days – because for four days he has hardly had a moment's rest, to say that that is a journalistic flourish. Have you ever heard such a statement?'

He repeated some of the factors to which he had earlier referred, which showed that the story was presented in various scenes as a true story. 'It is so much more real to people to be able to say "These people are still alive"' he said.

'For them to say that this man' (again indicating the Prince) 'did not do it, is beyond belief. Everyone who knows this story knows he did it, and what is the good of their getting people here to say these things: "I am not going to call before you the man who wrote this; I am not going to call before you the man who wrote the film; I am not going to call before you the man who produced the film, to say we never intended this lady and gentleman; we never intended that to be believed; I am not going to do that, but I will instruct counsel to say that it is not relevant to call them," which I say', said Hastings, 'is fundamentally wrong.

'...the issue which you are here to try', he continued, 'is this: do you think these thousands of people who see this film, and who know the story – not the details which are quite unnecessary – who know the story in this sense, would say, if they knew anything of Russian history, as thousands of them must: "The man who killed Rasputin, which we are going to see upon this film, is the Prince Youssoupoff; where is he? He is alive; everyone here has been killed except the Prince Youssoupoff and Princess Irina."'

He developed this theme for a short while, pointing out there were many features which left no doubt that it was a true story which was being enacted, and giving examples. He suggested there was no drama in presenting fiction (which seems an odd and inaccurate idea), but, he continued, 'when Prince Youssoupoff stood up there in the witness box and told you that story, there could not have been a living creature who heard it, who was not thrilled to the marrow; and that is what they wanted on the film, they wanted to say "This is the real story of how this man died"; it was a real person who killed him; that is the Prince and that is his wife, and now you know the real story; the real story is that he was furious with Rasputin because he defiled his wife, and then they say to you that this lady has not suffered damage.'

He explained that it was common practice in these cases when the plaintiff was in the witness box to ask her, 'What have you brought this action for?' He reminded them that the Princess had told them in evidence that she wrote to MGM to get the film stopped. She asked, he said, for nothing else. They refused. 'When the film came over here,' he said, 'she wrote to Mr Wright and begged it should be stopped. Their answer was "Do as you like, it will cost us too much to stop this film." Now,' he said, 'they come forward and say they cut it. They never told her that they cut it; when we were before the learned judge, trying to get it stopped, they never said they had cut it – not a word of it. They say "Go on" and then they come here and suggest – not to her but to her husband after she has left the box – that she had been exploited.'

Hastings told the jury that he had spoken long enough, but he was going to ask them to say that the Princess had been grievously wronged, and he asked them to give her very heavy damages. He was sure the fact that he had spoken for only three-quarters of an hour against the two hours spent by his opponent would not be allowed to weigh improperly in the minds of the jury.

He said he relied on two facts, (1) that Prince Youssoupoff was known as the murderer of Rasputin, and (2) that the Princess was his wife, and he coupled with it the fact that MGM had said it was a story of real people.

He began to sit down, saying, 'Members of the Jury, I am afraid I must put this case before you as one of serious damage and one in which I say there is no defence and that the damages should be very large.'

The summing-up to the jury by Sir Horace Avory was commendably short and to the point, and, as was not unusual with this judge, he left no one in any doubt as to the view he had formed of the case. He said the case had been described as a novel and unprecedented one but, in his opinion, there was nothing in it to which the established principles, applicable to every case of libel, could not be applied. A libel, he told the jury, is anything published of a person which is calculated to expose them to hatred, contempt or ridicule or to cause them to be shunned or avoided. In fact – or rather, in law – Avory was giving what was more a definition of defamation than of libel, which certainly would not normally include the spoken word.

He said the libel could be published in the form of writing or printing, or of a picture or effigy, and gave as an example, from an actual case, a figure in the Chamber of Horrors at Madame Tussaud's.

'On the other hand,' he explained, 'it could take the form of a virtuous woman, locked in a Chamber of Horrors in St Petersburg, with a brutal libertine named Rasputin, in circumstances which indicate that she has been seduced or ravished by that licentious man, whose character, if we believe one witness for the defence, was really ten times worse than it was depicted in the film. That', he continued, 'is the kind of libel of which the Princess Youssoupoff now complains: that she has been depicted on the screen as a woman who was locked in a room in these circumstances.'

The only question, he told them, which arose out of that was whether the evidence satisfied them that the character of Natasha in the film really represented her and would be understood by people who knew her, to represent her.

It did not matter, he said, whether the world who viewed the film would all recognize Natasha as Princess Youssoupoff. There was abundant authority, he confirmed, for saying that if a number of people who knew the plaintiff, believed it referred to her, an action could definitely be maintained.

If they were once satisfied, be continued, that a number of sensible people had the honest opinion that, when they saw the film, they understood that Princess Youssoupoff was indicated, then it afforded no answer that other people did not think so.

This was all clear, direct, no-nonsense stuff, as good directions to a jury must be if they are to command the respect of the jury and the public, although it is better for the judge to let the jury decide the facts, as they are expected to. No simpering, however, about the beautiful princess in distress; nothing about her fragrance; rightly or wrongly, he had made up his own mind, and they were to understand exactly what it was, even though they were free to ignore it.

'Sir William Jowitt', he reminded them, 'has suggested to you that everybody who knew the plaintiff, knew that she had never met Rasputin, and that therefore you ought to draw the inference that she could not be the person on the film, who obviously had met Rasputin. That seems to me to be a wholly fallacious argument. The essence of an actionable libel is that it is not true. If it is true, no action for damages can be brought. It is a complete answer to any action for libel to say that what was published was true.'

The judge, in a few sentences, had exploded the curious argument which Jowitt had advanced and which he should have realized at the outset was never sustainable. The judge, however, could not have meant to say it was a defence merely to say 'it is true', he must have intended 'if it can be proved it is true'.

Avory, however, rightly put this aspect even higher, in relation to the inaccuracy of the facts concerning Natasha. 'Does it not, in fact,' he asked, 'aggravate a libel, if you say the plaintiff was the person represented on the film? What is the result on the minds of people who see it? If they have once seen the person represented, they go away and say: "We have always been told that she never knew Rasputin; that she never met him. But this film shows that she did know him, and it shows that she did meet him!" In fact the libel is made worse.'

The judge reminded the jury of the various points which Hastings had made in his address, before turning to the Achilles heel which the unfortunate MGM supervisor, the luckless Bernie Hyman, had created for his employers when, with the best of intentions, and with a view to rendering the picture more attractive, he had added the caption at the beginning of the film. 'Probably,' said Avory, 'the most outstanding feature of the plaintiff's case is the announcement made on the screen as soon as the film begins. The film company start the exhibition by saying a few of the characters are still alive.'

Then, before inviting them to consider their verdict, he outlined some of the points on which the plaintiff relied: that she was, and remained, the only niece of the Emperor of Russia, and Natasha was depicted in the same way; between 1913 and 1916 the plaintiff was the only princess of the Imperial family of approximately the age of Natasha in the film; Prince Youssoupoff was the principal author of the death of Rasputin. Prince Chegodieff, in the film, was the principal – 'or it may be said, the sole' – author of the death of Rasputin.

He concluded with these words before inviting them to retire to consider their verdict:

'If Prince Chegodieff, in the film, was Prince Youssoupoff, then Natasha in the film must have represented Princess Irina. If you come to that conclusion, then the only question is one of damages. That question is entirely for you. Nobody can doubt that if this is a libel it is a gross and insulting and injurious one. It is difficult to imagine a worse libel upon a woman, who is happily married and upon whose virtue nobody had ever dared to cast a slur, that she had been seduced or ravished by such a villain as Rasputin.'

Thus, in a short summing up, in a clear and concise fashion, the judge had stripped the case to its essentials. That he thought the plaintiff had an unanswerable case, no one in court could doubt. The jury retired.

The nine men and three women on the jury were taken to a private room to decide that which so many were now eager to learn, but none so anxiously as the Prince and Princess themselves.

The jury was a 'special jury', which meant that they had to meet the requirement of the Juries Act, 1925, and be 'of the rank of Esquire or higher degree, or merchants or bankers'. The underlying theory was that, as they were more well-to-do than their neighbours, 'the common jury', they would be better equipped to understand and determine the more difficult cases. With the levelling-down which subsequently occurred, under what we like to think of as our democratic system, special juries were abolished for such cases by the Juries Act of 1949. Such a move was, and remains, balm to the wounds of those who resent class distinction, but the general deterioration in the mental, literary and numerative qualities of jurors which has resulted has done nothing to enhance the effectiveness of the system, and may well be contributing to the ultimate and unfortunate disappearance of the jury.

With the judge and jury gone, the court hummed with chatter, whilst those who were waiting outside strove more desperately to gain access.

Time seemed to pass very slowly. The Prince and Princess remained in their seats in the front of the court. They did not speak; the Princess sat, white-faced, with clenched fists, staring hard at the floor. No one dared leave the court for fear they would not be readmitted. After two hours – which seemed longer – the usher drew back the curtain over the judge's door, and the jury filed back into court. The atmosphere was electric. The judge returned and resumed his place, and the associate asked the jury whether they had reached a verdict. The foreman, a middle-aged bespectacled little man, stood up, cleared his throat and said, 'We have; we find for the plaintiff.' The silence in the court remained undisturbed; there was still an expectant hush. 'Have you assessed damages?' asked the associate. The foreman cleared his throat again and was evidently anxious to make a little speech. Avory intervened with, 'All we want to know is the amount you award in damages.' 'Twenty-five thousand pounds,' said the foreman in a loud voice. A gasp went round the court.

Avory said there would be judgment for the plaintiff in that sum, with costs and, on Hastings' application, granted an injunction restraining the film company from publishing the film in the manner complained of in the action.

Jowitt told the judge they would be considering an appeal to the Court of Appeal and asked for a stay of execution. This the judge refused, and the crestfallen expression on the faces of the defendants' representatives seemed a shade more despairing. The judge retired and the friends, mostly Russian, of the Prince and Princess crowded around them, offering congratulations. The Princess was at last smiling, as well she should have been. It was a vast sum, even by today's standards.

On the basis that over the last fifty years the value of money has risen from twenty to twenty-five times it would be the equivalent today of between half a million and six hundred thousand pounds. (The heated discussion, much of it misguided, concerning the large sums currently being awarded by juries in libel cases, disregards the fact that they are the last bastion for discouraging unwarranted intrusion into people's privacy for protecting their reputations.)

According to the *Daily Express*: 'The Prince and Princess were hurried away to one of the private rooms in the Law Courts. The Princess sank wearily into a chair and smoked a cigarette. "What a relief", she exclaimed, "I am tired – so very tired –." They made their way to a motor car in the courtyard. A crowd gathered as soon as they appeared. Strangers came up to the Prince and slapped him on the back. The Princess smiled and bowed to those who crowded around her, and, as she drove away, she waved her hand in acknowledgement of a burst of cheering.'

The Princess travelled down to Windsor for a fortnight's rest with her mother. 'These are the first moments of joy that have been given me for very many weary years,' she said. 'Oh, the relief', she told a reporter, 'of knowing the action is behind me. I never doubted I should win – how could I? But I am so very tired of having our misery and our private affairs held up to the public. I never go into society now. My recreation seems to be worry. Today's verdict is the first ray of light I have had. In spare moments during the case, I have been drawing and painting monsters out of my head. I hope I shall be able to sell them – perhaps for two guineas each. Painting has been my pastime as well as my livelihood for the past two years. I have painted since I was a child but never before have I put it to good use. I shall guard every penny of this £25,000 and put it in a trust fund for my daughter and her children, so that she and they shall never know the poverty I have endured.'

The Prince, for his part, was reported as saying: 'My cross-examination was a great trial for me. I know I could not have had fairer treatment than British justice; but you cannot imagine the torture I went through reliving the killing of Rasputin, before people who were not Russians. And so many came out of curiosity. The incident is especially harrowing to me as I believe my well-intentioned efforts to save my country by destroying the monk only released the devils concentrated in him. These were broadcast and resulted in the Revolution, causing the downfall of Imperial Russia. Then the defence had the audacity to suggest that I, Prince Youssoupoff, did not kill Rasputin, when I have suffered ever since for doing so. No one can calculate the damage of that.'

MGM took the case to the Court of Appeal; they were outraged by the amount of the damages. Curiously enough, they did not include in their grounds of appeal the very late amendment of the pleadings. They contended, instead, that there was insufficient evidence to justify the jury's decision that the film referred to the Princess, or that she had been seduced by, or had become the mistress of, Rasputin; they resurrected Jowitt's point as to it being a case of slander and the absence of special damage; they again contended that it was not actionable to say of a woman that she had been raped; they claimed the damages were excessive and unreasonable, and also misdirection by Mr Justice Avory in his summing up to the jury. However, they received short shrift from the Appeal Court.

The appeal was heard in July 1934 by a strong court, presided over by Lord Justice Scrutton, the only bearded judge to sit on the High Court bench for the last fifty years, and two Lord Justices, Greer and

Slesser. Scrutton, in giving judgment, referred to Avory as one of the most experienced judges on the bench and upheld his description of the law, quoting, in support, the case of Artemus Jones, and other cases. That being so, he said, regarding the question of identification of the plaintiff, it was for the jury to say whether reasonable people would take the character to refer to the Princess. 'It is not my business to express an opinion on the matter,' he said. 'There is obviously evidence, in my opinion, on which a jury might come to the conclusion that the Princess Natasha of the film is the Princess Irina Youssoupoff.'

On the second point, namely that if they were satisfied that it was the Princess portrayed, it was not defamatory, Scrutton, never a judge to mince words, said that 'it takes some courage to argue it'.

'If libel alone is for the jury,' he continued, 'why is it said that the jury in this case have come to a wrong conclusion? I desire to approach this argument seriously, if I can, because I have the greatest difficulty in approaching it seriously.' He referred to the provisions of the Slander of Women Act, and went on, 'from that we get to this, which was solemnly put forward, that to say of a woman of good character that she has been ravished by a man of the worst possible character is not defamatory. That argument was solemnly presented to the jury, and I only wish the jury could have expressed, and that we could know, what they thought of it, because it seems to me one of the most *legal* arguments that were ever addressed, I will not say to a business body, but to a sensible body ... I really have no language to express my opinion of that argument.'

'On the issue of damages,' he said, 'the constitution has thought, and I think there is great advantage in it, that the damages to be paid are decided by the jury.' He said it was well settled that the Court of Appeal would only interfere if they came to the conclusion that no reasonable body of people could have awarded the sum in question. He found it impossible to say this, and as for the summing up, he saw no ground for interfering at all. Lord Justice Greer was of the same view. He said he had at one time been in some difficulty as to whether they should interfere with the amount of damages, but had decided against doing so, and was impressed by the admission made by Mr Wallington, in the Court of Appeal, that 'the defendants were using the private story of this lady for the purpose of putting money into their pockets, and that they were unwilling to stop using this cinema picture when it was complained of, because they said they would lose £40,000 if they did, and a great deal more'. Those words have equal application today, and need to be borne in mind when some of the press complain about excessive damages.

Lord Justice Slesser had no doubt the action was correctly framed in libel and not slander. He thought the speech formed part of the total exhibition and had the purpose of explaining the actions. He followed the example of his brother judges and dismissed the appeal. Jowitt made noises about taking it to the House of Lords, but this never occurred, and the great case of *Youssoupoff* v. *MGM* was at an end.

Chapter **Eighteen**

Although the judges, both at the trial and in the Court of Appeal, were somewhat dismissive of the case, treating it as one which was little different from the ordinary run of libel cases, in fact it was a case of special interest, quite unusual in itself, and one from which many lessons can be learned which are relevant today. It is one of the peculiarities of certain High Court judges that they often adopt an inexplicable pose that the case with which they are dealing is, contrary to the arguments addressed to them, quite usual and simplicity itself.

In the first place, *Youssoupoff* V. *MGM* established that it was defamatory to assert of a woman that she had been raped. It needs to be remembered, however, that this case was decided in the 1930s, when outwardly, whatever occurred privately, public morality was far narrower than today, and when the views of the judges on such matters were even narrower than most. To have been raped was regarded as being only a rung or two above being born illegitimate. The fact that in neither case could the party concerned help it counted for little, and a parent would have been as outraged at the prospect of her offspring marrying someone illegitimate, as a mother would have been that her son intended to marry a girl who had been ravished. It may sound odd, but those were feelings which many entertained at that time. Scrutton, who presided in the Appeal Court, was notorious for his narrow moralistic views, and one of his brethren, Mr Justice McCardie, fell foul of him; McCardie being a judge who lived, not only before his time, but with a lady to whom he was not married, a situation of which Scrutton strongly disapproved.

Today, when society has suffered, and continues to suffer, from the consequences of the 'permissive society', it is open to question whether a woman suing because it has been said of, or written about, her that she had been raped, would succeed in the action at all. Today, the reaction would be that for which Jowitt unsuccessfully contended in 1934, namely one of intense sympathy and compassion, and one would be hard put to find anyone who would hold up a woman who had been ravished – or more correctly, of whom that was inaccurately said – to hatred, ridicule or contempt or shun her. It might, of course, be possible, had the victim previously been a virgin, this being a condition which, difficult as it sometimes is to believe, some still continue to regard as important. Thus, whilst a modern plaintiff might still succeed in such an action, it is by no means certain.

Another thing which the case demonstrates is the part which good advocacy can play in reducing the ever increasing, and often exorbitant, cost of litigation. It is only necessary to compare the advocacy of Hastings with that of Jowitt, and the succinctness of Mr Justice Avory with many others of our judiciary. Jowitt's ponderous and heavy-handed manner enormously extended the time taken by the trial; Hastings, as ever, reduced every effort to a minimum. Hastings won the day.

Moreover, what was Jowitt's purpose in calling much of the evidence which he adduced? He must have realized, as the judge later forcefully pointed out to the jury, that it mattered not how many people thought Chegodieff was not Prince Youssoupoff, if one or more reasonably and honestly believed he was. His evidence surely should have been limited to attacking the unreasonableness of such a belief, if that were possible.

The press at the time put the total costs of the action at £15,000. Today, that would be equivalent to £300,000. This is, as ever, largely guesswork, and, in any event, the greater part of the expense would have fallen on MGM, who had far more counsel employed than the plaintiff, and paid them a great deal more on their briefs. The fact that Hastings, in his address to the jury, several times adverted to the time which Jowitt had taken and, by implication, wasted, demonstrates that, at least in his opinion, much time had indeed been wasted, which always adds enormously to the costs of an action.

Another factor of particular interest is the question of contingency fees. This is another subject which is under active discussion today. At the time of writing, it is against the law, in Great Britain, for lawyers to act on the basis of contingency fees, which means they are paid nothing if the client loses the case, but receive a share of the damages if the action succeeds. Similarly, it is illegal, with a few exceptions which have no application here, for an agreement to be made which affords to a third party the right to share in the proceeds of an action at law brought by another. Of course, the plaintiff's English solicitors had made no such arrangements; they were to be paid on the usual basis, and as a result the bulk of their costs had to be paid by MGM. It was, however, otherwise with Fanny Holtzmann. There can be little doubt that she would have operated on a contingency basis, since it has long been permissible in America, to the great detriment of the administration of justice, and the integrity of the legal profession there.

Having lost the action in England, MGM set about settling the rest of the Princess's claims elsewhere. MGM's books recorded that of $185,000 (which was around £90,000 then and probably in excess of £1,800,000 today), $125,000 went to the Princess (about £1,200,000 today), and $60,000 went to Fanny Holtzmann (which would be about £600,000 today). Bosley Crowther, in his book *The Lion's Share* states: 'However, it was generally reported at the time that $750,000' (that is about £5,400,000 today) 'was paid to the Princess,' and Fanny Holtzmann's share being correspondingly increased, 'and the Company absorbed $380,000' (about £2,800,000 today) or more 'in costs'. He added: 'Miss Holtzmann remains cryptic on the subject. "The settlement", she says, "was for a lot more than they'll admit at Metro-Goldwyn-Mayer." It is quite possible that the company could have paid more than their books officially specified, out of an un-audited contingency fund of around $1,000,000, that it regularly noted on its report.'

The precise nature of the arrangements which the Princess made with Fanny Holtzmann never emerged, and probably never will. What is quite beyond question is that a firm of the high repute of J.D.Langton & Passmore, the English solicitors who acted for her, would not have been prepared to act on any basis other than the proper one, that is that she bore her costs in the usual way. If, moreover, the Princess was right and truthful when she said she was 'penniless', the costs must have come from somewhere. All the probabilities, therefore, are that, unbeknown to her English legal advisers, she entered into arrangements with Fanny Holtzmann that the latter would advance the costs in return for a share of the proceeds of the judgment or any compromised settlements. Indeed, were this not so, why did Fanny get any part of the proceeds? She did not act as lawyer for the Princess in the case. Fanny always thought they were on to a good thing, and although such an arrangement was illegal in England, this was probably not the case in America. The real occasion for surprise was that Jowitt never asked the Princess a single question about it. He was willing to suggest to the Prince that the Princess had acted under pressure from Fanny Holtzmann, and that she was ill advised to have done so, but missed the vital questions regarding Fanny Holtzmann's part in the litigation, although that part seems quite obvious. Hastings may well have tried to object to this line of questioning, on the grounds that what passed between the plaintiff and her legal advisers was privileged from disclosure, but Fanny Holtzmann was not her legal adviser in the English action, and in any event, if the arrangements were such as above described, and illegal in England, no privilege could have attached. Had the jury suspected that Fanny Holtzmann might be funding the action for a turn of a share of the spoils, the damages might have been very different, and perhaps even the outcome, since it would have struck at the very roots of the plaintiff's motives in bringing the proceedings.

Immediately following the trial, the press forecast that the jury's verdict might have a startling effect on the future policies of film companies, and that they would be more cautious about portraying, on the screen, the lives of real people. They would have to rethink their intention to cast George Arliss as Disraeli, and Matheson Lang as Marshall Hall, in *The Great Defender*. These forebodings, however, proved misplaced. Arliss certainly played 'Disraeli', and did so to such great effect that every film in which he subsequently appeared was treated by the film-going public as if the lead was being played by Benjamin Disraeli rather than George Arliss.

What the verdict did achieve is that no film maker ever again took the risk of saying that some of the characters were still alive. Indeed, as a result of the case, the well-recognized disclaimer appeared at the beginning of films and, where appropriate, has done so ever since. This states that any similarity between the characters portrayed and any living person is purely coincidental and not intentional. Presumably film makers still believe, equally misguidedly, that this announcement gives them full protection, which, of course, it does not. If the other requirements for a claim in libel are present, the disclaimer will be of singularly little value.

There is no reason to doubt that then, as now, the awarding of vast sums by way of damages was a reflection both of the jury's dislike of unwarranted invasion of the privacy of living persons, and the inadequacy of the law to protect them. It is little short of amazing that, fifty years on, Great Britain still has no law of privacy. The freedom of the press is a vital and essential factor in the freedom of the individual, but the invasion of privacy, whether in print, on film or by word of mouth, which is motivated by greed or the desire for financial gain, is indefensible, and the more so today when the gutter section of the press are hellbent on outstripping each other in the depths to which they are prepared to descend.

Following the case, the Youssoupoffs resumed their life in Paris, where they were later friends of the Duke and Duchess of Windsor. It has been written that the Princess invested the damages so as to produce £1,000 a year, on which they lived. That would today be between £20,000 and £25,000 a year and seems to indicate, if accurate, either that she had a change of heart about a trust fund for her children, or that the other accounts are accurate and she received vastly greater sums from MGM in settlement of her other claims, which enabled her to live on part, and put the remainder in trust. Certainly, she would hardly have had need to sell her paintings of monsters at two guineas each, which, it appears, she could not resist promoting in her interview with the press immediately following the verdict.

The Prince and Princess were not finished with litigation. They brought suit to recover a very valuable family château and were successful. Again, in 1965, the Prince sued in America, bringing an action against the Columbia Broadcasting System in respect of a play which featured once again his part in the killing of Rasputin. Fanny Holtzmann was once more in evidence, but on this occasion she honoured the court with her presence. The magic seems to have disappeared, and they lost. The Prince died on 27 September 1967 at the age of eighty. Princess Irina followed him when, at the age of seventy, she died of a heart attack in March 1970. We shall never know what part, if any, Fanny Holtzmann played on their behalf on the great Day of Judgement.

Bibliography

Lost Splendour by Prince Felix Youssoupoff – Jonathan Cape.
The Life and Times of Grigori Rasputin by Alex de Jonge – Collins.
The Lion's Share by Bosley Crowther – E.P.Watt & Co. Inc.
The Fall of the Russian Monarchy by Sir Bernard Pares – Jonathan Cape.
Letters of the Tsar to the Tsarina, edited by E.J. Bing–Nicholson and Watson Ltd.
Letters of the Tsar and Tsarina by John Lane – Bodley Head Ltd.
Rasputin by Henry Leipmann – Frederick Muller Ltd.
Rasputin by R.J.Minney – Cassell.
Prince Felix Youssoupoff by Christopher Dobson – Harrap.
Picturegoer Weekly.
Express Newspapers PLC.

Index

Wynyard, Diana, as Princess Natasha in *Rasputin*, 55, 64, 169, 185

Xenia, Grand Duchess, 35, 66, 86

Yar, 26
Youssoupoff, Prince Felix: and murder of Rasputin, 1–8, 40–42, 89, 95, 115, 118, 125, 128, 129, 131–2, 197; as author, 6, 37, 45, 89, 129, 130, 131, 132, 133; family history, 32–3; homosexuality, 33, 35, 36; death of brother, 33–4; at Oxford, 34, 109; first meeting with Rasputin, 34; marriage to Irina, 35, 87; anti-Semitism, 36, 46, 69; unlikely murderer, 36; avoidance of military service, 36, 111, 114; conspiracy against Rasputin, 36–9, 88–9; brief banishment, 42, 108; extravagant life in Europe, 43–5; disposal of jewellery and art collection, 44–5; chequered career of litigation, 44, 45, 134–5; business ventures, 45; financial straits, 46; alleged film portrayal as 'Prince Chegodieff', 54, 63, 89, 90–91, 114, 116, 117–18, 123, 125–6, 128, 133–4, 137–40, 142, 144, 148, 150, 155, 157–8, 168, 171–2, 174–6, 179, 183–4, 189–90, 201; first claim against MGM, 66, 99; Jowitt's 'pen picture' of, 109–11; evidence in court, 128–37; and verdict, 196, 197; later life and litigation, 204
Youssoupoff, Princess Irina: marriage to Felix, 35, 104, 171; extravagant life in Europe, 43–5; alleged portrayal as Princess Natasha in film, 67, 85, 90–92, 95, 97, 114, 119, 124, 126, 134, 137–8, 140, 143, 146–8, 156, 163, 170–1, 184–7, 188, 193–5; contact with Holtzmann, 67–8, 136, 202–3; instigates libel action, 68–72, 100, 124, 136; question of defamation, 69–70, 71, 153, 188–9, 193; and implied seduction, 71, 91–2, 96–7, 122, 126, 146–7, 150–1, 171, 182, 193; evidence in court, 94–122; claim to have never met Rasputin, 94, 98, 185, 194; cross-examination, 97–121; denial of financial motive, 98, 100, 102–3; admits distortion of facts in film, 111, 113–18; and verdict, 196–7; settlement, 202; later life, 204
Youssoupoff, Prince Nicholas, 33–4
Youssoupoff, Princess Zenaide (mother of Felix), 2, 20, 32–3, 34, 36

Zukor, Adolph, 48–9